PSYCHOLINGUISTICS
The Experimental Study of Language

Gary D. Prideaux

Department of Linguistics
The University of Alberta

CROOM HELM
London & Sydney

© 1984 Gary D. Prideaux
Croom Helm Ltd, Provident House, Burrell Row,
Beckenham, Kent BR3 1AT

Croom Helm Australia Pty Ltd, First Floor,
139 King Street, Sydney, NSW 2001, Australia

British Library Cataloguing in Publication Data

Prideaux, Gary D.
   Psycholinguistics: the experimental study
   of language.
   1. Psycholinguistics
   I. Title
   401'.9   BF455

   ISBN 0-7099-2069-5

Printed and bound in Great Britain by
Biddles Ltd, Guildford and King's Lynn

PSYCHOLINGUISTICS:
THE EXPERIMENTAL STUDY
OF LANGUAGE

CONTENTS

Contents

PREFACE

Students in an introductory psycholinguistics course need not only an overview of the central issues in the discipline but also some direct experience in carrying out experimental research. Designed to meet both these needs, the present work offers, through a set of exercises and laboratories, a "hands-on" approach to experimental psycholinguistics.

The book is designed for undergraduate students who have taken an introductory linguistics course, although prior laboratory experience is not required, nor is a knowledge of statistics necessary. Consequently, the laboratories are relatively simple in conception and design. At the end of each chapter is a short set of exercises plus an indication of which laboratories are appropriate for that chapter. The laboratories are gathered together at the end of the book, along with a section describing how to keep a laboratory manual. Following the laboratories are two brief sections dealing with the elementary statistics needed for a few of the labs.

Although intended as an introduction to the experimental study of language, this book makes no attempt at being exhaustive. Experimental phonetics and phonology are ignored, as are such important areas as reading, language pathology, and second language acquisition. I have instead adopted a more limited goal of trying to provide a survey of major issues. The text approaches issues in psycholinguistics in a relatively conventional manner, though my own biases are hopefully obvious throughout.

Preface

This book has benefitted from comments, suggestions, and criticisms from a number of persons. I am especially grateful to William J. Baker, Bruce L. Derwing, Joseph F. Kess, and Lois Marckworth Stanford for their suggestions on various parts of the manuscript, as well as for their clarifications or downright corrections when I was simply wrong. To my many colleagues and friends at the University of Alberta, the University of Victoria, and elsewhere, I am indebted for their sustained encouragement and assistance.

Both Mrs. Helen B. Hawkes, my administrative assistant, and Miss Nadia Ložkovova, my research assistant, have graciously read and re-read the manuscript in the unending search for typos and infelicitious expressions. They both found a bundle, but I must claim the remaining ones as my own.

Over the past four years, students in my undergraduate experimental linguistics course have responded to much of the material on which the book is based. Their questions and suggestions have prompted me to clarify issues, sharpen distinctions, and in general make the content more coherent and less polemic. Their reactions to the laboratories have resulted in considerable refinement and clarification. The "field testing" of the material and laboratories has, I feel, greatly benefitted the entire enterprise.

Finally, I am grateful to the Social Sciences and Humanities Research Council of Canada for their support of much of my own research reported in the book, through research grants 410-80-0343, 410-82-0153, and 451-83-1843.

Chapter One

INTRODUCTION

1.1 Linguistics as an Empirical Science

The scientific method. Linguistics is usually defined as the scientific study of language. The intent of the definition is to distinguish a *linguistic* study of language phenomena from a literary, philosophical, speculative, or purely subjective inquiry. In this spirit, the scientific study of language is understood to mean an objective analysis of some aspect of language. Moreover, it is generally assumed that particular languages (English, Urdu, Japanese, etc.) are instantiations of the general and universal phenomenon of "Language." Each specific language is assumed to be a highly structured set of systems, including phonology, morphology, syntax, and semantics. More recently, the separation of systems into various autonomous but interacting modules has become a popular research methodology, involving a "divide and conquer" strategy based on the idea that once systems have been properly isolated, they can be more readily dealt with individually than can the entire constellation of phenomena across all components.

While most people seem to have a high regard and even reverential awe for things scientific, a clear and precise specification of the scientific method is relatively difficult to formulate. We can, however, identify certain of its basic characteristics, including the requirements that data be public and replicable, that theories constructed to account for

1

the data be testable, and that the principles embodied in the theories be commensurate with other well-established principles in related disciplines. Indeed, many "theories" (e.g., creationism or Velakovsky's views of the origin of Venus) founder on the very fact that the "data" upon which they are built are highly suspect and non-replicable, while the theories themselves are both *ad hoc* and incompatable with other, well-established theories and principles.

Certain logical steps in the scientific enterprise can be delineated. The first involves the selection of a particular *domain* of inquiry. The astronomer might, for example, wish to study the behavior of double star systems, or the linguist might wish to investigate the various permitted word orders in Persian. When selecting an area of inquiry, the scientist usually has some prior notions about how things work in that domain, which he wants to explore and elaborate. Accordingly, he next gathers data relevant to his interests. It might be quite irrelevant, for example, for the astronomer to study the colors of binary stars if he is interested in their orbits, or on the other hand it might be quite relevant. Likewise, the linguist might have little interest in phonological stress and intonation patterns in Persian when studying word order, or he might find phonological considerations crucial to his investigation. Once data are gathered, they are organized so that preliminary *generalizations* can be drawn. Almost immediately after, if not simultaneously with, the gathering and organizing stages, the scientist begins to construct *hypotheses* to account for (describe or explain) the data. In describing word order in Persian, for example, the linguist wants to do more than simply create a *taxonomy* of possible word orders. In particular, he wants to specify the functions of such orders (e.g., signalling a question versus a statement, etc.), and inquire into how such word orders accord with other facts in Persian and with other languages.

Once the hypotheses are formulated, they must be tested against new data. As Popper (1962) has argued, it is in the scientist's best interest to construct the strongest and most vulnerable hypotheses imaginable so that testing may eliminate as many alternatives as possible as soon as possible. Upon testing the hypothesis, the scientist might find that all the predictions are borne out in the new data, in which case the hypothesis is not rejected, or that none are, in which case the hypothesis is rejected, or, perhaps most commonly, that some of the predictions are supported while others are not. In the latter case, the hypothesis must be revised and retested.

It is clear from this brief and oversimplified discussion that data collection and analysis interact with theory construction in an intimate and mutually supportive way. In this inductive-deductive spiral, the inductive aspect involves data collection and organization, while the deductive component refers to theory construction and testing. These two components, the empirical and the theoretical, constitute the two faces of the scientific enterprise.

Linguistic data. Linguistic data must meet the same conditions as data in any science. To qualify as scientific, data must be *public* and accessible to any qualified observer; they must not be privative and exclusively available only to some. They must also be *replicable*. If a scientist reports results which no one else is able to reproduce, those results are naturally going to be viewed with considerable skepticism. Finally, the data must be stated in a clear theoretical language in order be interpretable.

There are several sources of data available to the linguist. Traditionally, "text" data have been fundamental in linguistics. By this is meant not only those actual texts written in a modern or archaic language, but also the data collected by the linguist from his consultants or from himself acting as his own informant. While these are often referred to as "raw" data, it is clear than they are far from raw, since they are represented in a particular way (e.g., phonetically, in conventional orthography, etc.) which is itself only a representation of the spoken language.

A second kind of data consists of native speaker judgements ("intuitions") about linguistic forms. Speakers can make judgements about such matters as whether or not a given linguistic form is grammatically well-formed, whether it is semantically well-formed, whether it is ambiguous, whether it is paraphrase of another form, whether it is appropriate in some particular context, whether it belongs to some perceived "standard" dialect or not, what kinds of semantic functions are represented by various NPs, what its "speech act" function is (question, command, etc.), and a host of other judgements. These judgements and decisions about sentences, phrases, words, etc., are important because they provide a means by which we can uncover information about what the native speaker actually *knows* about his language as well as how he *uses* his language.

While native speaker judgements can be gathered in a variety of ways, perhaps the most common is for the linguist to serve as his own informant. Another is to ask a few other speakers about one's own judgements, and still another is to establish a controlled experimental context in which the data can be gathered. There are of course advantages and disadvantages with each of these.

When the linguist serves as his own source of data, there are at least three potentially serious problems which can arise. The first is that the linguist, having a particular theoretical bias, might make a judgement that another linguist with a different bias might not make. This is not to say that the linguist is deliberately contaminating the data, but rather that his bias might direct him unconsciously toward one or another judgement or interpretation which is not representative of a group of speakers.

A second danger, and one which is relevant to any data collection involving only a single source is the "N=1" problem. By this is meant that a particular individual's responses, judgements, or the like may be quite non-representative of the general population, or even of a segment of it. A third danger is that the linguist, quite unconsciously, might be highly selective in which forms he chooses to make judgements about, thereby inadvertently obscuring the real phenomenon and creating a false generalization. To illustrate these problems in concrete terms, let us consider the following three sentences:

1 a. To whom was it obvious (that) Max was a Hungarian?
   b. It is apparent (that) John will win.
   c. It was expected (that) Sue would arrive late.

Suppose that in all cases the linguist is to act as his own informant. Postal (1970) judged that (1a) was quite unacceptable, as it should be according to a particular theoretical issue he was promoting at the time. This judgement illustrates two of the pitfalls suggested above. First, Postal's theoretical bias apparently directed him to his judgement of the grammatical ill-formedness of (1a), and second, his judgement is clearly not representative of a large number of speakers and may, in fact, be quite idiosyncratic.

Another problem arises as follows. On the basis of the three sentences in (1), we might be led to conclude that the complementizer *that* is optionally deletable when the clause it heads is at the end of the sentence. Such a conclusion would be quite false, for while in a great many cases, *that* is optional, there are cases in which it is not, as Langacker (1974) has noticed and which are illustrated in the following:

1 d. *It has been shown rats are too plentiful.
   e. *It was established the dump is dangerous.

In these two cases, the complementizer's absence renders the sentences quite awkward, thereby demonstrating that *that* cannot be freely deleted. These examples illustrate the problems which can arise when the linguist serves as his own informant. The linguistics literature contains numerous instances where one person's intuitions serve as the basis of a strong theoretical claim, only to be met with someone else's counter-claims. The example in (1a), for example, was responded to by Limber (1970). Moreover, Spencer (1973) has found that linguists are in general less consistent with themselves than are naive native speakers! The moral which emerges here is that one must be careful to obtain

Introduction

representative and *replicable* data.

Within a given language there are invariably many dialects, and the study of dialects and how they differ constitutes a third source of data. Of course, this type of data might include either text or judgmental facts. For example, someone from certain areas of the Southern United States might well utter sentences like those in (2):

2 a. I might ought to go to the grocery store.
  b. Mary says that she may can go to the movie tomorrow.
  c. Jan wants for you to bring a salad to the party.

All three of these sentences probably sound quite awkward and even ill-formed to many native speakers, although they are all quite acceptable in certain dialects. Both (2a) and (2b) involve the "double modal" construction, which contrasts with standard English in that the latter normally does not permit a sequence of two modal verbs. Of course, to the speaker of the Southern dialect, these sentences are perfectly meaningful, and he will quickly explain that *might ought to* means "should perhaps," while *may can* means "may be able to." In (2c), the problem is that in the standard dialect, the complementizer *for* is forbidden immediately after the verb *want* and some other verbs as well. However, it is obligatory when other words intervene between *want* and the subject of the infinitive, as in:

2 d. Jan wanted very much for you to bring a salad to the party.

With dialect data, as with other kinds of data, care must be taken to ensure that reliability and replicability are satisfied. What kinds of conclusions can be drawn from such data? The answer to this depends, of course, on the kinds of hypotheses being tested. The examples in (2a) and (2b) clearly indicate that double modal structures are viable in a particular dialect, although the extent of the permitted forms is not addressed here. These are empirical questions which cry out for investigation. For example, the use of *can* in (2b) suggests that

6

speakers of the dialect in question permit substitution of *can* for the paraphrase "be able to" even when another modal is present, a construction not permitted in the standard dialect. Why this is permitted remains unexplained, but once some initial generalizations and hypotheses are constructed, further investigation can progress.

The example in (2c) is perhaps clearer. In all dialects, the complementizer *for* seems to be required in sentences like (2d), and it is only omitted in certain conditions in the standard dialect. In the Southern dialect, however, the omission is optional, suggesting that the condition for omission is relaxed, although what causes such a relaxation remains to this point unanswered.

There are potential problems lurking in dialect data too. For example, while many speakers of the Southern dialect might actually utter sentences like those cited above, some might refuse to acknowledge that they said them. That is, there might be a strong prescriptive injunction against such forms, arising perhaps from schooling or from a kind of linguistic inferiority complex, so that speakers might insist that they never use such constructions. This injunction acts as a kind of censor, even though it may be quite unconscious. Consequently, care must be taken to collect real utterances and not edited or contaminated ones.

We can see from these few examples that dialect data can be extremely useful. However, data like those cited above would be of interest only if there were important theoretical issues hanging on the formulation of a solution to, for example, the double modal problem or the complementizer problem. Otherwise, the facts would simply be isolated and not integrated into a theoretically coherent picture. It must be emphasized that linguistics, like other sciences, is constantly striving for a coherent theoretical perspective, and data are not simply accumulated for their own sake.

Historical data constitute another source for the linguist, and one which has methodological similarities to dialect data. Considerable insight can be gained as to how some aspects of language are learned and mentally represented by examining how forms change over time. It should be noted here that one major methodological problem with diachronic data, and especially text data from "dead" languages, is that there are no native speakers to whom the linguist can turn to check forms or from whom he can obtain judgements. He has, at best, the texts and his own intuitions about them.

A further problem in using text data from any source, and one which can also arise in using judgmental data, is the "editing" tendency alluded to above. That is, the linguist might unconsciously and inadvertently edit or revise text, eliminating such factors as mispronunciations, false starts, grammatical errors, and the like. In written texts, an attempt is generally made to force the material into standard forms, respecting orthographic, spelling, and other stylistic conventions. Accordingly, in "good" texts, one seldom finds run-on sentences, sentence fragments, and the like, although these are a common and natural part of the relaxed colloquial language. Consequently, when the linguist transcribes his data, especially if he knows the language well, he must avoid the trap of unconsciously editing and altering the text. In dealing with dialect data, for example, some nuances might be missed because of unconscious editing. The danger of sanitizing data is often present in experimental studies as well, and we shall return to this problem below.

Normal children, under normal conditions, learn the language of the community in which they are raised, and if that community is multilingual, the children often learn more than one language. The way children acquire language can provide considerable insight into the kinds of rules and structures that are learnable. Consequently, data from language acquisition provide a rich and varied source for the linguist. The problems associated with gathering language acquisition data are understandably numerous. Gathering linguistic data from children can be a trying business, and it takes considerable patience and rapport with them to make progress. Moreover, there is always the possibility that a child might comprehend more (and at an earlier stage) than he produces, forcing us to recognize a clear distinction between comprehension and production data. Various techniques have been developed in order to gather language acquisition data. Some involve no more than naturalistic observations, that is, simply watching, listening to, and recording the child's language production. Here, of course, the editing problem is quite important. For example, a child might say "milk" in one context to mean "I want some milk," while in another situation he might mean "No more milk!" Other techniques involve various games in which the child might be engaged. He might, for example, be directed to talk to toy animals, act out specific stories with puppets, and the like. Yet other techniques involve the child's attempts at imitating adult sentences. Both naturalistic and experimental techniques can be used to gather data from children, although with any such techniques unexpected pitfalls often abound.

One important source of data we have kept for the last, namely, experimental data, by which we refer to data collected in an experimental situation in which requisite controls and conditions are maintained. We shall discuss the nature of experiments below, but for the moment let us focus on the reason why experimental data are important. Primarily, the linguist, like any other scientist, is interested in testing his hypotheses, and considerable importance is attached to obtaining reliable information concerning native speaker judgements. Judgements of the sort discussed above, relating to well-formedness, anomaly, ambiguity, paraphrase, appropriateness, and many other factors, are crucial in testing linguistic hypotheses. However, such judgements must be secure from the bias which results when the linguist with a particular theoretical bent provides his own data, and they must also be safe from the "N = 1" problem. Properly constructed and executed experiments are one important means to gain such information. Along with experimental data, however, come an associated set of problems. One is that data collected in a laboratory situation may not be representative of natural language use. Another problem has to do with availability of subjects: in many university settings, only undergraduate students seem to serve as subjects, and yet it is always hoped that they are representative of a larger population. A third problem concerns data-analytic techniques. Many linguists seem to avoid experimental research if for no other reason than that they do not command the skills needed for data analysis. While this is an important concern, it is still one which must be faced head-on if experimental data are to be taken seriously.

In summary, there are numerous sources of data, in fact even more than have been mentioned here. For example, nothing has been said above about data from language pathologies, although this source is becoming increasingly important in some areas. Nor has mention been made of second language acquisition or sociolinguistics as rich sources of data. For our purposes, attention will be directed primarily toward experimental data, where this term is understood to include both adult and child language sources.

1.2 Methodological Issues

It is important at this early stage to discuss some basic methodological issues relevant to experimental linguistics. We will first examine naturalistic observations as an important source of data, and then we will turn to the nature of experiments.

Naturalistic observations are data collected through observation of a phenomenon in a non-experimental situation. For example, the linguist interested in so-called "slips of the tongue" might, like Fromkin (1971, 1973), simply take note of such instances when they occur, and even ask friends to do likewise. In this example, it would be important to gather information about the situation, the speaker making the error, the kind of error made, and perhaps much other information. In many instances, a speaker might not even be aware that he has made an error, or he might notice it and correct it in revealing ways. For example, if someone says "blond eyes" for "blond hair" (Fromkin, 1973), we might conclude that a semantic replacement has been made, while if someone said, as Spooner is reported to have, "blushing crow" for "crushing blow," we would recognize a phonological switch of /bl/ for /kr/, while at the same time producing a phrase of the form V+*ing* + N, consistent with the original form, and even semantically acceptable, although somewhat bizarre.

Naturalistic observations are of considerable importance to language acquisition studies, and many parents enjoy keeping a record of their children's language development, although it is frequently only the amusing or aberrant forms which they notice. From such diaries can be gleaned a wealth of information, not only about the stages the children pass through, but also the kinds of structures they try, then discard in favor of others. Of course, the editing problem can be significant here, too, but at least it cannot be claimed that naturalistic observation data are biased because of a laboratory situation.

A third area where naturalistic observation data can be gathered is in text analysis. Suppose, for instance, that one is interested in the frequency of occurance and the places in sentences where relative clauses appear in English. One might examine novels or other written materials and tabulate the locations and types of relative clauses for a given author or genre. It is conceivable that such a study can provide considerable information as to how certain structures are used to perform communicative functions. Perhaps differences in structures can be shown to correlate with differences in individual writers or even more generally in styles (cf. Marckworth & Baker, 1980).

In summary, naturalistic observation can be a rich and useful source of data, although it might be fraught with considerable problems of its own. For example, one might have to look long and hard before finding an adequate number of examples of the sort of phenomenon one is looking for, and even then the sample might be very skewed in one direction, for possibly quite obscure reasons. But in spite of such problems, naturalistic observations such as text counts or language acquisition studies are often extremely valuable (cf. Carden, 1982).

Experiments. Let us turn now to a discussion of the nature and purpose of experiments in linguistics. Scientists construct and carry out experiments in

11

order to gain reliable data relevant to a particular theoretical issue. As Zimney (1961, p. 18) points out, an experiment is an "objective observation of phenomena which are made to occur in a strictly controlled situation in which one or more factors are varied and the others are kept constant." Experiments are conducted in order to test the predictions made by particular hypotheses. Accordingly, the experiment must be properly designed so that it tests what the scientist wishes it to test. Although experimental design is a specialization in itself, we can nevertheless discuss informally some of the major components of an experiment in order to become acquainted with what experiments are and what they can and cannot tell us.[1]

Since experiments are expected to test empirical hypotheses, it is the scientist's first responsibility to formulate his hypothesis in a testable form. Accordingly, when he designs his experiment, its results should in principle either support or refute the predictions entailed by the hypothesis. For example, if the hypothesis states that one structure should be easier to comprehend than another, then the linguist should design the experiment to test this prediction. In order to do this, he must define the *independent variable*, that which he systematically manipulates in the *stimuli*, the forms (sentences, words, etc.) which are presented to the *subjects*, those persons who participate in the experiment. As he constructs his stimuli, he must insure that the independent variables represent those variations in the phenomena which he wishes to investigate. In designing the experiment, the scientist must also select a *dependent variable*, which will serve as a valid measure of the phenomenon he is interested in measuring. Measures of the dependent variable will be taken in the experiment. That is, subjects will carry out particular tasks, and aspects of their behaviour in those tasks will be measured. The hypothesis will predict that certain differences in the independent variable will cause certain changes in the dependent variable.

----

[1]An excellent introduction to the scientific method and to the nature of experiments in the cognitive sciences can be found in Christensen (1980).

For example, if the linguist hypothesizes that some structural type T_1 should be harder for subjects to comprehend than type T_2, then his stimuli will contain examples of both T_1 and T_2. The stimuli might also contain *distractors*, included so that subjects will not readily guess what the study is about and adopt an *ad hoc* strategy which might be unrelated to the phenomenon being investigated. The experiment might, for example, contain several *replications* of both T_1 and T_2, so that more than one measure is taken of each. Perhaps the linguist will choose response time as the dependent variable. If so, he will measure how long it takes a subject to respond in some particular way to the presentation of a given stimulus, perhaps under the assumption that the longer it takes to respond, the harder it is for the subject to comprehend the structure.

It is also important that in his design of the experiment, the scientist maintain control of his variables. He must not permit extraneous factors to enter into the experiment and contaminate the stimuli or the task, thereby rendering the results impossible to interpret. For example, if he hypothesizes that T_1 is more difficult to process than T_2, he must insure that the particular instantiations (replications) of the two types differ only in the ways he wishes. If, for example, he is comparing two different sentence types, he must be careful that the lexical items of one type are not radically different in kind from those of the other, since otherwise subjects may attend to nuances in lexical items and not to structural differences. The experimenter must also be careful that other factors do not *co-vary* with the independent variable, such that the results can be interpreted as supporting either the original hypothesis or an alternative hypothesis built from the co-varying variable. For example, if sentence length co-varies with structural type such that T_1 is always substantially longer than T_2, then length rather than type might plausibly be responsible for the subject variation in the experimental task.

The *subjects* are those persons who participate in the experiment and provide the data. Ideally, they should be naive as to the phenomenon under consideration, since otherwise they may have a tendency to behave in a biased manner. It is crucial that the subjects be representative of a particular population, and not be idiosyncratic in their behaviour. However, it may be that for a particular experimental task, some subjects will adopt a particular *task strategy*, which itself might, or might not, reflect the phenomenon under consideration, while another group might adopt a different strategy. Good will and honesty in subjects are crucial for any experiment, for otherwise the data may be useless. Since subjects can become confused and upset in some experiments, care must be taken that the task is completely clear and unambiguous, and that it is not threatening to the subjects, either physically or psychologically. There are ethical guidelines in place in most institutions for the treatment of human subjects, and these must always be respected.

Furthermore, care must be taken to insure that the dependent variable *validly* measures what the experimenter wants measured. This often calls for an *operational definition* of a phenomenon in terms of the dependent variable. For instance, in the example above, response time might be operationally defined as a measure of processing difficulty.

One of the challenging aspects of experimental psycholinguistics is the formulation of appropriate and useful methodologies for gathering data. Numerous experimental paradigms have been proposed and used, and in the course of the next few chapters we shall discuss some of these in detail. In any experiment, there may be unexpected pitfalls, unanticipated technical difficulties, or puzzling subject reactions, and learning to anticipate and avoid these is largely a matter of experience.

Finally, once the experiment has been designed and run, and the data collected, the problem of analysis remains. This usually involves specialized data-analytic techniques, including often elaborate statistical analyses. We will not delve into those arcane mysteries here, though it must be remembered when the experiment is designed that the data must be analyzable. Many a clever experiment has been carried out, with a large expenditure of time and effort on the part of both the scientists and the subjects, only to find that the design was not adequate for statistical analysis of the sort required to test a given hypothesis.

Summary. In this section, we have devoted considerable attention to the nature of linguistics as an empirical science. We have discussed sources of data, potential problems associated with those sources, and the nature of experiments. We have argued that linguistics can be treated as an empirical science. However, the question arises as to the source of hypotheses in this enterprise, and as a preliminary answer to that question, we turn to a discussion of the linguist's notion of grammar.

1.3 The Nature of Grammar

A *grammar* of a language contains, among other things, a syntactic description of the language. Among the "other things" are the *morphology* of the language, and in some linguists' view, *phonology* as well as *semantics*.

In order to provide an orientation for what follows, we shall adopt the familiar position that a grammar is a formal description of a given language, constructed in terms of a particular linguistic theory. Accordingly, the particular theory adopted will dictate both the form the grammar takes and what it includes and excludes. For example, in classical transformational theory, grammatical and semantic relations are not included as primitive terms, while in relational grammar (Perlmutter, 1980) and in some versions of functional grammar (Dik, 1978), grammatical relations are important basic terms. Moreover, in some versions of functional grammar and in case grammar (Fillmore, 1968), semantic relations are treated as primitives. Therefore, it is important not to view the notion of grammar as a monolithic edifice, but rather to recognize that there are indeed many different, often contending, versions of grammars, each with its own theoretical orientation and direction.

Descriptive syntax. In its broadest sense, syntax is the study of the structure of sentences and the relations within and among sentences. A central part of syntax deals with the *constituent structure* of sentences -- the hierarchical structure and linear ordering of the major constituents from which sentences are constructed. The major *phrasal* constituents include the sentence (S), noun phrases (NPs), verb phrases (VPs), adjective phrases (APs), prepositional phrases (PPs), and the like. This aspect of syntax also deals with the component parts of phrasal categories, namely the traditional parts of speech such as nouns (Ns), verbs (Vs), adjectives (As), adverbs (ADVs), etc., as well as other categories such as tense, aspect, number, gender, etc. The constituent structure of sentences is typically represented in terms of *phrase markers* or tree diagrams. For example, the constituent structure of (3) can be represented as in Figure 1.1.

3. John dropped a book on his toe.

The tree diagram in Figure 1.1 indicates that the sentence is composed of a major (subject) NP, consisting of a single noun *John*, plus a VP consisting of a verb, a NP (which functions as direct object), and a prepositional phrase. Each phrasal category has an internal constituent structure, while the tree diagram reflects the structural organization of the sentence. The theoretical perspective underlying the structure in Figure 1.1 suggests that structural representations consist of syntactic categories arranged in a hierarchical structure, but do not contain an overt specification of grammatical roles such as of subject, direct object, indirect object, and the like.

However, there is more to syntax than just constituent structure. For example, the study of syntax also involves the analysis of various *sentence types*, and the structural differences and similarities among them. For example, a syntactic description must address the fact that some sentences are declaratives, such as (3) above, while others might be imperatives, such as (4a) or interrogatives, such as (4b, c):

4 a. Please close the door.
   b. Did John drop a book on his toe?
   c. What did John drop on his toe?

==

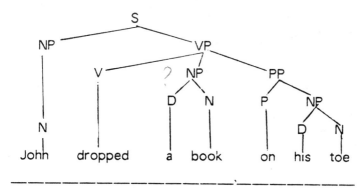

FIGURE 1.1 Typical Constituent Structure

==

Obviously, other types of structures could be enumerated as well. An important issue in the description of sentence types is the extent to which various sentence types are alike (e.g., the declaratives and interrogatives all have their subject NP to the left of the main verb *drop*), and the extent to which they are different (e.g, the imperative does not have an overt subject NP, while the other two types do). The statement of the specifics of similarities and differences in form across various sentence types is a second important part of syntax.

A third aspect of syntax deals with the relations among sentence types. For example, an active sentence such as (5a) seems at first blush to be very similar in meaning to its passive counterpart (5b)

    5 a. Sam kicked the ball.
       b. The ball was kicked by Sam.

while at the same time a regular syntactic relationship can be stated between actives and their corresponding passives. Likewise, a syntactic relationship can be stated between alternative dative sentences such as (6a) and (6b).

6 a. Sid sent some flowers to Chris.
 b. Sid sent Chris some flowers.

The syntactic relationship here can be roughly described as "The indirect object (*Chris*) and the direct object (*some flowers*) may change places, with an appropriate change in the indirect object's preposition." A further example is the syntactic relation which can be stated between extraposed and non-extraposed clauses within a complex sentence. For example, if we consider the pair of sentences (7a), and (7b):

7 a. That Sue was fired disturbed everyone at the party.
 b. It disturbed everyone at the party that Sue was fired.

we note that the embedded clause *That Sue was fired* may either be in subject position or at the end of the sentence, after *party*, leaving only the pronoun *it* in the subject position. Of course, there is a great number of such "related" structural types, and it is important not only to discover such relationships but also to formulate the relations in the most accurate and general way possible.

A further area of syntax deals with the specification and analysis of grammatical functions such as grammatical subject (SUBJ), direct object (DO), indirect object (IO), object of a preposition (OP), etc. For example, in sentences (6a) and (6b) above, the subject is *Sid*, which we can represent simply as "SUBJ=*Sid*," the direct object is *some flowers* (DO=*some flowers*), and the indirect object is *Chris* (IO=*Chris*). Classical transformational theory treats grammatical relations as *derivative* rather than *primitive* terms, while other theories such as relational grammar treat grammatical relations as basic terms within the theory. Interestingly, traditional scholarly grammarians, such as Jespersen (1965) did treat grammatical functions as part of the basic vocabulary of grammar, while certain of the structuralists tended to avoid including grammatical relations as part of the language of syntax on the grounds that such terms as subject and object were somehow too subjective.

Some linguists contend that the study of syntax should also include a treatment of *semantic roles* played by noun phrases within sentences. Such roles would presumably include *Agent*, *Patient*, *Objective*, *Experiencer*, *Recipient*, *Beneficiary*, *Location*, *Instrument*, *Time*, and possibly many more. For example, it might be suggested that in a sentence like:

8. Fred opened the can with a screwdriver.

the subject NP *Fred* serves as Agent, while the direct object *can* is the Objective, and *screwdriver* is the Instrument. However, defining semantic roles can be quite difficult. For example, in the sentence:

9. The wind blew the fence over.

it is not clear whether *wind* should be analyzed as an Agent, since Agents are typically animate nouns which intentionally initiate an action. This aspect of agentivity is not found in the subject NP of (9).

Classical transformational grammar. Many current grammatical theories are direct or indirect descendants of the theory developed by Chomsky and his associates in the mid 1960s and which reached its culmination in *Aspects of the theory of syntax* (Chomsky, 1965). Although few if any linguists still subscribe to that · theory, most later theories maintain some of its assumptions. Moreover, much psycholinguistic research of the 1960s and 1970s was carried out in the context of that theory. It is therefore useful to review the salient aspects of that "classical" theoretical position.

A classical transformational description of a language has four major components: a *base* component, a *transformational* component, a *phonological* component, and a *semantic* component. The *base* component is the generative component of the system; it is here that the "deep" structures for sentences are constructed. The base component contains a set of phrase structure rules and an elaborate lexicon. The phrase structure rules serve to generate a structural configuration, a hierarchical tree structure, into which lexical items can be inserted, given that each lexical item satisfies certain

TABLE 1.1 Sample Base Component

===

Phrase Structure Rules:

```
S      --->   (NEG) (Q) NP   AUX   VP
VP     --->   V (NP) (PP)
AUX    --->   T (M)
PP     --->   P  NP
NP     --->   (D) N
```

Sample Lexical Entries:

```
boy    [+N, +human, +animate, +common, -abstract]
Sue    [+N, +human, +animate, -common, -abstract]
dog    [+N, -human, +animate, +common, -abstract]
book   [+N, -animate, +common, -abstract]

run    [+V, +_,   +[+animate _] ]
smile  [+V, +_,   +[+human  _] ]
watch  [+V, +_NP, +[+animate _], [_-abstract]]

may    [+M]
in     [+P, +loc]
the    [+D, +definite]
```

===

strict subcategorization conditions (for example, only a transitive verb can appear in a structure containing a direct object NP) and *selectional* restrictions (for example, verbs such as *smile* may occur only with *human* subject nouns, while others, such as *elapse* may not). Some very abbreviated examples of base rules and lexical items are found in Table 1.1.

In principle, the classical model assumes that the base component generates all possible structures, the deep structures, underlying all well-formed sentences in the language. The deep structures serve as input to both the semantic component, which is supposed to provide a semantic reading or semantic interpretation for each such structure, and to the transformational component, whose job it is to convert the underlying structure into an appropriate surface structure. The distinction between the deep and surface structure of a sentence is extremely important in the classical model, since it is the deep and not the surface structure which feeds the semantic component. Moreover, it is at the level of underlying structural representation where similarities among paraphrases such as (6a) and (6b), or (7a) and (7b) are accounted for. As a case in point, let us consider pairs of sentences like those in (10) and (11):

10 a. Sam took out the trash.
   b. The clerk put away the shirts.
   c. Georgia cut up the steak.

11 a. Sam took the trash out.
   b. The clerk put the shirts away.
   c. Georgia cut the steak up.

The structures in (10) contain a verb plus a particle (V+PRT) to the left of the direct object NP, while those in (11) have the particle positioned at the end of the sentence following the direct object. However, the meaning of the pairs of sentences in (10) and (11) appears to be constant. The sentences in (11) are said to be derived and their deep structures have the particle in a position before the direct object NP as in (10), since in both kinds of sentences the V+PRT structure functions as a transitive verb. In order to derive the structures in (11), a transformational rule of PARTICLE MOVEMENT optionally moves the particle to a position after the direct object NP. Such a rule can be formulated roughly as:

PARTICLE MOVEMENT (OPTIONAL)

SD:	V	PRT	NP	
SC:	1	2	3	--->
	1	$\emptyset$	3+2	

In this formulation of the transformation, the structural description (SD) specifies the structure to which the rule may apply, while the structural change (SC) indicates what change is to be made. In this case, the SD reveals that the PRT must initially occur before the direct object NP, while the

21

SC indicates that the PRT (item 2) is deleted in its original position, and copied to the right of the object NP (item 3). The rule must clearly be optional; if it were obligatory, the particle would always be moved to a position after the NP, and accordingly there would be no surface instances of sentences like (8).

The transformational component consists of a list of (numerous) transformations, some of which are optional while others are obligatory. The following are typical examples:

DATIVE MOVEMENT (OPTIONAL)

SD:	V	NP	to/for	NP	
SC:	1	2	3	4	--->
	1	4+2	0	0	

QUESTION FORMATION (OBLIGATORY)

SD:	Q	NP	AUX	
SC:	1	2	3	--->
	3	2	0	

WH MOVEMENT (OBLIGATORY)

SD:	#	X	NP	Y	#	
SC:	1	2	3	4	5	--->
	1	3+2	0	4	5	

Condition: 3 dominates a *wh*-phrase
is a clause boundary

The rule of DATIVE MOVEMENT serves to move an indirect object such as *Chris* in (6a) to a position before the direct object, as in (6b), with the concomitant deletion of the preposition *to*. The rule of QUESTION FORMATION, applying in both yes/no and *wh* questions, moves the auxiliary verb to a position before the subject NP. The rule of WH MOVEMENT moves a *wh* phrase such as *which boys* to the front of a sentence. Questions like (12a) are presumed to have an underlying word order of (12b), in which *Q* indicates that the sentence being generated is a question.

12 a. Which boys was Fred chasing down the alley?
   b. Q Fred was chasing which boys down the alley?

Within classical transformational theory, the transformations are cyclic and ordered: they apply first to the most deeply embedded clause in a complex sentence, then to the next most deeply embedded, and so forth, until finally the set applied to the topmost (matrix) sentence. Since the rules apply in order, certain transformations create structures to which later rules automatically apply. The output of the transformations is also a tree diagram which itself serves as input to the phonological component, whose function is to provide the proper phonetic shape of the sentence.

Thus, the classical model is modular in structure, with each component having its own type of rules. There are several important assumptions associated with the classical model, one of the most important of which is that the transformations preserve meaning. This was the so-called "Katz-Postal principle" (Katz & Postal, 1964), which was adopted by Chomsky (1965). The effect of such a principle is that the deep structure of, for example, a declarative sentence and its corresponding yes/no question form, or its negative analogue, are not the same. Rather, an interrogative sentence is assumed to have in its deep structure a sentence morpheme *Q* (for "question"), marking it as an interrogative, while a negative sentence contains a deep structure morpheme *NEG*, indicating that it is a negative. A simple declarative affirmative sentence will lack both *Q* and *NEG* in its deep structure. However, paraphrase pairs such as those in (6) and (7) are assigned the same deep structure since they are presumed to be identical in meaning. According to the Katz-Postal principle, then, the rule of DATIVE MOVEMENT is meaning preserving and only serves to generate two stylistic variants representing the same meaning. An obvious question here is why a natural language would allow for two alternative ways of representing the same meaning. One obvious avenue to explore would be that the meanings are *not* identical, but rather that they differ in some important respect.

A second important assumption of the classical model, although one not often discussed, was that the deep structures should in principle be "surfacy" in nature; that is, no deep structure should be highly abstract, but instead should be of the same general form as surface structures. Thus, for:

13. Sue broke a glass.

the deep structure should not be a VSO structure, as McCawley (1970) suggested, but instead should mirror the surface order. Similarly, a relative clause should have the deep structure form of a simple sentence. Thus, in:

14. The man that the dog bit ran down the alley.

the relative clause "that the dog bit" should have the form "the dog bit the man" in the deep structure. Such a structure would be automatically be altered by two transformations, one of RELATIVIZATION, which replaces the repeated NP *the man* with the relative pronoun *that*, and a second of WH MOVEMENT which moves each relative pronoun (e.g., *who, which, where, that,* etc.) to the head of its clause, much in the same way as the rule which moves a *wh* phrase to the head of a sentence in a *wh* question. This sequence of operations, from deep to surface structure, for (12) is sketched in (15):

15. DEEP STRUCTURE:
    The man [the dog bit the man] ran down the alley.

    by RELATIVIZATION:
    The man [the dog bit whom/that] ran down the alley.

    by WH MOVEMENT:
    The man [whom/that the dog bit] ran down the alley.

A further assumption, and one which has actually served as a constraint on transformational grammar ever since the work of Chomsky (1957), is that in order for a grammatical analysis to be descriptively adequate, it must represent ambiguity in those cases where it is detected by the native speaker. To illustrate this, let us consider the ambiguous sentences in (16).

16 a. The thunder disturbed the old men and women.
   b. Sally enjoys entertaining men.

In (16a), *old* modifies either *men and women* or just *men*, and this fact must, it is claimed, be represented by two separate grammatical analyses for the sentence, one for each of the two meanings. Similarly, in (16b), either *entertaining* modifies *men* (i.e., "men who are quite entertaining"), or *entertaining* is a verb whose object is *men* (i.e., "Sally likes to entertain men."). The fact that such sentences are ambiguous is not in dispute, although it is commonly observed that such *potentially* ambiguous sentences are frequently not actually ambiguous in a particular discourse, simply because the surrounding linguistic and even non-linguistic context can provide a great deal of information favoring one or the other interpretation, such that the hearer usually does not even recognize the ambiguity.

A fourth assumption about the nature of the grammar which is found in Chomsky's work is that the grammar somehow represents the knowledge or "linguistic competence" that the native speaker has about his language. Moreover, Chomsky (e.g., 1965; 1975) intimates that the grammatical transformations represent the mental operations carried out by the speaker and hearer.

The issue of whether or not the rules are directly used in language performance has been hotly debated. On the one hand, Chomsky (1965) has claimed that a generative is only a representation of the ideal speaker-hearer's linguistic competence and does not represent the steps he goes through in language production or comprehension. One the other hand, he has stated,

in a discussion of the acquisition of a rule of
yes-no question formation, that the child

> ...analyzes the declarative sentence into abstract
> phrases; he then locates the first occurrence
> of "is" (etc.) that follows the first noun phrase;
> he then preposes this occurrence of "is,"
> forming the corresponding question (Chomsky,
> 1975, pp. 31-32).

Obviously, whether or not particular grammatical
rules are actually used in language processing is a
contentious one, and much exegesis of the
generative literature has been carried out with the
goal of supporting one position or the other. This
is a highly charged issue, and one to which we
shall return later in our discussion of the
derivational theory of complexity.

Revised transformational theory. So far, we
have dealt only with the classical version of
transformational grammar. However, in the several
years since this theory was articulated, many
revisions have taken place. In particular, Chomsky
and his associates have radically modified their view
of syntax. Under the modified versions, of which
there have been several, the tendency has been to
treat underlying structures as more and more
concrete, that is closer in form to surface
structures, than those found in Chomsky (1965). At
a time when some theorists were moving toward
very abstract underlying representations, Chomsky
(1970b) argued that some English nominalization
constructions, such as "the destruction of the city,"
were best treated not as transformed versions of
underlying sentences, but rather as "base generated"
NP structures. At the same time, the "X-bar" theory
of phrase structure was proposed, in which
similarities among various phrasal categories (NP, VP,
AP, PP, etc.) were represented in a uniform
notation.

Another revision of the classical theory, initiated
by Chomsky (1970a), was that some semantic
interpretation was held to take place at the level of
surface structure. This position was extended and
developed to the extent that when the "revised
extended standard theory" was developed, virtually

all semantic interpretation was assumed to take place at the level of surface structure, although this notion of surface structure was somewhat different from that of the earlier theory. In the revised theory (e.g., Chomsky, 1975), the surface structure is viewed as "enriched" in the sense that any time a transformation moves a constituent, the movement rule leaves behind a "trace" to which the rules of semantic interpretation (or rules of "logical form") have access in order to form a semantic interpretation. Accordingly, a sentence like "John was watched" would have an surface structure much like "John was watched t," in which the trace t is coindexed to the moved NP *John*. Thus, the rules of logical form could interpret the surface subject *John* as the logical direct object since the trace marks the normal position of a direct object.

More extensive revisions, such as those found in Chomsky (1982a, 1982b) have directed attention toward a specification of general principles governing the form of grammar. According to this perspective, the language system consists of a set of individual, relatively autonomous components or modules, including the lexicon, the syntax (base component and transformations), a set of filters, and those interpretive components which yield the phonological representation and the logical form for sentences. The role of transformations has, within this perspective, been somewhat reduced, even to the extent that it has been proposed that there is really only one remaining transformation, namely "MOVE α ," which is designed to move any constituent anywhere, with any ill-formed resulting structures filtered out by other components.

An interesting aspect of recent developments in the transformational tradition is a strong interest in formulating general principles and systems rather than attending to the details of particular rules, as characterized earlier work in this field (cf. Berwick, 1983). Thus, in the most recent versions of transformational theory, major emphasis is placed on articulation of the structure of the various components and the principles which govern them. At the same time, the phrase structure rules have come to be treated as derivative from properties of lexical representations via what Chomsky (1982a,

27

==

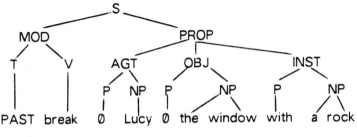

FIGURE 1.2 A Case Grammar Representation

==

1982b) has called the "projection principle."

Case grammar. In addition to revisions in transformational theory, other theoretical perspectives have emerged over the past several years, many of which have taken as a starting point some of the classical transformational assumptions. One important theory of this sort was Fillmore's (1968) case grammar, in which the Katz-Postal principle of the preservation of meaning was maintained. Unlike the classical model, however, case grammar assumed that semantic roles such as Agent, Dative, Instrument, Objective, etc. were treated as primitive terms. Thus, the underlying representation of a sentence contained nodes labelled *AGT, DAT, INST,* and the like. In the sentence

17. Lucy broke the window with a rock.

the underlying representation was much like that in Figure 1.2.

In case grammar, the underlying representations are quite abstract and distant from surface structures. This theory maintains that every sentence is made up of two basic parts, a proposition (PROP), consisting of a verb and its semantic arguments (AGT, OBJ, etc.), and a modality (MOD), consisting of verb tense, modals, aspect, etc. Furthermore, each semantic role is represented by a

28

TABLE 1.2 Fillmore's (1968) Cases

==

Agent: the (animate) initiator of an event or action.

Instrument: the physical cause, force, or object involved in the event.

Dative: the (usually animate) being affected by the action.

Factitive: the object resulting from the action.

Locative: the location or orientation of an action or event.

Objective: the remaining NPs.

==

preposition marking that role, plus a NP. For example, the preposition associated with AGT is *by*, the preposition appearing with the Agent in passives. A series of transformations convert the abstract underlying structures to appropriate surface structures. In spite of the relative complexity of case grammar, it has one very appealing characteristic: it unashamedly assumes a semantic basis for every sentence. Indeed, case grammar was the first generative theory to incorporate semantic cases directly into the grammatical rules. Definitions of some of Fillmore's (1968) cases are found in Table 1.2. As might be expected, the definition of semantic cases is a difficult matter, and numerous formulations other than Fillmore's have been proposed, among which are those of Chafe (1970) and Grimes (1975).

Relational grammar. One relatively recent theoretical position which has emerged from classical transformational theory is relational grammar (Perlmutter, 1980). This theory takes as primitive the grammatical relations subject (SUBJ), direct object (DO), indirect object (IO), plus several other "terms" such as locative, instrumental, etc. Under the various formulations this theory has taken, two basic levels of structural representation are maintained, one corresponding to deep structure and one to surface structure. The theory does not contain transformations, but instead each level is represented in terms of grammatical relations, though not in terms of linear ordering of constituents. Rules alter grammatical relations of constituents, restructure clause membership, etc., but it is only a late step which assigns linear ordering to constituents. Relational grammarians are deeply interested in syntactic universals. Accordingly, they are relatively uninterested in such language-specific aspects as word order in their formulation of rules such as Passive, which, in effect, simply advances a direct object (or a "2" as it is called by the relational grammarians) to subject (or "1"), with the concomitant displacement of the original "1" to a position of being a "non-term" or a *chômeur*. Even though relational grammar does not have transformations, it does contain relation altering operations analogous to transformations. Moreover, relational grammar, like the classical transformational theory, maintains the principle that meaning is preserved through the course of a derivation, even if the operations between underlying and surface are not called transformations. Finally, relational grammar draws a firm distinction between *grammatical* and *semantic* roles, arguing that linguistic rules are formulated only in terms of grammatical roles. This is another area where relational grammar is quite similar to its classical transformational ancestor.

Functional grammar. A different development in linguistic theory, but also one which adopts the position that semantics is fundamental, is the general area of functional grammar, such as developed by Dik (1879) and others. This theory, or more accurately, these theories, for there are several, are unlike transformational grammar in any of its forms or case grammar, in that they disallow in principle a distinction between deep and surface structure. Indeed there is only one level of syntactic representation in functional grammar, namely surface structure. At a level of functional representation, both semantic roles and grammatical relations are represented, as are more discourse-oriented notions of theme and topic. There are alternative versions of functional grammar (i.e., Kac, 1978; Prideaux, 1979b) in which syntactic structure is represented by the familiar constituent structure trees, while functional representations are treated as in terms of statements indicating what grammatical roles are played by each constitutent. In these versions, unlike Dik's, grammatical roles are elaborated and participate in functional statements, but semantic roles do not. Functional theories are concerned with more than the structure of sentences. They are also concerned with how the structures are used by speakers as coding devices for representing various kinds of information.

Lexical functional grammar. A further theoretical position which has emerged from the transformational tradition, but which rejects many of the basic principles of transformational theory is that of lexical functional grammar as articulated by Bresnan and her co-workers (e.g., Bresnan, 1981, 1982; Bresnan & Kaplan, 1982). This theory defines two levels of grammatical representation, a level of constituent structure ("c-structure") corresponding to the familiar notion of surface structure, and a level of functional structure ("f-structure"). The functional structure for a given sentence specifies the grammatical relations which each major constituent play, represented in a language-independent notation which is not tied to the syntactic form of the sentence. The grammatical functions are universal notions such as subject, object, and oblique.

An important aspect of lexical functional grammar is the role played by the lexicon. Each lexical item is formulated in terms of the *arguments* that particular item may or must take. Thus, for a sentence like (18), taken from Bresnan (1981):

18. Fred handed a toy to the baby.

the constituent structure would be of the familiar sort, namely a labeled tree. The functional structure assigned to the sentence would be determined in part by the lexical form of the main predicate, *hand*, which Bresnan (1981, p. 44) sketches as (19).

19. *hand* ((SUBJ), (OBJ), (OBLgoal)).

Introduction

According to the theory, each grammatical relation must be assigned a *thematic role*, so, for example, the subject of the verb *hand* may be assigned the role of semantic *source*, the object the role of *theme*, and the oblique the role of *goal*. That is, the verb *hand* requires the *predicate argument* structure of *"source, theme, goal."* Clearly, the pairing of a particular semantic argument with a specific grammatical relation is not unique, since for a sentence like (20):

20. Fred handed the baby a toy.

the same semantic arguments are present, but they are assigned to different grammatical roles, since in this latter case, the lexical form of the verb *hand* is (Bresnan, 1981, p. 45):

21. *hand* ((SUBJ), (OBJ2), (OBJ)).

In lexical functional grammar, the relation between (18) and (20) is not treated in terms of a transformation which alters constituent structure, but rather in terms of a lexical rule which relates the two lexical forms (19) and (21). Thus, lexical functional grammar rejects the traditional transformational notion that sentences must be assigned underlying "normalized" syntactic representations.

One of the motivations for the development of lexical functional grammar is the desire to construct a grammatical theory which is psychologically plausible and potentially "realistic." Like various versions of functional grammar, and to some extent like relational grammar, lexical functional grammar emphasizes the representation of functional information independently of constituent structure, although once represented, such information must be paired with the appropriate constituent structure for a given language.

Here, again, we find a theory which has developed out of transformational grammar but which has incorporated as primitive terms both grammatical relations and semantic roles, while at the same time rejecting the notion of transformation. More importantly, however, the evolution of lexical functional theory has been motivated at least in part by the recognition that linguistic theory must be responsible to psychological contraints. To this end, attempts have recently been made to provide evidence for the theory from both the realms of language acquisition (Pinker, 1982) and language processing (Ford, Bresnan, & Kaplan, 1982; Ford, 1982).

1.4 Some Important Distinctions

Before closing this chapter, it is useful to draw some basic distinctions in order to facilitate discussion in the following chapters. First, the position adopted here is that a grammar of whatever kind (transformational, functional, etc.) constitutes a description of the *language product*. That is, the grammar describes the structure of sentences and their relationships. The grammar is not a description of the *processes* through which the speaker goes as he utters a sentence or through which the hearer goes as he engages in his task of comprehension. Whether or not the grammar somehow characterizes such steps, either directly or indirectly, is an empirical issue.

Moreover, a distinction must also be drawn between a *grammatical* process, such as a transformational rule, and a *psychological* process, which deals with how a language user employs his knowledge of his language. A grammatical process does not necessarily represent a psychological process.

A further distinction will be drawn between *grammaticality* and *acceptability*. These two terms are often used interchangeably in the linguistic literature, but for the sake of clarity, we will define *grammaticality* operationally as follows: A particular linguistic form (e.g., sentence) is *grammatical* if it is generated or described by a particular grammar. If not, the form is *ungrammatical*. Thus, according to this definition, grammaticality is a binary notion, defined in terms of a particular grammar. If, for example, a given grammar does not deal with passive sentences in Japanese, then any particular Japanese passive sentence will by definition be ungrammatical with respect to that grammar. *Acceptability*, on the other hand, refers to native speaker judgements about particular linguistic forms. Acceptability judgements may reflect grammatical well-formedness, appropriateness in a given context, and a host of other factors. For example, the sentence "John gave Sue a flower" might be judged acceptable in isolation, but in response to the question "What did John bring to the party?" it might be judged inappropriate and unacceptable. According to this operational definition, acceptability is not a binary notion predicated upon a particular grammar, but is instead a matter of native speaker judgement as assessed against a variety of criteria. Consequently acceptability is a relative matter.

Finally, a distinction must be maintained between *competence* and *performance*. *Competence* refers to what one knows about his language, including his implicit knowledge of the grammar, the rules of use and convention, the rules of discourse, and the like. *Performance* refers to how that knowledge is put to use. Thus, when one comprehends a particular sentence, he must *know* the grammatical structures, and their functions, and he must *execute* various psychological processes as he constructs the meaning representation for that utterance.

These distinctions have all played important roles in linguistic discussions over the past decade or so, and all are highly charged and often controversial. We will return to many of these in our discussion of the experimental research in the following chapters.

1.5 Summary

In this chapter, we have adopted the position that linguistics is an empirical discipline with a commitment to empirical facts from a variety of sources. We have argued that experimental evidence constitutes a primary source of data for the linguist committed to an investigation of psychological processes, states, rules, and representations. We have furthermore explored a variety of problems associated with experimental data, as well as with data from other sources. We have discussed in some detail the nature of experiments and have informally defined certain terms involved in their design.

A second function of this chapter has been to outline in relatively brief terms some current aspects of linguistic theory. We have touched briefly on transformational grammar as well as on case grammar, relational grammar, and various kinds of functional grammar. All of these proposals constitute grist for the empirical mill to the extent that they provide hypotheses which can be empirically tested. The remainder of this book is devoted to an examination of such empirical questions from a variety of areas, including morphology, syntax, and semantics.

EXERCISES

1.1. Define, with examples, (a) independent variable, (b) dependent variable, (c) confounding variable, and (d) replication.

1.2. Results of a study designed to assess relative acceptability of various sentences indicated that subjects found the (a) members of each of the following pairs to be less acceptble than the (b) members. For each pair, offer an explanation as to why this might be the case.

1. a. Judy anticipated exciting sailors at the party.
   b. Judy expected interesting sailors at the party.

2. a. Fred hated visiting relatives.
   b. Fred expected visiting relatives.

3. a. The stewardess stopped smoking in the aisles.
   b. The stewardess forbade smoking in the aisles.

4. a. Sally cut up the steak which Fred had cooked.
   b. Sally cut the steak which Fred had cooked up.

1.3. Construct an experiment to test the hypothesis that longer sentences are relatively harder to comprehend that shorter sentences. Use an operational definition to quantify sentence length. Explain your independent and dependent variables. Construct some stimulus sentences, and on the basis of these suggest some potentially confounding variables.

1.4. Dialects are generally associated with geographical distinctions. However, dialects may also be defined in terms of social levels, situational contexts, sex, etc. Suggest some ways in which social differences in politeness levels are reflects in the language we use. Offer some lexical and structural examples of the differences between the language of men and women.

1.5. Ask a friend to let you tape record his brief oral description of a movie he has recently seen or a book he has read. Transcribe the oral version faithfully in conventional orthography, but preserving all hesitation forms, pauses, false starts, etc. Then edit the transcript, reducing it to conventional written English. Enumerate the differences you find between the oral and written forms. Are the two really different versions of the "same language" or not? Why?

1.6. For what reasons would you be suspicious of accepting texts from a dead language as truly representative of that language as it was spoken?

1.7. A sentence like "Scots like spaghetti more than the Irish" is presumably at least two ways ambiguous. What are the two meanings? In what way could the linguistic context for such a sentence remove the ambiguity? Give examples.

1.8. Enumerate as many factors as you can think of which could contribute to our judgement as to the acceptability of a sentence. Indicate why each factor is important.

1.9. Why should a distinction be drawn between grammatical roles and semantic roles? Are these just different names for the same notions or not? Give examples to justify your answers.

LABORATORY

Laboratory 1. Variation   in   Acceptability
                   Judgements

Chapter Two

THE DOMAIN OF EXPERIMENTAL LINGUISTICS

2.1 Introduction.

In this chapter we shall explore three major areas of concern for experimental linguistics, namely language comprehension, production, and acquisition. We shall attempt to uncover the kinds of problems the language user faces when he is involved in the task of language comprehension as well as the processes he unconsciously employs as he constructs meaning representations for sentences. Then we shall turn to language production and try to specify the steps and stages which the speaker must execute as he produces language. Since an understanding of how children learn their first language is informative and indeed crucial to discovering the rules, structures, and representations the human language processor actually uses, we shall finally delve into the issues of first language acquisition. In each of these three major sections, we shall direct major attention to a specification of the logically necessary kinds of conditions which must be satisfied in order for language processing to take place.

2.2 Comprehension

In this section, we attempt to establish the kinds of processes that must take place and the kinds of goals that must be satisfied in the act of language comprehension. The remarks which follow are concerned with the insights about comprehension which can be gained by serious reflection and introspection, and as such they can at best constitute only starting points for empirical investigation. They are not themselves answers, but rather questions which provide directions and guidance when we search for an understanding of the actual nature of comprehension.

An important point to be kept in mind during the following discussion is that language comprehension is a dynamic, active process in which the hearer is engaged as he constructs a semantic representation in his mind. He takes as input the noise he hears, plus a vast array of other linguistic and extralinguistic information. He is aware of the preceding linguistic context and the topic under discussion. He is aware, for example, of the roles of various participants in the discussion. He has a vast stock of extralinguistic information and world-knowledge to which he can constantly advert. He has expectations built up from the conversation. He has an idea about what the other participants know in relation to the discussion. In short, the hearer has a multitude of resources to aid him in constructing a mental representation of the message. Of course, he relies heavily on his knowledge of the language in interpreting the incoming phonological signals, but the fact that he has other and varied cues must not be lost sight of. Clearly then, language comprehension is not a passive act in which the hearer's mind is written upon by the speaker but rather an active, highly involved set of processes.

When we hear someone speaking a language we do not know, we are immediately struck with the complexity of its sound system. We notice those aspects which are unlike our own system, and generally we form a quick impression as to what that language sounds like. Arabic may be heard as "gutteral" (whatever that means), while Chinese may be labelled "singsong," for example. But in order to understand a message, which after all is the final goal of comprehension, the hearer must somehow execute a phonological analysis of the incoming stream of noise. He must quickly form an acoustic image in his mind -- a representation on which he can operate. That is, he must construct an appropriate phonological segmentation for the incoming utterace.

A second task is for the hearer to carry out a rough and ready morphological analysis. This is only possible if there exists a phonological representation, along with at least a preliminary mental chunking of the utterance. Obviously, the morphological segmentation and analysis takes place concurrently with the incoming noise analysis. It makes little sense to suggest that a complete phonological analysis takes place before any morphological analysis begins. Suppose, for example, that we hear the sentence:

1. Germans like beer more than Spaniards.

We notice immediately that the sentence is ambiguous, although in a particular context one meaning or another may be virtually automatic in the hearer's mind simply because it is congruent with the discourse as it has developed to that point. The point of the example, however, is that even if we carry out a complete phonological and morphological analysis, there is still much more to be done. That is, the hearer must also assign some further linguistic structure beyond that of morpheme classification.

The example in (1) suggests that some measure of grammatical structure must be assigned by the hearer to a sentence he is processing. Whether the structure assigned mentally by the hearer is similar to that which the linguist posits is itself an important empirical question. For example, in the instance cited above, does the hearer simply assign functional information to the sentence, so that in one reading of the sentence, *Spaniards* is understood as the subject of an implicit ("understood") verb phrase *like beer*, while in the other interpretation it is the direct object of an implicit *like* whose subject is still *Germans*? Or, alternatively, does the hearer actually construct mental constituent structures, one for each reading of the sentence? Here again, the question cannot be answered in the absence of empirical evidence.

As a second example of the hearer's need to assign grammatical structure to sentences, let us consider Chomsky's (1964) celebrated pair of sentences:

2 a. John is eager to please.
 b. John is easy to please.

It is with these examples that Chomsky argues that surface structures may be very similar while the meanings are very different. The native speaker, for example, recognizes that (2a) may mean that John is eager to please somebody, or even anybody. More explicitly, *John* is the logical (deep structure) subject of both *eager* and *please*, while *please* is a transitive verb with an empty or unspecified direct object. However, (2a) can be paraphrased as

3 a. It is easy (for someone) to please John.
 b. (For someone) to please John is easy.

These last two examples reveal that *John* is the logical object of *please*, while an unspecified NP is the subject. However, it is not at all clear from these examples that the hearer assigns grammatical relations to various lexical items or whether he actually constructs a constituent structure representation for each, or perhaps both. The matter is an empirical one, and to conclude from the fact that the native speaker can make the judgements represented in (2) and (3) that he must *necessarily* assign deep and surface constituent structures to these (and all) sentences he hears is to engage in a dramatic leap in logic.

Nevertheless, the examples cited so far suggest that in the act of comprehension, at least phonological, morphological, and some form of grammatical analysis must take place. What else is needed? Clearly, some sort of lexical look-up is also required. The hearer must find a given lexical item in his mental dictionary, along with its various meanings, and integrate these into the sentence. He must execute such lexical searches very rapidly, and he must also assess the appropriateness of certain lexical items in relation to others. Let us consider the examples in (4):

4 a. Fred elapsed for an hour.
   b. Fred slept for an hour.
   c. To sang the quickly all Fred frogs.

It is immediately obvious that something is wrong with (4a), and this suggests that the hearer must be able to recognize semantic (and grammatical) anomaly. He must be able to make at least two kinds of judgements here: he must recognize that a sentence like (4a) is syntactically well-formed, having as it does a word order of NP V PP, paralleling the syntactically and semantically well-formed (4b). However, (4a) is semantically ill-formed, since the verb *elapse* does not select a human subject noun, while *sleep* does. Moreover, this is a different kind of judgement from that which allows him to recognize that a string of words like (4c) is simply not structurally well-formed, quite independent of the meaning of the various words.

We have seen that the assignment of grammatical relations such as subject and direct object seems to be required in sentence comprehension, but what about the assignment of semantic relations? Surely, these are needed too, since the goal of the hearer is to comprehend, or more accurately, to *(re)construct* the message. Accordingly, it is important that in his formulation of the message, the hearer must establish the semantic roles of various participants and events in the discourse. He must know, in short, who is doing what, to whom, when, where, why, etc. This suggests that the hearer must assign not only semantic roles to various nouns, but also that the lexical meanings of the various nouns, verbs, adjectives, etc. are involved in this assignment. For example, the hearer knows that the verb *kiss* normally requires an animate, probably human, Agent, and in the Active voice, this is typically represented in the subject NP. Accordingly, he can assign the role of Agent to *Sue* in the sentence

5. Sue kissed the old dog sitting beside her.

However, the hearer would be reluctant to assign the role of Agent to *Sue* in the sentence:

6. Sue is a lovely young lady.

simply because the adjective *beautiful* does not represent an action and does not select an Agent subject. In addition to semantic roles for various constituents, the hearer must also discern the differences among various sentence types simply in order to recognize the distinction between a statement, a command, and a question.

It is clear from this cursory survey that the hearer engages in a great deal of constructive activity when comprehending language. To this point we have discussed only the comprehension of single sentences, but obviously each sentence must be integrated into a larger discourse structure, and how that is done is also a complex issue. Moreover, the steps outlined above are at best only minimal constraints which need to be satisfied if language comprehension is to take place. These steps are *not* to be taken literally as a set of operations executed sequentially in real time. They are not an algorithm for the comprehension processes themselves.

Problems. Some interesting problems and questions associated with this view of comprehension are immediately apparent. One of the most obvious concerns the issue of time-sharing. If steps involving phonological, morphological, syntactic, and semantic analyses are all a part of the active comprehension process, do they go on simultaneously or are they sequential? How much attention is paid, for example, to a close and detailed phonological analysis, and how much to lexical look-up? Only a moment's reflection is needed to reveal one important point: the hearer does not wait until he has an entire sentence represented phonologically before he begins other steps. The time-sharing aspect of the problem can be graphically illustrated by considering what happens when we first listen to the speech of someone with a distinct foreign or otherwise unexpected accent. At first, the accent itself, that is, the phonological system of the speaker, demands considerable attention, often to the extent that the meanings of utterances are lost as we try to cope with the phonology. In such a case, much more time and attention are devoted to the phonology than is normally the case, and consequently less time and attention are available for the other processes required for comprehension. However, once we have adjusted to the accent, our comprehension increases; now we might begin to notice syntactic pecularities or strange lexical choices, but at least the phonology is somehow accommodated. In short, the time-sharing problem is real. We would expect that the more familiar the hearer is with the speaker's phonology, the less of a problem that will be. Similarly, the more familiar he is with lexical items or grammatical structures, the less difficulty these pose. In short, the more familiar we are with the structural properties of the message, assuming some viable notion of "familiar," the easier it is to begin to construct the semantic representation for an utterance.

A second major issue concerns the nature of the structure which a hearer must construct in his comprehension process. This issue is particularly important since the kind of grammatical structure which the hearer constructs will serve to guide and constrain the linguist's description. Does the hearer construct a phrase structure representation for sentences, and if so, is it of the form postulated by linguists? That is, does the hearer construct a mental representation corresponding to a surface structure phrase marker? To a deep structure phrase marker? To both? To neither? And most importantly, how do we know? Just because a particular linguistic theory postulates a particular kind of syntactic representation, such as a surface structure tree, in the description of the language product, does it necessarily follow that the hearer also constructs such a representation?

To give this issue empirical content requires empirical evidence about what the hearer, and not just the linguist as analyst, actually does. Such evidence may come from a variety of sources, but it must crucially reflect actual language processing and not just the linguist's analytic notions as to how a particular theory would structure the sentences. If we consider this issue as it relates to phonology, we can ask if the linguist's phonological representation is what the hearer adverts to in his phonological analysis, or whether he perhaps makes use of syllables or other even larger chunks such as phonological phrases. Of course, the hearer may use several units, including segments, features of segments, and larger, syllable-like units as well. There is no *a priori* guarantee that only one unit is used at the phonological level, or at any other level, for that matter. The issue of the nature and size of units involved in comprehension is again an empirical one. Just because a particular theory opts for one kind of unit, possibly on the grounds of simplicity or economy of representation, does not ensure that the hearer is doing the same.

In summary, the issue here is the extent to which the structures and rules postulated by the linguist are actually learned and used by real live speakers and hearers. The relation between the linguist's postulated constructs and the language user's actual structures will be explored in detail in Chapter Four.

A third problem with the view of comprehension set out above is the extent to which hearers might use various short cuts or heuristics in their analysis of sentences. If, for example, certain structures, or structural properties, are extremely common, then these might serve as templates such that when a part of a sentence seems to fit a template, the hearer could anticipate with a high degree of confidence that some other properties of the template are coming. That is, he could make educated guesses -- predictions that a certain kind of structure is involved and that certain kinds of constituents should appear at particular places. For example, upon hearing the definite article *the* in English, we expect that we are moving into a noun phrase, with the further expectation that, for example, an adjective may be coming and that a noun must eventually appear to head the phrase. If a preposition is encountered, a NP object is expected; if a transitive verb is identified, a NP direct object is anticipated somewhere. Surely the hearer can expect such structural signals to aid in his construction of semantic representations for sentences. Moreover, it may be the case that some of the cues are language-specific, such as those just mentioned, while others may well be far more general. For example, in the sentence:

7 a. The man expected to win the election died.

we notice that after *election* there is a natural stopping place, even though the sentence goes on. The stopping place is a result of the fact that English is basically a subject-verb-object (SVO) language. In (7a), *election* is the direct object of *win*, and it appears that *expected* is the main verb, with *man* as its subject. However, once we encounter *died*, we are forced to reassess the sentence and interpret *expected* as a passive participle as in (7b):

7 b. The man who was expected to win the election died.

Examples such as (7a) are often called "garden path" sentences, since the hearer is led down the garden path toward one interpretation, only to be brought up short when the sentence does not end where he expects it to. Our treatment of such sentences suggests that there may be a general strategy which leads us to anticipate the completion of a sentence at the earliest possible point. This strategy generally serves the hearer quite well, and it is just in those cases where the strategy does not work that we are even aware of the existence of our anticipation of early closure. Again, the issue here is two-fold: what are the possible strategies which might be expected to be a part of the hearer's battery of comprehension heuristics, and how do we determine empirically whether or not a particular strategy does indeed exist and is operating? This issue of cognitive strategies is also addressed in Chapter Four.

Another problem, and one with enormous scope, involves the question of how the hearer utilizes his own knowledge of the world and his awareness of the contents and direction of both the preceding linguistic and extralinguistic context as aids in comprehension. Suppose, for example, one hears the following:

8. It was great fun. I especially enjoyed the last murder.

Obviously the hearer would give such an utterance one interpretation if the speaker were discussing a movie he had recently seen, but quite another if he had recently participated in a prison riot. Just how is the hearer's awareness of the context integrated into the construction of the meaning of the utterance? He must have certain expectations resulting from his knowledge of the topic under discussion, but an explicit hypothesis as to how he accesses such knowledge, and how he uses it to facilitate the interpretation of the sentence is difficult to imagine. Or consider a situation in which two people are gazing out the window onto a snowcovered winter landscape, and one says to the other:

9. It is really a great day.

Under certain conditions, such a statement may be taken for irony, but if both are ardent skiers, then it may be a simple statement of enthusiastic anticipation. In such a case, it is the hearer's knowledge of his companion which permits one or the other interpretation.

Knowledge of the linguistic context and its effect on the interpretation of a given utterance is crucial in assessing the contribution that discourse makes to sentence comprehension. In the usual cases, where discourse flows smoothly, we are generally unaware of the vastly important role played by our assessment of the surrounding linguistic context, but once that context seems to be violated, even in subtle ways, we are at once aware of the disruption. It is often the case that a sentence which seems perfectly acceptable in isolation, and which even appears thematically related to a particular discourse, may cause us to trip up mentally when it is inserted into the discourse. For example, the sentence

10. He opened the door and quickly came in.

appears perfectly acceptable, so long as we can find an antecedent for *he*. However, if we consider the following context, (10) does not seem to fit as a final sentence.

11. The shabby young man was standing across the street, gazing through the plate glass window into the brightly lighted restaurant. He looked to the left and the right, saw that no one was walking on his side of the street, and quickly pulled a gun from his pocket. He ...

Why does (10) not fit? What would make it fit? The problem seems to lie with the verb *come*. If the sentence had read as in (12a) or (12b), all would have been well:

12 a. He opened the door and quickly entered.
   b. He opened the door and quickly went in.

The problem with the appropriateness of (10) as a last line to (11) is simply that the "camera angle" or perspective set up in (11) is violated by (10). The passage in (11) establishes a perspective from the point of view of someone standing across the street from the restaurant. The movement of the shabby young man into the restaurant is therefore *away* from the imagined narrator, not toward him, and movement away from the speaker's point of view is represented by *go*, not *come*. This matter of *deixis* is implicit in the two verbs, but it is neutralized in a verb like *enter*, in which either movement toward or away from the speaker is allowed. Such contextual issues become especially noteworthy when they are violated.

These are only a few of the problems which must be addressed in an empirical study of the processes involved in language comprehension. Let us now turn to an examination of language production and try to formulate, via introspection and reflection, what must go on when a speaker produces a sentence.

2.3 Production

What does the speaker do when he utters a sentence? We will attempt to answer the question by sketching some of the operations which the speaker must logically execute, although again we must bear in mind that these are not necessarily sequential, such that one is completed before the

49

next begins, nor are they all independent. Indeed, some of the proposed steps may in fact overlap or interrelate.

It is only charitable to assume that before a speaker utters a sentence, he has something to say. That is, he presumably has at least the rough idea of a *message* which he wishes to convey. What the shape of the message is, whether it is initially represented in some linguistic or extralinguistic form, is open to debate. Moreover, we shall not belabor the issue of why one particular message rather than some other is encoded. We are not concerned with the various circumstances in which the speaker finds himself such that he wishes to communicate some piece of information, nor with the issue of why such information is important. We simply take as a starting place that the speaker has something to say.

At some point, either initially or early in the logical sequence of events, the message must be represented semantically, possibly in terms of a set of propositions or the like, with semantic roles assigned, predicates selected, and even various lexical items, or sets of semantic features, chosen. Suppose, for example, the speaker for some reason wants to say:

13. Sam chased away the dog.

At some point, the semantic representation associated with (13) must contain at least something like:

14. *Sam* = AGT *(chase away)*
    the dog = PAT *(chase away)*
    Speech Act = Statement
    Time of Action – Past

The semantic representation of the sentence might also be represented propositionally as something like:

15. Prop = *chase away* (AGT(*Sam*), PAT(*the dog*)).

Of course, additional information is required stating that the semantic tense is "past," the Speech Act function is "Statement," etc. The notation in (15) is intended to indicate the make-up of the basic *proposition* of the sentence, which consists of a *predicate*, in this case the verb *chase away*, and its two *arguments*, namely an Agent, *Sam*, and a Patient, *the dog*. The two representations of (14) and (15) are just alternative means of spelling out the semantic representations in a convenient notation.

Some sentences represent more than one semantic proposition and may, for example, contain relative clauses or other kinds of structures. Sometimes, such semantically complex sentences are not syntactically transparent; that is, there is no reason why a syntactic representation should necessarily have the same number of clauses as semantic propositions. Consider, for example, the following two sentences:

16 a. I expected Sue to leave early.
   b. I expected to leave early.

In both these sentences, the semantic object of the main clause predicate *expect* is itself a proposition. That is, if we call P_1 the proposition associated with the main clause and P_2 the proposition associated with the subordinate clause, and if we treat the subject NP *I* as the semantic Experiencer (EXP) of the psychological verb *expect*, we can represent the propositional semantic structures of the two sentences in (16) as (17a) and (17b) respectively.

17 a. P_1 = *expect* (EXP(*I*), OBJ(P_2))
      P_2 = *leave* (AGT(*Sue*), TIME(*early*))
   b. P_1 = *expect* (EXP(*I*), OBJ(P_2))
      P_2 = *leave* (AGT(*I*), TIME(*early*))

It is clear from the two representations in (17) that the only difference in the two sentences is that in the second, the Agent of the second proposition is *I* while in the first sentence the Agent is *Sue*. This difference is reflected in the difference in grammatical functions assigned for the two sentences. In both, the grammatical subject of the main verb is *I* (i.e., *I* = SUBJ (*expect*)), but in (16a) the (overt) subject of the embedded clause is

Sue (*Sue* = SUBJ (*leave*)), while in (16b) the subject is implicitly *I* (i.e., *I* = SUBJ (*leave*)). The grammar of English treats these two cases differently in terms of structural assignment: if the subjects of the two clauses are not the same, both NPs must be overtly present in the surface structure, but if the two functional subject NPs are identical, then the second is not represented at the surface. In transformational terms, the subject of the embedded clause is, under certain conditions, deleted when it is identical to the subject of the main clause.

This brief example illustrates just how very complex semantic representations can be, and, more importantly, it demonstrates that there is no strict requirement for a one-to-one mapping between a proposition and a surface constituent structure. A similar exercise could be carried out with the *easy*/*eager* sentences in (2) and (3). At any rate, for our present purposes this exercise suggests that once a semantic representation has been formulated, it must be converted into a grammatical representation, perhaps in terms of functional statements or of phrase markers. Once the functional information has been formulated, a (surface) constituent structure can then be assigned. This structure is of course a matter of language-specific rules. For example, English as a SVO language generally has the subject before the verb and the object following, while an SOV language like Japanese has a different constituent structure.

One factor not to be lost sight of in the present discussion concerns lexical selection. It would appear from our discussion above that the semantic representation itself must somehow incorporate lexical items, or at least the meanings of lexical items. That is, the meanings of the words which enter into the sentence must be present very early in the formulation of the sentence. With the construction of a surface structure phrase marker containing lexical items, various morphophonemic rules come into play to assign the phonological shapes to grammatical morphemes such as tense, number, etc., and any irregularities must also be taken care of. Thus, if the sentence is to contain the plural of *dog*, the form *dogs* must be selected, although such irregular plural forms as *men* and *feet* must also be taken into account.

Finally, it should be clear that a final logical, if not real-time, step is needed to convert the phonological sequence into a phonetic representation, to send appropriate messages to the vocal system, and to have appropriate noises emitted. Moreover, during the emission of noises, and indeed during the entire process of language production, a constant feedback monitoring is taking place, such that the speaker can alter, reroute, or even restart the processes. All in all, the speaker's activities in producing language are highly complex and very involved.

Problems. Here, as in the case of comprehension, some obvious problems arise as a function of the choices we have made in partitioning the production processes into separate steps. We must, however, again stress that the various steps outlined above are not to be understood as taking place in a sequence such that one step is completed before the next begins. Rather, it is entirely plausible to assume that a great deal of time-sharing goes on, such that some aspects are being carried out at the same time as others. Moreover, a moment's reflection indicates that we do not work out the entire plan for a sentence before beginning it, although such a strategy may be fairly common for people just beginning in a second language. Clearly, if we first devote attention to establishing a message, and then consciously focus on how to execute it, we would have no time or attention for what others are saying. The very fact that discourse takes place so rapidly is support for the time-sharing aspects involved.

A second problem, and one alluded to above, concerns the role of lexical search or lexical look-up in relation to the formulation of a message. For example, it is an empirical question whether or not the actual lexical items are selected when the semantic representation of the message is being formulated or whether just some aspects of their meanings are involved. If the latter is the case, we

53

are forced to make precise what we intend by the notion of the meaning of a word -- do we intend a complete, precise, and exhaustive specification, a rather vague and general aspect of the meaning, a network of several lexical items bound together by semantic commonalities, .or what? This is a most difficult question, but one which cries out for an answer if we are serious about the empirical nature of the enterprise.

A further problematical issue in the formulation of the steps for sentence production involves the kind of syntactic constituent structure assigned by the speaker. Does he really need to assign constituent structure, or is this only necessary in comprehension, if even there? Can the speaker satisfy his goals by simply assigning grammatical functions to lexical items and then linearizing them without access to or need for the assignment of a hierarchical structure? What would count for evidence one way or the other? This question is directly related to one we discussed with respect to comprehension, namely, to what extent is the structure proposed by the linguist required by the speaker?

Yet another problem involves the speaker's incorporation of his knowledge of the world and of the current linguistic and extralinguistic context in the formulation of his utterance. If a great deal of information is assumed by the speaker to be shared by the hearer(s), then certain shortcuts become possible, while if little information is presumed to be shared, more elaboration is required. For example, (18a) would be appropriate in some contexts, but as a first sentence in a conversation, it would be bizarre. However, (18b) could be a natural conversation initiator.

18 a. I really enjoyed it too.
b. When did you get back to town?

Each of these maxims guides the speaker as he formulates and executes his sentences. Moreover, he accommodates his speech in such a manner that the thread of discourse is kept alive. To illustrate this, consider the question in (19a), along with the possible responses (19b) and (19c), and the inappropriate response (19d):

   19 a. Who broke the clock in the hall?
       b. Jason broke it.
       c. It was Jason who broke the clock / it.
       d. It was the clock which Jason broke.

What is wrong with (19d)? It is a perfectly good, acceptable sentence in isolation, but it is not a good answer to the question. Presumably, the reason for the inappropriateness of (19d) resides in the fact that the question itself is asked under the assumption that the hearer knows that someone broke the clock. That is, the statement "Someone broke the clock in the hall" is *presupposed* by the question. Both answers (19b) and (19c) are formulated in terms of that presupposition, since they provide answers to the *who* part of the question. However, (19d) does not share this presupposition; rather it presupposes that "Jason broke something." That is, (19d) does not fit into the exchange appropriately simply because it violates a presupposition of the question. Native speakers are quite aware of such disruptions as that resulting from (19d) when they occur. Otherwise, things move smoothly along, with the presuppositions being well-linked in the discourse. Just what aspects of sentence production, and in particular what aspects of sentence planning, are involved here? This and similar questions can be addressed empirically, as we shall show later, but it is first necessary to demonstrate that we have a reliable phenomenon, and then attempt to discover what underlies it.

Yet another problem in the study of language production is that of the nature of the rules which the native speaker knows and uses in his production. We must establish on an empirical basis those rules which the speaker uses to relate the meaning of a sentence to its form, even though we recognize that the chain of rules may be long and complex. Moreover, we must be able to construct experimental contexts which allow us to choose from among various hypothesized rules. Techniques for accessing such information are often complex and difficult to establish, although the challenge of devising appropriate methodologies and experiments is paramount. In the absence of such methodologies, we are destined to remain in the thrall of unstructured introspection, both as a source of hypotheses and as a source of data.

Before leaving the discussion of language production entirely, one final issue needs to be addressed, namely whether language comprehension might not simply be the reverse of language production. Since in comprehension we begin with a phonetic input and move toward formulation of a message, while in production we start with a message and move toward the phonetic representation of that message, is it not plausible that the two processes are just mirror images of each other? If so, once we have established the empirical content of the comprehension process, we have automatically solved the production issue too.

However, a moment's reflection will indicate why comprehension and production cannot be mirror images. First, in production, the speaker has a message to communicate, and he wishes to encode that message for his hearer. But the hearer does not have a message, just a set of noises. His goal is to decode the signal and reconstruct the message. He uses quite different strategies from the speaker, along the lines discussed above. The hearer may make skillful guesses as to where the speaker is headed in his utterance, and of course those guesses may be incorrect. For example, the ambiguity of a sentence like (1) or (7) above is problem for the hearer, not for the speaker. Moreover, the speaker's intended messager may not be fully realized by the hearer, who, in constructing a semantic representation, builds up his perceived message. It is even plausible that the hearer never actually gets the exact message intended by the speaker. Strategies for the speaker and hearer may be quite different; lexical items may have very different flavors for the two; one may favor certain syntactic ways of delivering messages which the other finds difficult or off-center. In short, the two activities of speaking and listening are quite different and appear to involve very different processes.

2.4 Language Acquisition

Preliminaries. Normal children in normal circumstances learn the language of their community with ease and with little or no tutoring. In fact, child language acquisition is such a natural and normal phenomenon that we often pay little attention to it other than to inquire politely of our friends if little Johnny is talking yet. Yet language acquisition provides an important source of data for the linguist. The way in which language develops in the child, the kinds of errors he makes (errors from the adult point of view, at least, but probably not from the child's), the stages through which he passes, his use of specific words in ways strikingly different from adult use, and a host of other factors provide the linguist with a vast array of information. Acquisition data are so important simply because if a person uses a specific word, rule, or structure, then that word, rule, or structure must have been acquired. The child's acquisition processes reflect his struggles and strategies in coming to terms with his language. As he passes through various stages, he may try, then reject, some form or structure in favor of another. An understanding of language acquisition can shed light on which segments and forms are learned, which rules are learned, and what steps, stages, or sequences the child passes through as he develops a growing command of his language.

There are various quite distinct views about the nature of language acquisition. Some scholars have felt that language acquisition is best represented as the learning of individual words and patterns which take place in accordance with behaviorist principles of learning theory. Such a view eschews a complex mental structure and instead opts for a stimulus-response view of learning. This position is now seldom championed, since it has become obvious that language knowledge and use involves highly complex mental operations and activities.

A second, cognitivist, view of language acquisition assumes that the human is born with a highly enriched cognitive structure, in which some, or much, of the language faculty is "pre-wired" or innate. The problem with this position is just how much of the language facility is indeed innate and how much must be learned. According to the view held by Chomsky (i.e., 1965; 1975; 1982a) and his followers (e.g., Lightfoot, 1982; Tavakolian, 1981), a very large amount of the language faculty is innate, with a restricted range of possible variation along certain dimensions (e.g., word order, possible rules, etc.) which is fixed within the child through his exposure to the language of his community. The motivation for the nativist position is found in the assertion that the principles and systems involved in grammars are so abstract and complex that they could not possibly be learned, given any coherent theory of learning. This view rests on the claim that the formal principles of grammar offered by the linguist are necessarily isomorphic with those represented mentally.

Alternative mentalistic views of language acquisition are also possible. One such suggests that there is no highly specific and autonomous language faculty at all, but instead language arises from the interaction of quite general cognitive processes. According to this view, language is not substantially different from a host of other cognitive skills, and indeed the appearance of a unique language faculty arises through the intersection of several general cognitive domains.

Another alternative position, and one which stands as a kind of middle ground between the two extreme mentalist versions, suggests that the innate structures, while necessary, are quite general, with far less detailed structure than Chomsky would require. Given any position, it is of course necessary to determine just how much of the language faculty is innate and what its structure is like. Within any mentalist version of language acquisition, however, great importance is placed on the cognitive basis for language and on the specific details of what is actually learned and used.

Two further aspects of a cognitivist approach to language acquisition should also be mentioned here. The first is that most such approaches, with the possible exception of the view denying the existence of a particular language faculty, opt for a more or less modular view of language in which various autonomous components are postulated. According to this view, a grammar, itself consisting of several components, constitutes just one of several interacting modules. Others might be belief systems, discourse constraints, world knowledge, and the like. One advantage of adopting a modular view is that it permits a research strategy in which particular phenomena can be studied in isolation. But a concomitant disadvantage is that a correct understanding of the phenomenon might be blurred by considering only one aspect and ignoring other, potentially crucial, factors.

A further aspect of a cognitivist approach to language acquisition centers on where one wishes to place major research effort. In the approach developed by Chomsky and his colleagues, major effort is directed to an articulation of the formal properties of various grammatical systems. Others, while still holding to a cognitivist perspective, direct their attention to the kinds of strategies children employ as they develop their linguistic systems (cf., e.g., Derwing, 1973; 1977; Slobin, 1979). The latter approach focuses attention not so much on a detailed development of the abstract properties of a formal system, but rather on the surface structures actually manifest in children's language behavior. Here, the child's strategies, along with the pragmatic factors defining the larger context of his language environment, are given primary attention. According the the former view, the child is often viewed as a "little linguist" going about the task of hypothesis testing and theory construction (cf. Kiparsky & Menn, 1977), while in the latter perspective, the child's primary task is seen as one in which he is learning to communicate, with the development of his grammar subservient to that more pressing need (cf. Derwing, 1977).

In the early 1960s, when much important basic research in language acquisition was being carried out, a commonly held view was that the child was indeed a "little linguist," learning grammatical structures via hypothesis testing heuristics. Such a view was explicitly adopted, for example, by Klima and Bellugi (1966, p. 191), who were primarily interested not with semantic or grammatical relations but instead with the way in which the child

"...handles lower-level syntactic phenomena like position, permutability, and the like." Similarly, McNeill (1966, p. 99) argued that the child acquires the abstract relations manifest within a transformational grammar, including such notions as base rules and transformations. Today, that attitude has given way to a more eclectic view of language acquisition which recognizes the crucial importance of not only the grammatical structure of a language, but also such aspects as discourse phenomena, semantic categories, grammatical relations, and pragmatic concerns. While some linguists still maintain that the child is a little linguist in his approach to the acquisition of his language, with syntax at the heart of his activity, this view is by no means shared by all researchers working in the area of language acquisition.

In this section, we shall address issues which enter into virtually all discussions of language acquisition, including the view that the child passes through various *stages* in his linguistic development, and that he makes overgeneralizations as well as differentiations. We shall also discuss various methodologies used in obtaining data from children, along with potential pitfalls and problems.

Stages. It is often observed, by parents as well as linguists, that children pass through various *stages* in their acquisition of language. One often hears, for example, of the "one-word stage" or the "babbling stage." What do these terms really mean, and how are they characterized? It is clearly convenient to adopt some notion of language stage in order to chart a child's linguistic development and to compare his development with that of other children.

Obviously, the notion of a stage can be operationally defined in a host of ways. One of the most obvious, but perhaps least reliable, criteria is that of chronological age. We might for example, choose to define stages as six-month intervals, measured from the date of birth. Accordingly, we can then specify at what age a particular linguistic phenomenon emerges. One advantage with age as a defining criterion for stages is that it is obvious and easy to employ. But a disadvantage is that all children do not develop their linguistic skills at exactly the same age, even though the general developmental trends appear fairly constant and fixed. That is, all children appear to manifest one-word utterances before they produce full-blown sentences, and all appear to control simple, one-clause sentences before they learn complex sentences. But they do not all learn any of these at exactly the same time.

Another commonly used criterion for the definition of stages is the "mean length of utterance" or MLU (cf. Brown, 1973; Klima & Bellugi, 1966). Under this definition, data are collected from children, and the mean length of the utterances being used by the children is calculated. Utterance length can be measured in a variety of ways. For example, the number of words can be counted, and the MLU calculated in terms of average number of words per utterance. Or the number of morphemes can be counted and a MLU calculated. In both of these cases, there are potential problems since what counts as a word for the child might be quite different from that which the adult uses. Similarly, if one wishes to base the MLU on a morpheme count, one must have an adequate analysis of the child's morphological system. To illustrate these problems, let us consider the following actual utterances taken from Taya, a child of age one year, eight months (or 1,8 as it is often indicated in the acquisition literature).

20 a. I sleep
   b. make cookie
   c. make milk
   d. no go
   e. Taya breakit (=break it?)
   f. commere (=come here)

If the number of words is used as a basis for calculating the length of an utterance, then in (20a), the number is apparently two. In other cases, however, the number is not so clear. Does Taya treat *commere* as one word or two? Does she treat *breakit* as a single lexical item? Her mother thinks that in both cases Taya treats these as single words, although the adult does not. Clearly, the MLU based on number of words must be carefully assessed and consistent and appropriate evaluations made.

If the MLU is based on the number of morphemes per utterance, one must similarly decide on what counts as a morpheme. For example, if no third person singular affixes appear on a verb, as in (20e), do we count or not count this fact? Do we count only those affixes which overtly appear? If so, do we count the "zero" affix of the third person plural present tense verb suffix? Do we count the zero suffix on singular nouns? Do we count the imperative form as having a suffix or not? Depending on answers to these questions, the length of a particular utterance like (20e), when based on number of morphemes, could range from three to six. Moreover, the meaning of an utterance is important in assessing the MLU. If (20d) means that someone did not go, then one length value might be assigned, but if it is a negative imperative, then another assignment might be appropriate, and if it means that Taya does not want to go, then yet another length might obtain. Accordingly, the criteria for MLU assignment in determining stages must be not only clear but rigorously applied if such an operational definition of a stage is to be of any value.

In an extensive series of studies, Roger Brown and his colleagues and students (e.g., Brown, 1968, 1973; Brown, Cazden, & Bellugi, 1969; Klima & Bellugi, 1966) employed the word definition of the MLU as a criterion for the definition of stages. In these studies, the speech of three children was charted over a period of several months, and an extensive data base was assembled on the development of the children's linguistic systems. Indeed, these pioneering studies are among the most important in the area of first language acquisition, and even though they utilize only a small number of children in a detailed longitudinal study, a great deal of information was gleaned. It appears from this and other studies, that although children develop at different individual rates, the general profile of development is the same across all children. They all appear to go through the same sequence of stages, although at individually different rates.

Stages can also be defined in terms of the child's mastery of some particular grammatical phenomenon, such as the formal distinction between declaratives and imperatives or in terms of the acquisition of certain of the regular plural suffixes. In any case, the operational definition must be clearly specified. However we define stages, they are extremely useful in charting a single child's linguistic development over a long period of time (a "longitudinal" study) as well as in comparing various children with each other at the same stage. In dealing with the convenient notion of stages, however, it must be kept in mind that language development is more or less continuous, and while a concept of sequential stages is useful for the organization of data, it does not mean that there are discrete and sharp discontinuities between one stage and another.

Language acquisition processes. Among the processes which characterize children's language acquisition, those of *overgeneralization* and *differentiation* are among the most important. By *overgeneralization* is meant the child's tendency to extend a form or rule to a broader domain that it would have in the adult's grammar. For example, it is commonly observed that many children, once they learn a form like "doggie," tend to use it for all sorts of other animals, including cats, horses, and the like. That is, the child is generalizing the form to mean something like "animal" perhaps, and from the adult's point of view, this is an *overgeneralization* of the word. Or the child might learn at some stage that the regular English plural suffix for nouns is represented by /s/, /z/, or /Iz/, which he then uses for all nouns, including the irregular ones, and produces forms like *foots* and *mouses*. Or he may learn that the regular English past tense is represented by /t/, /d/, or /Id/, and he may then form such regularized past tenses as *goed*, *breaked*, or *hitted*.

Overgeneralization of words has been discussed in detail by E. Clark (1973), who concluded that most such cases deal with referents which somehow look like the target word, and the child is basing his overgeneralization on cognitive and perceptual grounds, treating as the defining semantic feature for "doggie" something like "four-legged animal." She suggests that as the child develops his lexicon, he adds one feature at a time, until he differentiates among referent classes and reaches the adult form. This perspective has been challenged by others, including Palermo (1978), who argues that the feature approach logically requires the child to know the abstract features before the more concrete ones. Moreover, Clark's theory does not allow for the possibility of *undergeneralization*, in which the child would fail to use the general term, e.g., "doggie," for particular instances of dogs. However, Anglin (1977) has argued that such undergeneralization does take place, and furthermore it has been argued that comprehension and production differ in terms of overgeneralization (Huttenlocher, 1974). Thus, Clark's feature is not universally accepted. This is an important topic which will be discussed in further detail in Chapter Five.

Not only is the child able to generalize and form classes of objects in his environment, but he is also able to differentiate among the classes. That is, while he might, much to the distress of his father, call all males "Daddy" at one stage, he later learns to distinguish among them. This, like overgeneralization, is a cognitively complex task, although it may well appear simple to us as adults. The child may even *overdifferentiate* to the extent that he may call all dogs "doggie" except his own, which he may call by its proper name.

The cognitive processes of generalization and differentiation are therefore of great importance in language acquisition, and these continue to play a role throughout the child's development, with more and more detail being given structure, such that more subtle distinctions are drawn and more elaborate and complex generalizations constructed.

One of the reasons for attending to the child's overgeneralizations and differentiations, as well as to any *simplifications* he might make, is that his "errors" can reveal the specific rules he is learning and the structures and forms he is constructing. That is, the area of child language provides a very informative window into the creativity of the language user. For example, it is highly unlikely that the child will have heard a form like "getted" from his parents or other mature speakers of the language, but when he uses such a form, it reveals to us that the child is applying in a perfectly creative and regular way the English past tense morphology to a verb stem, and that he is not aware of, or at least able to produce, the correct irregular form. That is, the production of such forms tells us that the child is operating with a very general rule. Similarly, when the child uses a sentence like "Did Mommy didn't go?" we recognize that he is using the auxiliary *do* both as a signal for the question and as a tense carrier for the negative, but that he has not yet learned that standard English permits only one instance of the auxiliary.

In summary, the processes of generalization and differentiation are of extreme importance in language acquisition, and they suggest that, details aside, the child begins with rather global forms and moves into specifics of his language with an overriding concern for communication. He has access to a vast arsenal of contextual and pragmatic resources, as well as language, in his acquisition process.

Methodologies. In their study of language acquisition, linguists employ a variety of methodologies including both naturalistic observations and experimental techniques. One of the most important sources of data from the perspective of naturalistic observation is diary studies, in which a parent records aspects of the utterances of his child. Important contributions in this area include the works of Leopold (1939-1949) and Weir (1962). More recently, of course, tape recording and even video recording have become commonplace, although while perhaps more faithful to actual utterances and devoid of the editing problem, these recordings are non-selective in terms of what is reported. Many parents record in diaries just those special utterances which are either amusing or somehow stand out as unusual, generally those which are assumed to be mistakes. An advantage of such data is that they are taken in a naturalistic situation with no laboratory constraints. One problem associated with such studies, however, is that of interpretation.

In particular, does the observer view the language forms with the same structure or meaning as the child? This is a complex issue, with pragmatics usually playing a crucial role in indicating what the child means. In Taya's utterances in (20) above, for example, only the context and situation could possibly reveal just what Taya means when she says "no go."

One general problem in language acquisition studies is whether or not the child comprehends certain forms, even if he does not produce them. Consequently, a technique of elicited imitation (Slobin & Welch, 1973) is often used in which the child is asked to repeat the utterances of the experimenter, who can vary his sentences in systematic ways. He might even offer the child grammatically ill-formed sentences for imitation to see if the child corrects him. Of course, just because the child does not repeat a sentence correctly does not mean that he does not comprehend it. For example, if a child is given a sentence with a relative clause as in (21a), he might respond with (21b).

21 a. The dog that chased the cat ran away.
   b. The dog chased the cat and it ran away.

If the child responds with (21b), and if it can be determined that *it* refers to the dog and not the cat, then apparently the child has understood the sentence correctly. But if *it* refers to the cat, then the child has not understood the sentence correctly. Elicited imitation is a powerful tool in assessing children's comprehension and production skills.

Other experimental techniques often involve children as participants in little games. For example, H. Brown (1971) and Sheldon (1974) have used a toy moving task to test children's comprehension of relative clauses. In such a task, the child has before him a set of toy animals, and when the experimenter utters a particular sentence, the child's task is to act out the sentence with the toys. Another technique involves the child in a puppet show (T. Derwing, 1979), in which the child talks to the puppet, giving instructions, asking questions, and the like. This technique, when coupled with elicited imitation, can be very revealing since it engages the child in a play situation in which he tends to respond very spontaneously. One of the most famous techniques employed in language acquisition studies is that of Berko (1958), in which pictures of imaginary creatures are shown to children. Each creature is given a .nonsense form name, and then a similar picture of two of the creatures is presented, with the child's task to provide the plural of the nonsense form.

In all such techniques, it is of paramount importance to engage the child's attention not only to encourage his participation in the experiment, but to sustain his interest so that the experiment can be completed. It is also important that the child is doing what the experimenter wants, and that the experimenter is interpreting the child's behavior correctly. Although the construction of experimental methodologies for dealing with children is often difficult, it is nevertheless well worth the effort when a new method provides rich data.

2.5 Summary

In this chapter we have examined language comprehension, production, and acquisition from an intuitive perspective. We have detailed some necessary conditions which must be satisfied in order for comprehension and production of language to take place, while at the same time recognizing that neither of these aspects of language use is simple. We have also attempted to enumerate the kinds of problems associated with a serious study of language use.

A second function of this chapter has been to suggest, albeit at times obliquely, that a cognitivist, mentalist approach to language use is essential, even though there is a broad spectrum of approaches available.

Now that the broad conceptual issues have been sketched, we can turn to empirical issues in language use. The remainder of this book is devoted to an assessment of the empirical issues involved in the study of morphology, syntax, and semantics.

EXERCISES

2.1. The two sentences "Fred is hard to please" and "Fred is anxious to please" both contain two distinct propositions. Construct propositional semantic representations for these two sentences along the lines suggested in (17) above.

2.2. Specify, for each of the following sets of sentences, which presuppositions are shared and which are not.

1. a. The one who proved the Mach theorem was Fred.
   b. What Fred proved was the Mach theorem.

2. a. Why did Mary leave the party early?
   b. When did Mary leave the party?
   c. When did Mary arrive at the party?

2.3. When Sandy first heard her new friend speak, she found his accent was so different from hers that she was not able to understand what he meant. After a little practice, however, she could understand him much better. Explain, with examples, what this sort of experience can tell us about the issue of "time sharing" in comprehension.

2.4. When one wishes to communicate some "message," is this "thought" expressed in linguistic terms or not? In other words, do you think that thought is internally represented in language or not? Give examples and reasons for your view.

2.5. Consider the following utterances from the child Jennifer:

   a. I want eat it.
   b. Mommy goed outside.
   c. Jenny breakit good.
   d. No go bed now.
   e. What Daddy bring?

Find the MLU of these utterances in terms of (a) words and (b) morphemes. Make explicit the criteria you employ to decide on what counts as a word and as a morpheme, with special attention to "zero" morphemes.

LABORATORIES

Laboratory 2. Interference Phenomena

Laboratory 3. Phonological Stages in Language Acquisition

Chapter Three

EXPERIMENTAL MORPHOLOGY

3.1 Introduction

Morphology, the study of the structure of words, occupies an important place within linguistics, sandwiched as it is between phonology and syntax. Linguists typically define the morpheme as a minimal unit of meaning, realized phonologically by one or more allomorphs. *Free* morphemes are those which can stand alone as separate words, and English manifests a host of these (e.g., *cat, go, pretty, from*, etc.), while *bound* morphemes are those which cannot stand alone but must instead be attached to either a free or another bound morpheme (e.g., the plural suffix, the *pre-* of *prefix*, the *un-* attached to adjectives as in *unhappy*, etc.). Languages vary greatly in their morphological typology. Some, like English, have an abundance of free morphemes, while others, such as Halkomelam, show a great deal of affixation.

Morphemes may also be partitioned into lexical and grammatical classes (cf. Francis, 1958). In English, lexical morphemes are generally free, while many of the grammatical morphemes are bound. The free grammatical morphemes in English include the prepositions, determiners, and the negative marker *not*.

During the halcyon days of structural linguistics, when structural methodologies were being widely applied to a variety of languages and when grammars for a number of different languages were

71

being written, a major part of each grammar was a description of that language's morphology. With the advent of transformational grammar, however, morphology seemed to loose its privileged position, and in the earlier versions of the theory (e.g., Chomsky, 1957; 1965) morphology was treated largely as a part of syntax. Inflectional morphology tended to be analyzed in terms of base-generated nodes, while derivational morphology was handled transformationally (cf. Lees, 1960). Allomorphy was sometimes treated as syntax, sometimes as morphophonemics, and sometimes as phonology. For example, the three English regular past tense forms /d/, /t/, and /ld/ were at times treated as three allomorphs and at other times as derivable via phonological rules from a single underlying representation.

More recent developments in transformational theory, however, have once again emphasized the importance of morphology, initially in terms of investigations into the nature of the lexicon and lexical representations, with emphasis on the question of how best to represent similar, presumably related, lexical items (cf. Chomsky, 1970; Jackendoff, 1972). Morphology fully reemerged as an important focus of attention in generative theory with the work of Siegel (1974) and Aronoff (1976). A representative statement of the current view of morphology from the generative perspective is that of Zwicky (1983), who proposes separate components of word formation rules, allomorphy rules, and morphophonemic rules, along with a rather highly structured lexical component.

Inflectional morphology is usually characterized as a set of paradigmatic variations associated with a particular part of speech (noun, verb, adjective, etc.) which is both systematic and productive. Moreover, the allomorphs of a particular inflectional morpheme are usually fairly regular, that is, phonologically conditioned. Examples include the English past tense allomorphs (e.g., *kicked*, *petted*, *smiled*), the English plurals (e.g., *hats*, *dogs*, *churches*), the Japanese verb tenses (e.g., *taberu*, *tabeta* "eat, ate," *hasiru*, *hasitta* "run, ran"), and the Spanish verbal suffixes in each tense (e.g., *trabajo*, *trabajas*, *trabaja*, *trabajamos*, *trabajais*, *trabajan* "I, you, he/she, we, you, they work"). Of course, inflectional morphology may also involve morphologically conditioned allomorphs, as in the irregular past tense forms (*slept, drank, ran*), or irregular plural forms (*feet, sheep*).

Derivational morphology tends to be less productive and less regular than inflectional morphology. There is also a greater tendency in derivational morphology for a change in the part of speech, as for example, the various English nominalizers which convert verbs to nouns, such as *-tion* (e.g., *act, action, produce, production*), or adjectives to nouns, such as *-ness* (e.g., *eager, eagerness, helpful, helpfulness*). It appears, for example, that one must know that the adjective *eager* requires the nominalizer *-ness* and not *-ity*, as in *productivity* or *activity*.

Perhaps because of the rather ambiguous status of morphology in earlier transformational theory, there was relatively little experimental work done in this area, even though it provides an ideal domain for the empirical investigation of the psychological reality of various proposed rules and relationships among lexical items. One notable exception, however, was the classical and pioneering work of Berko (1958), who explored the status of various English morphemes, their allomorphs, and the rules relating them as reflected in the speech of children. Indeed, much of the empirical research in morphology has been carried out in terms of language acquisition studies.

In this chapter, we shall first address issues in inflectional morphology and then turn to topics in derivational morphology. In each of the following sections we shall first attempt to formulate the fundamental problems or issues from an empirical perspective, after which we shall review the more important studies done in those areas.

3.2 Issues in Inflectional Morphology

The non-uniqueness problem. It is frequently possible to describe the allomorphs of a particular morpheme in a variety of ways, all of which successfully account for the data. Often, one particular description may seem preferable on some *a priori* grounds. For example, one description may be simplier (i.e., shorter or more economical) than another, or one analysis might be preferred because it involves only phonetically plausible (i.e., "natural") rules. Or perhaps one analysis might involve three independent allomorphs while its competitor requires only one basic allomorph, with other variants accounted for entirely in terms of phonological rules. Derwing (1979) has called this common situation, in which several competing analyses are available for one morphological phenomenon, the "non-uniqueness" problem.

Because of the non-uniqueness problem, some decisions must be made concerning what will constitute criteria for selecting the prefered analysis. Within generative theory, the issue of correctness is usually formulated in terms of the two interrelated criteria of simplicity and naturalness. One analysis is often judged to be simpler than another if it is shorter, more ecomomical, more widely applicable to other cases, more elegant, etc. than its competitors. A solution is usually judged more natural than another if it involves only natural rules, where paradigm instances of naturalness in phonology, for example, involve such phonetically plausible alternations as voicing assimilation, nasal assimilation, vowel harmony, or maintenance of syllable structure. However, criteria such as simplicity or naturalness, while they might offer descriptive utility, are not necessarily also psychologically operative. That is, it is logically possible that a description might be very economical and elegant when expressed in some particular notation, while at the same time failing to represent what the native speaker actually knows or does.

From our perspective, then, the fundamental issue of correctness is an empirical one. We must formulate empirical means to assess which, if any, of the alternative descriptions for a set of allomorphs is the correct one.

Alternative analyses: an example. To illustrate the non-uniqueness problem, we turn to the regular English plural morpheme and, following Derwing (1979; 1980) outline several alternative descriptions.

TABLE 3.1 Regular English Plurals

==

/-z/	/-s/	/-ɪz/
dogs	cats	judges
birds	maps	messes
mobs	socks	dishes
cars	pits	matches
trees	cops	churches
songs	stacks	mazes

==

The allomorphic alternations found in the regular English plurals are exemplified in Table 3.1, in which the suffixes /s/, /z/, and /ɪz/ are found in complementary distribution. The most familiar analysis for the regular English plurals is one which states that the three allomorphs are distributed as follows:

1. PL --->
$$\begin{cases} /z/ & \text{after final voiced consonants except sibilants} \\ /s/ & \text{after final voiceless consonants except sibilants} \\ /ɪz/ & \text{after final sibilants.} \end{cases}$$

According to this analysis, the three allomorphs are phonologically conditioned by properties of the final segment of the noun stem to which the plural morpheme is attached. Following Derwing (1979), we call this the "Feature" analysis, since it depends on a set of phonological features of the final segment of the stem.

A different analysis, but one which also accounts for the facts, refers to three allomorphs just as the Feature analysis does, but which states that the conditioning factor is the final segment itself, and not a feature or features of that segment (cf. Francis, 1958, p. 180). This "Segment" analysis simply states that, for example, the allomorph /s/ is selected when the stem ends in one of the phonemes /p, t, k/, with similar distributional statements for the allomorphs /z/ and /ɪz/. The Segment analysis is usually rejected as lacking generality, though such a criticism is based on

75

simplicity arguments rather than on empirical evidence. The native speaker may in fact learn his allomorphs on the basis stem-final segment identification, and until empirical evidence is provided to the contrary, the Segment analysis must still be considered a logical possibility, even if not a very plausible one.

A further "Phonotactic" analysis is also possible, according to which there is only one basic allomorph, namely /z/, with the /s/ and /lz/ forms derived from the /z/ form by the following two purely phonological rules:

2 a. null ---> /l/ between adjacent sibilants
  b. /z/ ---> /s/ after a voiceless consonant.

The first of these rules simply inserts the lax vowel /l/ after a final sibilant and before the sibilant /z/ suffix, while the second devoices the /z/ after a voiceless consonant. One advantage claimed for the Phonotactic analysis is the fact that the two rules of (2) can also be used to account for the third person singular verb suffixes, as in *washes* and *kicks*, under the assumption that the basic allomorph of the third person singular present tense morpheme is /z/. Moreover, this analysis invokes natural rules such as maintenance of syllable structure and voicing assimilation.

There are then at least three plausible competing analyses for the regular English plurals. With the Phonotactic analysis is usually championed on grounds of economy and naturalness, these factors alone do not necessarily cinch the case for the psychological correctness of that proposal.

If three analyses were not complicated enough, there are even more possibilities, and although these may be less linguistically sophisticated, they still have a chance of being correct. One such is the "List" analysis, which simply states that there is *no* regular English plural rule at all; instead the plural form of each noun stem is learned as a separate item, with the learner drawing no generalization other than the semantic one of pluralization. This analysis requires that just as the speaker must learn "exceptional" plurals such as *feet* and *mice*, he also treats what the linguist regards as regular plurals as separate items as well. Although practically no one would subscribe to such an analysis, it is still logically possible, given the fact that our mental lexical storage space is so great.

Another somewhat more clever analysis is the "Rhyme" proposal, which claims that the child learns a few basic plurals such as *dogs, cats, matches,* etc., and then when encountering a new item, he forms its plural from a rhyming scheme based on the final vowel plus consonant(s). For example, according to the Rhyme analysis, when the child encounters a new form like *cog,* he forms the plural on the basis of a rhyming word he already knows, such as *dog,* yielding *cogs.*

One other analysis, the "Whole Stem" analysis, should also be mentioned. According to this proposal, there are three allomorphs of the plural morpheme, just as in (1) above, but in this case the conditioning factor is the entire stem. Thus, the child supposedly learns that the /z/ suffix is added when the stem is *dog, mol, ear,* etc., while the /s/ suffix is used with *cat, stick, cup,* etc. In the Whole Stem analysis, the entire lexical item and not just the final syllable, segment, or feature of the last segment, conditions the choice of allomorphs.

There are conceivably even more analyses for the regular English plural system, although we have cited only six candidates here. Admittedly some of these seem so bizarre as to be excluded *a priori,* but what is really needed is an empirical test or tests by which we can eliminate one or more of the competitors and focus attention on the remaining and potentially viable candidates.

The existence of often quite straightforward competing analyses leads one to suppose that the regular English plurals should be an ideal area to explore experimentally. However, as is to often the case with conceptually simple issues, other complexities intervene. For example, inflectional morphology is such an integral and fundamental part of a language like English that the native speaker seems to have gained almost perfect control over the system quite early. Even though there are contending analyses, all describe the same forms, and accordingly just asking an adult to produce the plural of some word will not serve as a test to differentiate among the analyses on empirical grounds. If we ask him to tell us the plural of *aardvark*, for example, and he offers *aardvarks*, which of the six potential analyses has he actually used? We don't know. Since the adult seems to have mastered and habituated his inflectional morphology to such a high degree, subtle and ingenious means are needed to differentiate empirically among the predictions made by alternative descriptions.

For this reason, the psycholinguist often turns to the development of inflectional morphology in the child. Language acquisition studies have provided a rich testing ground for alternative analyses, and therefore this is the first area we shall explore.

Testing alternative analyses. Jean Berko (1958), in her pioneering work in language acquisition, set the stage for a great deal of experimental work by providing both conceptual and methodological orientations which have proven extremely valuable and productive. Berko wanted to determine whether or not children could be shown to be using certain rules of English morphology. She focused attention on the regular English plurals, past tense, progressive (*ing*), third person singular, possessive, and certain compounds. Her insight was the realization that when asking subjects, either children or adults, to produce a particular plural form, a "correct" response (from the linguist's or adult's perspective) could arise in one of two ways: either the subject had acquired a rule of morphology or he had memorized the plural form. These two explanations of subject response correspond to the Feature and Whole Stem analyses discussed above.

In order to confront the non-uniqueness problem, Berko introduced her now classic *wug* test. As stimuli, she constructed a set of nonsense forms, all of which were phonologically well-formed (such as *wug*), but all were novel and meaningless. She then had pictures drawn of imaginary creatures, one for each of the nonsense forms. In her plural test, she showed a child a picture of a creature and told him that "This is a picture of a *wug*" (or some other nonsense form). Then she showed the child a picture of two of the creatures and said "Now there are two of them. There are two _." The subject was to respond with a plural form, such as *wugs*. With Berko's methodology, any response would automatically rule out the Whole Stem and List analyses, since the forms were novel, The children responded with what by and large amounted to the "correct" adult plural forms, with the exception being those stems ending in a sibilant. This led Berko to conclude that the children had pretty well learned the rules of the English plural (and past tense, etc.) morphology.

From a retrospective position, it can be observed that Berko's results failed to rule out several other alternative analyses, such as the Rhyme analysis, for example. Moreover, there were some important methodological problems associated with her study. For example, she pooled the results from her subjects, whose ages ranged from four to seven years, thereby obscuring any developmental trends which might have been found in the data. Furthermore, her stimuli did not contain instances of all final English segments, and consequently the results do not exclude the Segment or Rhyme analyses as possible explanations. Yet in spite of these problems, Berko's work constitutes a landmark in language acquisition research. It set the stage for a series of studies employing her basic methodology, or variations on it, which have reaped rich rewards over the past several years.

Later studies tended to support Berko's conclusions. For example, Ervin (1964) found that the /Iz/ allomorph is learned later than either the /s/ or /z/ suffixes. In an extensive language acquisition project, Miller and Ervin (1964) noted that children appear to learn some specific plurals first and then only later do they generalize, and even later yet do they sort out the regular and irregular forms.

Anisfeld and Tucker (1967) addressed both production and recognition of the plural forms in the child. In three production experiments employing Berko's methodology, they found that the /Iz/

suffix was far harder for six-year old children than either the /s/ or /z/ forms, while in a series of recognition tasks, the /z/ was the most easily identified, with the /s/ and /lz/ forms both significantly harder. These results were attributed to the factor of relative frequency. It was noted, for example, that stems requiring /lz/ are far less frequent in Engish than are stems selecting the other two forms, suggesting that the lower exposure to /lz/ could account for its relatively poorer performance in production. It seems plausible that the more often a particular type of form is heard, the more readily it should be mastered. Frequency, however, is often ignored as a relevant factor in language acquisition, even through from the child's perspective it would seem to be crucial. Further studies, such as those of Koziol (1970) and Natalicio (1969) also tended to support Berko's early results.

In order to address two shortcomings of Berko's original study, Innes (1974) used the *wug* test in a study of the developmental aspects of the English plural. Her stimuli covered the full range of final English segments, and her subjects were 120 children from two to eight years of age, with a balance of ten males and ten females in each of six groups. Innes found considerable variation in performance among subjects in each group, as would be expected since the groups were defined in terms of chronological age. However, when a criterion of shared performance was used to assess the data, clear and interpretable results emerged. Innes found that at the earliest stage, children could not pluralize nonsense forms at all, much as Miller and Ervin (1964) had noted. At the next stage, however, the children tended to exhibit mastery of the plurals for all nonsense stems except those with a stem final fricative, including the affricates. At the third stage, the children had mastered all plurals except for the final sibilant stems. Next they mastered all the plurals except for final /z/ stems, for which they appears to feel there was already a plural marker present. And finally, at the last stage, they mastered all the forms. As Derwing and Baker (1977) point out, these results suggest that the children adopt a fine-tuning approach to the plural forms in which the correct distribution of the /lz/

suffix is achieved by a progressive identification of appropriate phonetic features defining the target stem-final segment.

In a much more extensive analysis, Derwing and Baker (1976) tested some 112 children, aged three to nine, on 67 nonsense stems, again using Berko's methodology. They found that the order of acquisition of those English morphemes they studied was, from earliest to latest, (a) progressive, (b) plural, (c) past tense, (d) possessive, (e) third person singular. Derwing and Baker (1976; 1979) provide extensive evidence to show that the three allomorphs of the English plural are not all mastered at the same time or with equal facility, and their work supported the developmental trends found by Innes (1974). The most frequently correct form is /z/, while the /s/ was less often correct. In Derwing and Baker (1976), nonsense words with no English rhymes were included in the stimuli, and accordingly the Rhyme analysis was eliminated as a viable candidate, since the children did not treat these forms in any way different from others. Moreover, the children's errors were revealing. If, for example, the Final Segment analysis is actually used, errors of substitution of /s/ for /z/ or vice versa should occur, since if only the final segment and not features of that segment was the governing factor, confusion would be expected among forms with different final segments. But none did occur. Instead, errors tended to be based on phonological properties of the final segments, thereby lending credence to the Feature analysis as the most plausile. The Rhyme, Whole Stem, List, and Final Segment analyzes were eliminated, at least for the cases of the regular plurals. Moreover, a developmental tendency emerged based on the child's attention to phonological features of the conditioning stem. Similar results were obtained for the past tense and third person singular forms.

It should be kept in mind in assessing this research, however, that the Feature analysis has not been supported for all English plurals. Presumably, the irregular plurals (*oxen, feet, sheep*, etc.) and irregular past tenses (*got, swam, ran*, etc.) must to some extent be learned individually, although even among these there may be systematic subgroups which are linked via a set of phonological properties.

Irregular Inflectional Morphology. Not only does English possess an extensive set of regular allomorphs for its morphemes, it also exhibits an interesting set of irregular allomorphs as well. It is with the irregular forms that the child's propensity to overgeneralize most obviously shows up, thereby providing evidence for the kinds of rules he is learning. Brown (1973) noted that overgeneralization in the English past tense seems to last a long time, so the child might say *eated* for *ate* for an extended period. Kuczaj (1977) noted that two types of overgeneralizations tend to occur in the English past tenses: forms like *eated*, based on the present tense stem *eat*, and forms like *ated*, based on the past tense form *ate*. Observing spontaneous speech in children, Kuczaj found the the relative frequency of these two forms varied with age. Younger (three year old) children tended to produce more forms like *eated*, while the older (five year old) children produced more like *ated*. Kuczaj hypothesized that this was due to the fact that younger children tended to avoid semantic redundancy, which is apparent in forms like *ated*, while older ones did not.

Kuczaj (1978) reports the results of two experiments, both of which support this contention. In the first, 45 children served as subjects in a task in which puppets sometimes made "errors" such as *eated* and *ated*. The children were to determine when and if an error was made. The younger children (three and four year olds) accepted *eated*, while the middle aged children (five and six year olds) accepted both forms, and the older children (seven and eight year olds) accepted neither. In the second experiment, the acceptability of *eated* was found to decrease with age. These results not only provide a useful illustration of overgeneralization, but they also demonstrated two distinct kinds of overgeneralization distinguished by a semantic factor of redundancy.

In their investigation of English irregular verbs, Bybee and Slobin (1982) focused attention on two large classes, one with a three member paradigm (e.g., *swim/swam/swum*) and one with a two member paradigm (e.g., *spin/spun*). When adults were given irregular verbs and instructed to create the past tense as quickly as possible, a variety of errors was found, the most common of which was to regularize the past tense (e.g., *swimmed*). However, many errors involving a vowel change were also found, and there was a tendency for the past tense of three-member verbs to be treated as if they were two-member verbs. For example, the past tense of *swim* often was given as *swum*. In a second experiment, children were given sentences to complete, with the past tenses of irregular verbs as targets. The children also tended to give responses based on the two-member paradigm.

Bybee and Slobin's important finding is that speakers seem to employ a schema or generalization about the shape of a lexical item in a particular category rather than relying on either rote memory or rule learning. They suggest that subjects adopt a prototype member for each irregular verb class, although such prototypic forms are based on shared phonological properties of members of that class rather than based on one specific member.

In a subsequent study, Bybee and Modor (1983) further explored the productive two-member class exemplified by *string/strung*. After noting that this class seems to be phonologically defined in terms of a prototypic member, they attempted to determine the specific shape of the class prototype. Subjects were given sentence frames in which the past tense of the verb was elicited. They found that the prototype for this class is /sC(C)lŋ/, and they noted that the closer phonologically a verb is to the prototype, the more likely it is to be absorbed into the class.

While much of the experimental research in inflectional morphology has dealt with language acquisition, more and more is now focusing on the adult. One conclusion which seems to emerge from much of this research is that inflectional morphology tends to be treated according to phonological properties with a concomitant minimization of list learning. This is especially in the Bybee and Modor (1983) results. In addition to phonological properties of forms, however, such factors as frequency and saliency might also play important roles in the acquistion of inflections.

3.3 Issues in Derivational Morphology.

Unlike inflectional morphology, derivational processes tend to be less productive, less phonologically regular, and often involve a change in the part of speech. For example, English contains a host of "nominalizers" which change verbs or adjectives into nouns, as well as other derivational morphemes which permit the conversion of nouns to adjectives or nouns to verbs. Some of these are illustrated in Table 3.2. Other derivational processes are also possible in English, including those which employ prefixes (e.g., *impossible, unlikely, antimissile, preconceive*, etc.). One troublesome aspect of derivational morphology is that it is often impossible to select the appropriate derivational suffix on the basis of the phonological shape of the stem alone. For example, the verb *refuse* is nominalized by the suffix *-al*, perhaps leading one to speculate that the final segment of syllable of the verb is the conditioning factor. However, this is clearly not the case, since *confuse* has the same final syllable, yet is nominalized as *confusion*, not **confusal*. It appears that the specific suffix must be learned in association with the stems to which it is to be added, almost in a list-like manner. However, other suffixes suggest quite the contrary. For example, the highly productive nominalizer *-ness* seems freely attached to adjectives (e.g., *smallness, happiness, sadness*, etc.), although there are some exceptions such as *undecidability* rather than the questionable *undecidableness*. Even in these cases, however, the *-ness* forms seem somehow more "Englishlike" than an inappropriate *-al* form such as **confusal*. In such instances, the *-ness* formation is said to be more productive than the *-al* formation, since proportionally more forms of the former sort are possible than of the latter.

To answer the question of whether or not two forms should be described as derivationally related, two descriptive criteria are usually employed, although often only implicitly. These are the extent

TABLE 3.2 Some English Derivational Morphology

===

Verb to Noun		Adjective to Noun	
refuse	refusal	tiny	tininess
confuse	confusion	monstrous	monstrosity
record	record	happy	happiness
teach	teacher	red	red
accept	acceptance	foreign	foreigner
wonder	wonderful		

Noun to Adjective		Noun to Verb	
child	childish	trauma	traumatize
joy	joyful	man	man
cat	catlike	victim	victimize

===

of semantic similarity and phonetic similarity between the forms. For example, in the *refuse/refusal* pair, there appears intuitively to be a great deal of meaning similarity and at the same time much phonetic similarity. In fact, the stem *refuse* appears phonetically unaltered in *refusal*. Empirically, of course, the extent of phonetic and semantic similarity admit of degrees, and it is possible that the native speaker will regard one pair of forms as semantically closer than another, and likewise for phonetic similarity.

For example, in a pair such as *opaque/opacity*, the phonetic similarity seems less than in the *refuse/refusal* pair, while the semantic similarity between the two pairs might be judged as very close. In the pair *class/classic*, native speakers would presumably find a considerable phonetic similarity but very little semantic similarity.

Considerations such as these suggest that all derivational morphology ought not be treated in the same way. In particular, the question arises as to whether, in a specific instance, the speaker actually learns a single stem plus a derivational affix or whether he learns two distinct forms. For pairs like *tidy/tidiness* and *refuse/refusal*, considerable semantic and phonetic similarity might be expected in speakers' judgements, and if that is indeed the case, it seems plausible that the mental representation of such pairs involves a single lexical item plus an affix. Of course, an additional piece of information would also be needed, namely the coding which links certain forms with their appropriate suffixes.

For pairs like *class/classic*, however, we would expect that two distinct and semantically unrelated lexical items would be stored by the speaker. But how are we to treat pairs with some, but not very great, semantic or phonetic similarity? In the pair *wonder/wonderful*, what is the extent of semantic similarity? For a pair like *write/author*, we recognize a great deal of similarity in meaning but virtually none in form. Or how should we handle a pair like *shirt/skirt*, for which there is a historical connection, but one which is apparently no longer recognized by speakers of Modern English? The answer to this last question at least seems clear: if there is no perceived semantic similarity, then there is no reason to conflate a pair of forms into a single lexical representation.

These questions are empirical and accordingly empirical means are required to answer them. To this point, we have identified phonetic and semantic similarity as basic criteria for establishing the relatedness of pairs, and we now need recourse to an empirical means to assess these factors. Accordingly, we must operationalize our definitions of semantic and phonetic relatedness to the extent that we can explore their consequences empirically.

One way to sharpen the notion of phonetic similarity is to invoke a concept of phonetic transparency (cf. Cutler, 1980; 1981). As an operational definition, we assume that if, in a pair of words, the shorter stem is found phonetically unaltered in the longer form, then the relationship is transparent. Thus, in a form like *refusal*, the stem *refuse* is found unaltered, and accordingly the relationship between the derived form and the stem is phonetically transparent. In a form like *confusion*, however, the stem form *confuse* is altered such that its final consonant is altered, thereby rendering the pair somewhat, but not very, opaque. In a pair like *opaque/opacity*, there is even more variation in the stem, while in a pair like *monstrous/monstrosity*, the stem is altered by both vowel changes and accent movement. Accordingly, we can speak of complete transparency or relatively more or less opacity in pairs of words. Presumably something like the transparency notion also obtains for semantic similarity, although in this area it is difficult to operationalize the distinction with the same precision possible in phonetics.

It is possible to quantify the notion of "morphological relatedness" for pairs of forms in terms of the two independent parameters of semantic and phonetic similarity and to graph native speakers' judgements of these similarities. Derwing (1976) adopted just this approach in attempting to determine the extent of native speakers' abilities to assess morpheme relatedness among pairs of words. He asked a large number of adults to rate 115 pairs of words on a five-point scale of semantic similarity and then, independently to rate the same pairs of words on a seven-point scale of phonetic similarity. Such data can be represented graphically as in Figure 3.1, where each point represents a pair of words. While the specific details of subjects' judged similarities on the semantic and phonetic axes determine when each pair falls, four interesting quadrants can be discerned. These are labelled A, B, C, and D in Figure 3.1. Derwing (1976) found that certains pairs, such as *quiet/quietly dirt/dirty*, and *teach/teacher*, tended to fall in the A quadrant. These forms are typically judged as highly similar both semantically and phonetically. Indeed, many such pairs are phonetically transparent. Thus the members of the A quadrant would presumably be treated by native speakers as closely related and could be represented as having a single lexical stem plus an affix. Items in quadrant B, which were judged to have high semantic similarity but low phonetic similarity, included pairs like *kitty/cat* and *wild/wilderness*. There seems to be no strong reason to treat such pairs as having the same stem form, but instead it is preferable to treat them as two distinct lexical entries with some semantic

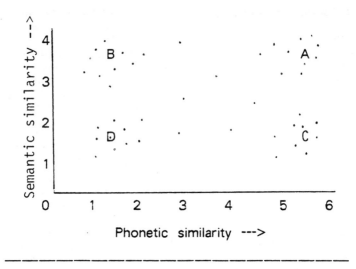

FIGURE 3.1   Morphological Relatedness

===

linkage. Quadrant C represents those forms with high phonetic and low semantic similarity. Included here are pairs like *live/liver* and *ear/eerie*. Presumably, such pairs should be treated as independent lexical items with no semantic linkages. Finally, quadrant D contains pairs with low semantic and phonetic similarity, including such forms as *carpenter/wagon* and *ladder/lean*. Although a few pairs fall between the cracks in the four quadrants, the technique is useful in supporting the major distinctions among what Derwing (1976) called the "degrees of morpheme recognition."

In another experiment designed to evaluate subjects' recognition of morpheme relatedness, Derwing (1976) employed the "comes from" test, in which subjects are given pairs of words and asked to indicate on a five point scale whether they think one form "comes from" the other. They were also asked whether they had ever thought of the relationship before. The results of the "comes from" test correlated highly ($p < .0001$) with the semantic similarity results, but less highly ($p < .002$) with the phonetic similarity results.

It appears, then, that the extent of perceived morpheme relatedness in the area of derivational morphology is one of considerable variation. Some pairs are clearly perceived to be closely related, while others are much less so. One important lesson to be learned here is that since derivational morphology exhibits so much variation, it is a mistake to treat all derivational morphology in the same way.

In addressing the development of derivational morphology in the child, Derwing and Baker (1974) and Derwing (1976) employed a Berko test to determine the relative productivity of six derivational suffixes, including the *-er* agentive nominalizer (e.g., *teacher*), the *-er* instrumental nominalizer (*eraser*), the *-ie/y* diminuitives (*doggie*), the *-ly* adverbs (*quickly*), the *-y* adjectives (*muddy*), and some noun compounds (e.g., *birdhouse*). In this study, children, adolescents, and adults were tested. The most productive suffix was found to be the *-er* agentive nominalizer, which although formally identical to the instrumental *-er* suffix, was considerably more productive. In general, the young children treated only the agentive *-er*, the *-y*, and the noun compounds as productive. The dimunitive suffix exhibited low productivity for all groups. As expected, adolescents scored higher than children, and adults scored even more highly, suggesting an increase in productivity of these derivational morphemes with age. The distinction in productivity between the *-er* agentive and instrumental suffixes highlights the fact that formal identity alone is insufficient to determine morphological relatedness.

In an attempt to test the relative productivity of two competing derivational suffixes, Aronoff and Schvaneveldt (1978) employed the "lexical decision task," a technique in which subjects must choose which of two forms they consider to be more English-like. It has been shown (Rubenstein, Lewis, & Rubenstein, 1971; Taft & Forster, 1975) that the closer a nonsense word is to an English word, the more likely it will be accepted in the lexical decision task. Aronoff and Schvaneveldt defined productivity in terms of the ratio of actual words of a given pattern to the total possible words of that pattern. Thus, since there are more actual words of the form *Xiveness* (such as *decisiveness*) than of the form *Xivity*, the former is more productive than the latter. Aronoff and Schvaneveldt used three types of words as stimuli: actual words (e.g., *objectivity*, *decisiveness*), possible words whose bases occur in the *Webster Collegiate Dictionary* but which are not themselves cited there (*reflectiveness*, *reflectivity*), and nonwords. Subjects preferred forms in *-iveness* over those in *-ivity*, and morphological productivity was offered as an explanation for this. However, as Anshen and Aronoff (1981) point out, there could be an alternative explanation for this result, namely that the *-iveness* forms are more transparent than the *-ivity* forms.

In order to determine which factor is directing subjects' choices, Anshen and Aronoff (1981) carried out a further experiment, again using the lexical decision task, but in which productivity and transparency made different predictions. *Xible* base forms were used as stimuli, to which both the suffixes *-ity* and *-ness* can be added. The *-ity* suffix is more productive since it can be added to more *Xible* forms, but the *-ness* suffix is more transparent. In this study, subjects preferred the *-ity* forms, supporting morphological productivity over transparency. The results of these studies suggest that while both transparency and productivity are important, when they work against each other, productivity is dominant.

The last word is yet to be uttered on this issue, however. In a clever experiment, Cutler (1980) showed that when subjects turn adjectives like *splendid* into verbs, they tend to use the *-ify* suffix and produce forms like *splendify*, on the analogy of *liquid/liquify* rather than producing forms like *splendidify*, in which the stress is retracted one syllable. That is, when faced with the conflict between maintaining the main stress on the stem form and losing a final consonant versus retracting the stress but keeping the consonant, subjects tend to prefer the former. Culter (1981) argues from those results that the notion of transparency must be modified. Since the perservation of the initial portions of the base word appears to be more important than the preservation of the final portions, she concludes that so long as a derived word preserves the segmental structure and relative syllable prominence of the base word up to what she calls the "recognition point," it will be treated as transparent. The recognition point is, following Marslen-Wilson (1980), that earliest point at which the word can be uniquely identified and distinguished from all other words in the language beginning with the same sequence of phonemes.

Presumably, words are mentally represented with linkages other than phonological ones, for otherwise such unrelated forms as *man* and *manner* would be stored together on the basis of sound alone. To test the hypothesis that morphological relatedness contributes to the way we store forms mentally, Murrell and Morton (1974) carried out a word identification study in which subjects initially learned a list of 12 words, such as *man* and *car*. Phonologically and orthographically similar words were then flashed briefly on a screen. Some were morphologically related to the list forms (such as *manner*, *cars*) while others were not (e.g., *manner*, *card*). In an identification task, subjects made significantly more errors on non-related words than on words related to the initial list forms, leading Murrell and Morton to conclude that related forms are stored with morphological links.

It thus appears from a wide variety of studies that both sound and meaning similarity play important roles in the perception of morphological relatedness. A third factor which might also seem relevant to the notion of morphological relatedness is frequency.

In order to address both frequency and productivity, Aronoff (1983) examined what he called "potential" as well as actual words. An actual word is one which is attested in the language, while a potential word is one which could exist according to the rules of word formation but which happens not to be attested. Aronoff asked if the productivity of a form could be attributed to, or correlated with, its frequency. He calculated the mean frequency of the *Xivity* and *Xiveness* forms, as well as the mean frequencies of their base words. He found that the former are significantly more frequent than the latter, and the base words of the *Xivity* class are also significantly more frequent than those of the *Xiveness* class. Yet Aronoff and Schvaneveldt (1978) had found that subjects preferred the latter over the former. To explain this discrepency, Aronoff invoked the notion of "foregrounding." He suggested that the less transparent *-ity* forms tend to become more specialized and foregrounded in their meanings than the more transparent *-ness* forms, as in *productivity* versus *productiveness*. The foregrounded forms are, he claims, more likely to be expropriated to specialized use and jargon.

On the basis of this result, Aronoff expected to find that *Xibleness* forms, which are less English-ike and less productive, would be more frequent than *Xiblity* forms. However, the results of his frequency count indicated that both forms have very low frequency counts and that they are not significantly different from each other. To try to understand this result, Aronoff searched the dictionary for citation dates for both forms. He found no citations for the *Xibleness* forms in the last two centuries, leading him to conclude that this formation is no longer operative in English. The only remaining *Xibleness* forms are apparently viewed by native speakers as archaic and residual (cf. *forcibleness, apprehensibleness*).

In an experiment in which subjects judged the relative acceptability of pseudo words formed from a stem, plus an optional suffix, plus *-ity*, Randall (1980) found that those words in which *-ity* was adjacent to a latinate morpheme (e.g, *obliquity*) were judged more acceptable than those in which it was not (e.g., *earthicity*). She also found that familiarity and homogeneity of morpheme types were influential in subjects' acceptability judgements. This study suggests that speakers are sensitive to whether or not a particular form has a "classical" (i.e., Greek or Latin) or native source.

It appears then that frequency, productivity, phonetic similarity, semantic similarity, historical source, and familiarity all contribute to the perceived degree of morphological relatedness among pairs of words which the linguist might wish to describe as formally related. The complex interactions of these various factors present a complicated picture of derivational morphology, although this same complexity provides support for the earlier observation that all instances and types of derivational morphology should not be forced into the same mold: speakers treat different kinds of pairs differently, depending on a host of factors.

There are likely to be yet other factors which enter into morphological relatedness but which have not been considered here. For example, when two pairs of words exhibit the same formal morphological relationship, but differ in salience, how will this affect the native speaker's perception of the relationships? The pair *dirt/dirty*, for example, might be more salient than the pair *louse/lousy*, thereby causing the mental representation of the two pairs to be different. Another possibly relevant factor might be that of sociological distinctions among subjects. A higher level of education or a greater degree of specialization in some particular area might be an important determinant of different mental representations. It would be only natural to expect considerable individual differences across a wide spectrum of the population, and accordingly variation might be expected in terms of a large number of factors, including age, education, social group, occupation, and others. If this is the case, then it is clear that one cannot speak of "the" degree of morphological relatedness among forms, but instead the relationships established must be in part based on properties shared by groups of subjects. Indeed, such a conclusion supports the often expressed claim that meaning does not reside in the language, but in the language users.

3.4 Summary

In this chapter, we have examined both inflectional and derivational morphology from an empirical perspective. We have attempted to isolate those factors involved in the acquisition and use of both kinds of morphology. In the area of inflectional morphology, the approach initially undertaken seemed relatively simple and straightforward: we would simply test alternative analyses for particular inflectional morphemes. While this approach has exhibited some measure of success, we still have not zeroed in on the one correct analysis for even the relatively simple regular English plural or past tense morphemes, though several competing analyses have been eliminated. However, the situation is not as bleak as one might think. We have been able to chart some important aspects of the child's acquisition processes and we have noted that such properties as the formal complexity of forms, phonetic structure, natural classes of phonemes, and frequency of occurrence, all play a part. While some of these factors are of more interest to the linguist than others, none may be safely ignored.

In derivational morphology, things are even more complex. This area is generally less productive than inflectional morphology and contains considerable variation in terms of internal productivity. Here, the factors of phonetic and semantic similarity play important roles, as do productivity, frequency, and perhaps salience.

Methodologically, we have encountered in this chapter several useful techniques which have allowed psycholinguists to obtain a wide variety of data on morphology. These include Berko's *wug* test, along with the many variations on it elaborated by numerous researchers, the semantic and phonetic similarities tests, the "comes-from" test, and the lexical decision task. These techniques and any others we can devise are of great importance, for if we are to understand how morphology is acquired and used, we must exploit all the methods we can.

EXERCISES

3.1. English has a host of irregular plurals such as *foot/feet, goose/geese, mouse/mice,* all of which contain vowel changes in the plural forms. If a child produces plural forms like *lice, meese,* or *reef,* what kinds of explanations can be offered for each form? What type of analyses (List, Rhyme, Feature, etc.) are consistent with these forms and which are not?

3.2. Some English words, such as *record* and *contract,* can function as either nouns or verbs, although the pronunciation changes. List five or six other such words which vary like these. What phonological factors characterize the noun forms? The verb forms? Which member of each pair do you consider to be "basic" and which the "derived"? Why? Comment on the semantic similarity or difference between the members of each pair in terms of constancy, specificity, and other relevant factors. Which member of each pair has the wider range of meaning?

3.3. For each of the following pairs of words (taken from Derwing, 1976), ask yourself if the second "comes from" the first. Rate your answers on a five-point scale defined as follows: 1 = absolutely not, 2 = unlikely, 3 = uncertain, 4 = possibly, 5 = absolutely. Into which quadrant of Figure 3.1 would you place each pair? Why?

thirst / thirsty	dine / dinner	holy / holiday
hide / hideous	limb / limber	bull / bully
bash / bashful	range / rangy	pink / pinkie
fire / fiery	sis / sissy	skin / skinny

3.4. At a particular stage, Sammy says *getted* and *runned* rather than *got* and *ran.* Is the Rhyme, Phonotactic, or Feature analysis consistant with each of these forms? Explain why (not).

3.5. Consider the following data taken from Jeff over four consecutive stages.

Stem	Stage 1	Stage 2	Stage 3	Stage 4
hat	hats	hats	hats	hats
toy	toys	toys	toys	toys
dog	dogs	dogs	dogs	dogs
mess	messes	messes	messes	messes
match	matches	matches	matches	matches
nose	noses	noses	noses	noses
hose	hoses	hoses	hoses	hoses
mouse	mice	mouses	mices	mice
foot	feet	foots	feets	feet
sheep	sheep	sheeps	sheeps	sheep

a. Explain what the child seems to be doing at each stage.

b. Chart the differences between each pair of stages. Include in your description such factors as overgeneralization, the confusion of regular and irregular plurals, and the conditioning factors for the suffixes.

3.6. Some linguists and psychologists have suggested that irregular forms, such as irregular verbs, are maintained as irregular over long periods of time in the history of a language because of frequency. That is, the more frequent an irregular form is, the more likely it will be maintained as irregular, while less frequent irregular forms will tend to become regularized. In support of this contention consider the following verbs:

Regular	Irregular
lurk	eat
jab	run
excite	see
provoke	sing
punch	run
summarize	go

a. Turn the suggestion above into a testable hypothesis (the "frequency hypothesis") relating the frequency of a form with its regularity or irregularity.

b. Check the frequencies of each of the verbs

above in a frequency list such as Thorndike and Lorge (1944). Is the frequency hypothesis supported for these forms?

c. Try to construct counterexamples to the frequency hypothesis and test these in terms of frequencies as found in Thorndike and Lorge (1944).

d. To what extent do you consider the frequency hypothesis plausible? To what extent do you think it could play an important role in maintenance of irregular forms? Why?

LABORATORIES

Laboratory 4. Morphological Relatedness

Laboratory 5. The Acquisition of the English Past Tense

Chapter Four

EXPERIMENTAL SYNTAX

4.1 Introduction

In this chapter we examine a vast array of studies devoted to experimental research in syntax. A persistent theme running throughout the chapter is the extent to which grammar is directly or indirectly involved in language use. Involved with the issues of comprehension, production, and acquisition discussed in Chapter Two are the questions of what rules a language user actually knows, how those rules are used, what knowledge states and mental representations are involved, and what empirical means we have to garner evidence about such issues. In this chapter we shall review numerous experimental studies and attempt to draw conclusions as to the current state of knowledge. Since an understanding of language processing is rapidly advancing, the best we can hope for here is a relatively up to date progress report.

We shall first examine the classical "derivational theory of complexity" with its assumption that a transformational grammar is directly involved in language comprehension and production. Next we examine the "processing strategies" approach to langages use, and finally we turn to some recent proposals for parsing strategies which the language user might employ as he constructs rather detailed syntactic representations for sentences.

Throughout the chapter, both theoretical and methodological issues are explored, since we adopt the view that fundamental issues in linguistics cannot be addressed without a clear understanding of the empirical content of particular theoretical claims. We will notice from time to time that a particular experiment may seem to support a particular hypothesis at one point, while a later reexamination of the results may yield quite a different interpretation, depending on theoretical advances or the emergence of new perspectives. Empirical results do not simply speak for themselves but instead must be interpreted and often reinterpreted. Moreover, while introspection and thoughtful reflection about an issue may provide the scientist with a starting place, his introspection alone does not suffice as both a source and a testing ground for hypotheses.

4.2 The Derivational Theory of Complexity.

Foundational preliminaries. What is the relationship between the linguist's formal grammatical description and the actual processes employed in the production and comprehension of language by real language users? This question has attracted much attention over the past two decades, and it has been of special importance since the advent of transformational generative grammar. Most linguists assume that the construction of a grammar is not just an arbitrary exercise, but instead requires the formulation of a coherent theory which not only generates the sentences of a given language but also assigns to them "correct" structural descriptions. But what constitutes "correctness"? In Chomsky's (1965) view, a description is assumed to be "correct" if it mirrors or "characterizes" the native speaker's knowledge of his language. Needless to say, the issue of a grammar as a representation of the native speaker's "linguistic competence," has generated a great deal of debate.

One of the most contentious issues within the debate focuses on a relatively simple point: What constitutes *empirical evidence* for the claim that a particular description (or even a particular rule or structure) does in fact mirror the knowledge of the native speaker? Two relatively distinct approaches to this question may be discerned. On the one hand, Chomsky and his followers seem to feel that if a particular theory is highly constrainted and well-developed, such that the resulting grammars properly generate acceptable sentences along with "insightful" or "interesting" representations of the sentences and the relations among them, then such grammars at least approach the goal of being the "correct" mental representations of the native speaker's knowledge.

Under this view, the linguist is primarily interested in theory construction and in testing his theories against his own intuitions. There is no principled requirement to go beyond the domain of the formal theory to secure other kinds of evidence for the relative correctness of the postulated description. This places the speculative linguist in a unique position: he can make claims about mental reality without the need to provide the sort of evidence which in virtually all other sciences would be considered "empirical." If experimental evidence happens to emerge supporting his theory, he might be pleased, but he need not feel threatened. If such evidence fails to support his theory, he can simply attribute this to the particulars of the empirical study, to the subjects used, to the experimental design, or the like and thereby preserve the theory from external disconfirmation. It is probably safe to say that few linguists today would publicly admit to such a radical position (but cf. Matthews, 1979). Indeed most linguists claim that their theories are responsible to data from such areas as dialect variation, historical change, language acquisition, and experimental psycholinguistics. With the possible exception of the work of Bresnan (1981, 1982) and her colleagues, however, there is little indication that research results from any of these domains has played a significant role in fostering theoretical changes.

The other general approach to the issue of the "correctness" of a linguistic description takes quite a different stance. This view takes the position that if claims are made that a given description is psychologically viable ("psychologically real"), then it is encumbant on the scientist making such a claim to provide empirical evidence. From this perspective, evidence from psycholinguistic experiments, language acquisition, language pathology, language change, dialectal variation, etc. are all highly relevant. Such a view does *not*, it must be realized, require that every theoretical construct have some sort of observable counterpart in the "real world." Such an extreme positivist position would scarcely be adopted by any working scientist. Yet this position does acknowledge the central importance of empirical evidence from external domains. This view weds the rationalist position, which is so crucial for theory construction, with the empirical methodologies required for the testing of predictions made by theories. This rationalist-empiricist amalgam combines theoretical and experimental aspects into an on-going and mutually reinforcing (and challenging) scientific activity. Such is the nature of the scientific enterprise. The fact that a combined rationalist-empiricist view is adopted here should not be interpreted as suggesting a disregard for theory construction, since neither component of the scientific enterprise can advance without the other.

The issue of how the linguist's theoretical constructs, his grammatical descriptions, are involved in actual language use, gave rise in the 1960s to the so-called "derivational theory of complexity." One of the earliest explicit formulations of this position (Chomsky & Miller, 1963, pp. 481ff) raised the following questions: (a) How is a generative transformational grammar related to language use? (b) Are the levels of a transformational grammar (deep structure and surface structure) and transformational rules actually employed in language comprehension, production, and acquisition?

These questions must be seen against the backdrop of Chomsky's (1965) assertion that a generative grammar is *not* to be understood as a model of either language production or comprehension, but is rather a model of the abstract linguistic *competence* of the native speaker. However, Chomsky further maintained that any model of language performance must somehow *incorporate* a generative grammar. How is such an incorporation to take place? This is a crucial question, for if it is assumed that a generative grammar is somehow *directly utilized* by the speaker or hearer, then the derivational theory of complexity follows naturally. This theory can be formulated as follows:

THE DERIVATIONAL THEORY OF COMPLEXITY

A. There is a direct correspondence between the formal *levels* represented in a transformational grammar (i.e, deep and surface structures) and the mental representations constructed by the language user in comprehension and production.

B. There is a direct correspondence between the transformational rules and the mental steps carried out by the language user to "encode" (produce) or "decode" (comprehend) sentences.

The derivational theory of complexity can be treated as a hypothesis which states that during language processing, the number and complexity of mental operations performed by the speaker or hearer is a function of the number and complexity of formal transformations represented in the grammatical derivation of that sentence. In short, the more complex the formal derivation of a sentence is, the more difficult it is for the speaker to produce or comprehend.

A position analogous to the derivational theory of complexity has also been formulated to account for language acquisition. In this "cumulative theory of language acquisition" (Brown & Hanlon, 1970), children are assumed to learn transformations as an important part of their linguistic development. Accordingly, the child is assumed to begin his acquisition process with relatively basic structures and, as he develops linguistically, he augments his grammar with new rules. On occassion he is forced to restructure his entire grammar. His long-term target is considered to be the adult grammar, which he approaches slowly at first, then very rapidly.

Early experimental studies. At first blush, the derivational theory of complexity seems natural and obvious. Although it involves the direct incorporation of a transformational grammar into the language processing system, the theory is quite at odds with Chomsky's disclaimer to the effect that the grammar is an abstract characterization of the speaker's knowledge. Nevertheless, the derivational theory of complexity is such a natural projection of grammatical theory onto the domain of language use that it would be absurd not to explore it. If it could be shown that the theory is empirically justified, we would have learned a great deal about language processing, and we would also have discovered that our theory construction has been on the right track. Positive results would constitute a great advance in our understanding of natural language, would provide firm empirical underpinnings for generative linguistic theory, and would solve a host of questions about the nature of language production and comprehension. One issue which would be quickly settled if the derivational theory of complexity were correct is that of the centrality of syntax. Since the derivational theory of complexity maintains that syntax is at the heart of comprehension and production, supporting evidence for the theory constitutes supporting evidence for the centrality of syntax, perhaps at the expense of such factors as semantics, pragmatics, and discourse.

The derivational theory of complexity has been explored through an examination of what has come to be called the "PNQ Sentence Family" exemplified in the set of eight sentences in Table 4.1. These sentences all contain the same basic lexical items with the same semantic relations. The coding before each sentence represents the three syntactic parameters along which the sentences vary. The first letter refers to the grammatical voice of the sentence (Active or Passive), the second letter to the mood (Declarative or Interrogative), and the third to the modality (aFfirmative or Negative). Thus there are four active and four passive sentences, four declaratives and four interrogatives, four positives (affirmatives) and four negatives. According to a formal transformational derivation of the sentences, an ADF sentence would have undergone only the usual "housekeeping" rules such as affix hopping, etc. and would be the closest surface form to the underlying representation for the entire family. In particular, it would not have undergone the NEGATIVE, QUESTION, or PASSIVE transformations. The relevant transformations associated with the

TABLE 4.1 The PNQ Sentence Family

==

Type	Sentence	Transformations
ADF	Sam saw the dog.	none
ADN	Sam didn't see the dog.	NEGATIVE
AIF	Did Sam see the dog?	QUESTION
AIN	Didn't Sam see the dog?	Q + N
PDF	The dog was seen by Sam.	PASSIVE
PDN	The dog wasn't seen by Sam.	P + N
PIF	Was the dog seen by Sam?	P + Q
PIN	Wasn't the dog seen by Sam?	P+N+Q

==

derivation of each sentence are also represented in Table 4.1.

According to the derivational theory of complexity, the ADF sentence should be the least complex of the set to produce or comprehend since no major transformations have applied in its formal derivation. Similarly, a PIN sentence should be the most difficult to produce and comprehend, since it is the most transformationally complex, having undergone three transformations in the course of its formal derivation. The relative order of difficulty, from most difficult to least, should be: PIN > PIF, PDN, AIN > AIF, PDF, ADN > ADF. This prediction is valid so long as there is no distinction among the three transformations of PASSIVE, NEGATIVE, and QUESTION. Under such an assumption, each transformation carries the same processing "weight." However, a more elaborate version of the theory could be formulated in which each transformation is assigned a weight in terms of such factors, for example, as whether or not it rearranges major constituents (such as PASSIVE), or whether it maintains the meaning of a sentence (i.e., a passive sentence might arguably have the same meaning as its active counterpart, while a negative is clearly different in meaning from a positive). Other possibilities also exist: perhaps a transformation involving several "elementary operations" such as movement and deletion should be weighted heavier than one involving fewer such operations. All these are questions, and in order to test any version of the derivational theory of complexity, initial operational definitions must be established as to how to weight each transformation. In the early experimental research in this area, all that was really expected was that "the more transformations, the more processing complexity." Such a view simply hypothesizes a *monotonic* relation between number of transformations applied and processing difficulty.

Next, a way must be found to measure "processing complexity," with experiments designed to test the predictions of the theory in those terms. An early and influential test of the derivational theory of complexity was that of Miller and McKean (1964), who reasoned that if processing complexity is carried out in real time, then the more processing steps necessary, the more real processing time would be consumed. The Miller and McKean "chronometric" study employed the PN sentence family members as stimuli, with subjects' reactions times as the dependent variable. Their major experiment involved several subtests. In each, the subject was instructed as to what kind of transformations he was to make to sentences. He was then shown a sentence, and his task was to construct mentally the required transformed version. He then activated a list of sentences and found his target among them. His mental computation and his search times were measured.

Miller and McKean's results looked encouraging for the derviational theory of complexity. Interestingly, the passive change, averaging .91 seconds, took considerably longer than the negative change (.41 seconds), but for the derivational theory of complexity, this only suggests that the passive transformation should be weighted heavier than the negative. A plausible reason for differential weighting might be that the passive rule moves two NPs around, and also changes the verb morphology, while the negative transformation only places the negative morpheme in its correct surface position. Moreover, the operation of the two rules together (1.53 seconds) is roughly the sum of their independent components. This early study provided positive impetus for many further tests of the derivational theory of complexity, even though alternative interpretations of the results are possible. One alternative explanation relates to the factor of sentence length. The simple declarative (ADF) is the shortest member of this sentence family, the simple negative is the next longest, the simple passive is next longest, and finally the passive negative is the longest. Consequently, sentence length covaries with transformational complexity and is also a monotonic function of search time.

The study could also be criticized for quite a different reason, namely that it required subjects to convert one sentence to another in a conscious, deliberate manner. Yet this is quite an unnatural task, and there is no evidence that in ordinary language use speakers actually execute such mental gymnastics when producing sentences. Therefore it might be argued that the experiment was not tapping a natural language process but rather a special skill peculiar only to the experiment. It quickly became obvious that more indirect methods were needed to assess the possibility that transformations are directly involved as mental processes in actual language processing.

Another early study investigating the hypothesis that a generative grammar is directly involved in language processing was that of Savin and Perchonock (1965). In this experiment, the PNQ sentence family was used to define the stimuli, and a recall task was employed. The assumption underlying this experiment was that different amounts of memory storage space would be required for different members of the PNQ family, depending on transformational complexity. Subjects were presented (aurally) with a PNQ sentence, followed by a list of unrelated words. If the sentence was recalled correctly, the number of correctly recalled words from the list was taken to reflect the amount of unused memory storage space remaining after the sentence had been processed.

These results indicated that the more transformationally complex a stimulus sentence was, the fewer words correctly recalled words there were, giving further support to the derivational theory of complexity. However, there is an obvious potential confounding here between *processing* and *memory*. This particular experiment really focuses on some notion of memory space into which both a processed sentence and the list of words is placed, with the assumption that this is a fixed space. There is consequently no real assessment here of the relative *processing* differences among the sentences.

Interestingly, Savin and Perchonock found that the NEGATIVE transformation took up *more* space than the PASSIVE, while quite the contrary result is implied by the Miller and McKean results, where PASSIVE took *longer* than NEGATIVE. Consequently, even though both of these two studies independently appeared to provide initial support for the derivational theory of complexity, they do not provide mutually consistent results, possibly because very different kinds of cognitive processes (overt grammatical change versus memory) are being called upon in the two studies.

A third experiment which also offered early support for the derivational theory of complexity, but again with results not so clean as had been expected, was that of Clifton and Odom (1966). The PNQ sentence family again served as the basis for the stimulus materials, and a recognition task was employed. A list of eight sentences, one representing each of the PNQ types, but all differing in lexical content, was presented several times to subjects. Then, the eight "target" sentences were embedded in a larger list containing the other seven variants of each of the targets, plus additional "filler" sentences. The total test list consisted of 64 sentences plus fillers. The subjects' task was to pick out of the test list just those sentences which they felt to have been in the original target list. Obviously, if a particular sentence contained the same lexical items as a target sentence, but differed from it by some transformation, such a sentence would be confusable with a target sentence. The general expectation was that the closer transformationally a given sentence is to a target sentence, the greater the potential confusability.

Upon examining subjects' errors, Clifton and Odom found that the closer transformationally a sentence was to a target, the more "false positive" errors were made, errors in which the subject thought the sentence belonged to the target, but in fact it did not. However, there was a higher error rate associated with PASSIVE than with NEGATIVE, leading Clifton and Odom to conclude that a relation does exist between the transformational complexity of a sentence and comprehension, but that some transformations (e.g., NEGATIVE) are more heavily weighted than others (e.g., PASSIVE). Again, this result contradicts the weighting suggested by the Miller and McKean study. It must be borne in mind, however, that this experiment involved a recognition task, so that once more there is no direct, on-line assessment of processing, but rather both memory and a matching routine are needed.

In summary, these early studies seemed promising, although there were still some troublesome details to work out. They all shared the common goal of trying to establish viable psychological measures (e.g., processing time, memory storage space, confusability) of independent formal linguistic variables, namely transformations. However, there was in all this work a frequent confounding of processing, memory, recognition, and a variety of other cognitive operations. Accordingly, while some of the studies might have been interpreted as being relevant to processing, they might in fact have had more to say about the nature of memory, for example.

At the same time, other studies were being carried out addressing the issue of the psychological reality of deep and surface structures. One of the most influential of these was that of Fodor and Bever (1965). In this study, sentences such as:

1. That he was happy was evident from the way he smiled.

were presented aurally and, employing a technique first explored by Ladefoged and Broadbent (1960), a "click" was superimposed on the sentence. The click was placed in various positions in the sentence, sometimes near a major constituent boundary and sometimes well before or after a boundary. The subjects' task was to indicate where the click was heard. The results indicated that the subjects tended to perceive the click close to a major constituent boundary, regardless of its actual location. The gravitation of the click toward a major boundary, for example after *happy* in (1), supported the notion that major constituents form psychological chunks for processing. The reasoning here is that while working within a major constituent, the hearer does not tolerate an interruption (i.e., a click), and therefore mentally displaces it toward a position where no constituent processing is in progress, namely at a major boundary.

This study appeared to support the existence of constituent structure as relevant to language comprehension, and the "click paradigm" came to be one of the most cited in the psycholinguistic literature of the period. In other click migration studies, Garrett, Bever, and Fodor (1966) and Bever, Lackner, and Kirk (1969) concluded that click migration occurs because the hearer's mental segmentation of the sentence is determined in large part by his knowledge of the language and not because of such acoustic cues as pauses. These researchers suggest that their results provide evidence for the psychological reality of constituent structure representations at both the underlying and surface levels.

Another group of experiments carried out during this period attempted to give empirical content to the theoretical notion of deep structure by examining ambiguous sentences. Within classical transformational theory, an ambiguous sentence is assigned a separate deep structure for each meaning. Accordingly, if an ambiguous sentence is psychologically assigned two different deep structures, one for each meaning, then such a sentence should be more difficult to process than a non-ambiguous sentence. In a series of studies, three types of ambiguity were distinguished: lexical, surface, and deep. Lexical ambiguity simply resides in two different meanings of a word in a sentence (e.g, "She can't *bear* children."). Surface structure ambiguity arises when different surface bracketing are possible for a given sentence (e.g., "Old men and women love rocking chairs."). Deep structure (or "relational") ambiguity obtains when two different grammatical relations can be associated with a given constituent (e.g., "Germans like beer more than Italians.").

To investigate the psychological effect of ambiguity in sentence processing, MacKay (1966) employed a sentence completion task in which subjects were given a partial sentence and instructed to complete it. The stimuli contained all three types of ambiguity as well as non-ambiguous partial sentences. It was found that it took subjects longer to complete the ambiguous sentences than the non-ambiguous ones, although their attention had not been directed toward ambiguity, leading MacKay to conclude that ambiguous sentences involved more processing complexity than non-ambiguous ones.

In a similar study, MacKay and Bever (1967), used all three types of ambiguity in stimuli and had subjects indicate when they recognized the ambiguity within a sentence. They found that the recognition of ambiguity was fastest for lexical ambiguity, next fastest for surface structure ambiguity, and slowest for deep structure ambiguity. The three types of ambiguity definable within transformational theory therefore appear to have behavioral analogues in sentence processing. At this point, then, the derivational theory of complexity appears to have wide support both in the incorporation of transformations into the processing mechanism and in terms of the reality of underlying and surface levels of constituent structure.

Later studies. The heady success of the early studies was shortly tarnished, and from two different directions. On the one hand, a closer inspection of certain transformations appeared to yield counter-intuitive predictions about what should be more or less complex, thereby undermining the theoretical foundations of the theory, while on the other hand experimental results began to accrue to refute the theory empirically.

111

To illustrate the first point briefly, we can consider a "truncated passive" sentence (2a) which presumably has a deep structure associated with (2b):

2 a. John was kicked.
  b. Someone kicked John.
  c. John was kicked by someone.

To derive (2a), the transformations of PASSIVE and AGENT DELETION, which erases the *by someone* of (2c), must apply. Yet it seems intuitively plausible that (2a) is *less* complex than (2c), although (2a) has undergone *more* transformations than (2c). Moreover, truncated passives appear to be more frequent and more natural in the spoken language than full passives. The derivational theory of complexity, it seems, makes an intuitively incorrect prediction here.

As a further example, let us consider a prenominal adjective within a NP, as in (3a), which, according to the classical transformational arguments, was to be derived from a full relative clause structure as in (3b):

3 a. the happy boy
  b. the boy who is happy.

Here, (3a) is intuitively much simpler to process than (3b), even though (3a) has undergone more transformations in its formal derivation than (3b). In particular, (3a) has undergone a transformation of WH BE DELETION, which deletes the relative pronoun plus the verb *be*, and a rule of ADJECTIVE PREPOSING, which moves the stranded adjective (or adjective phrase) resulting from the deletion of *who + be*, to a position before the noun. Once again the derivational theory of complexity makes counter-intuitive predictions, even in the absence of empirical evidence.

However, empirical evidence was forthcoming. In their attempt to replicate Savin and Perchonock (1965), Glucksberg and Danks (1969) noted, as we have above, that in the PNQ sentence family, sentence length co-varies with transformational complexity, and consequently the Savin and Perchonock results can also be explained by sentence length. In an interesting experiment reported in Bever (1968), it was found that a sentence with an initial adverb and a final particle ("Slowly the operator looked the number up.") was simpler to recall than the untransformed version ("The operator slowly looked up the number."). In cases like this, sentence length does not change, although transformational complexity does, and the results indicate that the transformed versions are *easier* to process, as measured by a recall task, than the non-transformed versions.

Baker and Prideaux (1980) reexamined the original Miller and McKean (1964) chronometric task using all members of the PNQ sentence family as stimuli, yielding 8 x 8 = 64 latencies collected for 64 subjects. Two distinct models of language processing were tested. One was the derivational theory of complexity and the other was a "direct performance" model which assumes that subjects convert a stimulus sentence directly into a response form without detouring through the deep structure. It was found that the response latencies were not clearly related to either of the models. During the experiment itself, if an incorrect response was obtained, that stimulus type was presented again later so that each had given a correct response for each stimulus. There were 4,096 correct responses (64 x 64) plus some 1,261 incorrect responses. These errors were examined in terms of the stimulus to response sentence types as formulated in terms of elementary operations (of deletion, addition, or substitution). A strong correlation (r = .81) was found between the frequency of errors and the performance model, suggesting that this model was more predictive of errors than was the derivational theory of complexity.

In an earlier paper, Baker, Prideaux, and Derwing (1973) used a "concept formation" paradigm to investigate the syntactic relations among members of the PNQ sentence family. The 32 high school students serving as subjects were presented with a sentence and directed to form a concept of a target set (which was one of the eight PNQ types). They were able to categorize sentences on the basis of syntactic form, but an analysis of the errors they committed in the course of "learning" their individual targets suggested that it was the semantic aspect of the various types which contributed to the ease of learning. For example, mood and modality were approximately equally easy to learn, but voice was some four time harder to learn than either mood or modality. Clearly both mood and modality forms signal semantic differences, while voice typically does not, especially for sentences in isolation. The derivational theory of complexity fails to predict the relative difficulties of the various structures. Recognizing that such results might be attributed to written stimuli, Reid (1974) replicated this study using aural stimuli. Although the aural concept formation task was more difficult for Reid's 64 subjects than the earlier written version, the results were the same: subjects were able to focus on mood and modality changes with relatively little difficulty, while voice changes were extremely difficult to detect. Again the derivational theory of complexity was refuted empirically.

In their attempt to replicate the click results of Fodor and Bever (1965), Reber and Anderson (1970) obtained contradictory results and claimed that intonation was a major factor in explaining the click migrations, while syntax made little or no contribution. Reber (1973) suggested a further twist, namely that the click superimposed on a sentence really constitutes a "separate message" from the content of the sentence, so that the subject's attention is constantly shifting between one message and the other. Such a shifting of attention, in addition to being quite unnatural as a language processing task, might account for the perceived click migration. In his review of the click paradigm research, Patel (1973) claimed that both intonation and semantic content contribute to an explanation of the click results. Consequently, the centrality of underlying and surface syntactic constituent structure representations as the major factors must be seriously questioned.

The importance of the psycholinguistic research on ambiguity, like the click research, takes on a rather different flavor when examined in terms of factors additional to those considered in the original work. While the early research purported to demonstrate that underlying constituent structure was very important in explaining subjects' behavior in the comprehension of ambiguous sentences, later research undercut that position. The three factors of context, bias, and surface structure complexity all appear to be significant in explaining subjects' treatment of ambiguous sentences.

Let us first deal with the problem of context. It has often been pointed out that while an isolated sentence may be ambiguous, within a particular context the ambiguity may vanish. The context itself can and usually does serve to direct the hearer's expectation toward one particular meaning. In terms of actual language processing, the issue immediately arises as to whether the language user first constructs one meaning of the sentence, and then tries it out against the context or constructs the two or more meanings simultaneously and then selects from among them. Within the literature there is apparent support for both the single reading at a time processing (e.g., Foss, Bever, & Silver, 1968; Cairns, 1973; Bock, 1978) and multiple readings processed simultaneously (e.g., Carey, Mehler, & Bever, 1970; Mistler-Lachman, 1972). In their comprehensive review of the psycholinguistic literature dealing with ambiguity, Kess and Hoppe (1981) deal with the apparent conflict between these two views in terms of what they call the "ordered access approach" which suggests that the hearer/reader invokes various kinds of cues or strategies in dealing with ambiguity, including judgements of what sorts of situations, and therefore sentences, are more plausible, and what kinds of structures and lexical items are more frequent. If this is the case, the hearer may represent the meaning of a sentence as ambiguous and discard various options in terms of context, expectations, bias, and perhaps even canonical form.

This observation immediately leads to the second important factor, namely bias. It is clear that many ambiguous sentences do not have equally likely alternative readings. For example the two ambiguous sentences in (4) have the same structure but differ in lexical items, and also in bias for expected meaning.

  4 a. The mayor instructed the police to stop drinking in the mall.
  b. The principal instructed the students to stop smoking in the hall.

The most natural reading for (4a), and therefore the one with strongest bias, requires the police to *prevent* drinking in the mall. The reason for this bias no doubt has to do with the hearer's perception of the role and function of a policeman, along with the fact that a policeman is not normally expected be drinking on the job. On the other hand, the normal expectation for (4b) is that the students have been smoking in the hall and are being ordered to cease. Even though two sentences have virtually identical structures, the choice of lexical items can play a large role in which of two meanings is more expected.

Finally, the issue of actual syntactic structure, and in particular, surface structure, is often overlooked in assessing results of the experiments dealing with ambiguous sentences. For example, while MacKay and Bever (1967) argued that their results could be explained in terms of underlying and surface structure representations, Prideaux and Baker (1976) showed that the results could also be explained in terms of (a) the fact that all but one of the so-called "deep structure ambiguous" stimulus sentences had two surface clauses, while virtually none of the "surface structure ambiguous" stimuli did and (b) the former sentences were all significantly longer than the latter. Moreover, the location of ambiguity in either the first or second clause was not controlled in the MacKay and Bever study. With sentence length, surface clausal complexity, and location of ambiguity controlled for, Prideaux and Baker (1976) were not able to replicate the earlier results. Instead they found that structural ambiguity of both kinds was more difficult to detect that lexical ambiguity, but that there was no significant difference between deep and surface ambiguity.

Consequently, the early results from the study of ambiguity which appeared so promising in support of the psychological reality of underlying constituent structures can quite plausibly be explained in terms of such factors as context, bias, and surface structure. Again, evidence fails to support the psychological viability of deep structure.

Before leaving this section, let us examine briefly some research dealing with subjects' direct assessment of constituent structure. One method for eliciting subjects' perceptions of surface structures was developed by Levelt (1967; 1969), who had his subjects provide an indication of the strength of relatedness among pairs of words in sentences. For example, Levelt (1970, pp. 110ff) noted that for a sentence like:

5. The too expensive food was tasteless.

subjects tend to feel that a stronger link obtains between *the* and *food* than between *the* and *too*. Various methods can be used to gather subjects' judgements as to relative relatedness, and across several such methods, at least for simple sentences, there is remarkable consistency. But the real question is the extent to which those judgements reflect the linguist's proposals for constituent structure. They should, of course, if there is any psychological reality in the constituent structures offered by the theorist. Under Levelt's hypothesis, "relatedness judgements are mainly determined by underlying structural relations of the sentence" (Levelt, 1970, p. 112). Levelt found considerable agreement between subjects' judgements of relative relatedness of words and constituent structure for the stimuli he used.

However, Martin (1970), in using a word-sorting technique, did not obtain such neat results. He explored the "subjective phrase structure" assigned by subjects to English SVO sentences, some of which were relatively simple while others contained relative clauses. Examples are:

6 a. Parents were assisting the advanced teenaged pupils.
b. Children who attend regularly appreciate lessons greatly.

Martin found that while a transformational grammar would assign a grouping of S-VO for all types of sentences (since the VO constituents are part of the syntactic category VP), his subjects did not behave so regularly. For relatively compact sentences like (6a), subjects assigned the structure SV-O, and for those like (6b) they assigned the structure S-VO. It might be concluded that in sentences like (6a), with a relatively "heavy" direct object phrase ("the advanced teenaged pupils"), this heavy unit is treated separately from the relatively "light" subject NP and verb, thus yielding the SV-O result. In (6b) the subject NP is itself quite heavy, and therefore is bracketed as a single item, with the two lighter verb and direct object NP constituents treated as a unit. The results of this study indicate that subjects do not necessarily take the linguist's proposed constituent structure as psychologically sacrosanct. It may be that subjects are only concerned with major constituents such as NP and V, and are not sensitive to such higher level constituents as VP. If this is the case, then the linguist's proposed constituent structure is more elaborate than required psychologically.

It should be noted that experimental research in language comprehension has dominated the field of psycholinguistics simply because in comprehension studies, the experimenter can control the structures and can therefore examine just those structural properties he is interested in. In production studies it is far more difficult to obtain data containing the kinds of structures targetted by the experimenter for investigation. One method is to use text materials (novels, etc.) but these are clearly somewhat contrived since they must conform to the rules of the written language, rules which may be quite at odds with those of the spoken language in certain respects. A second method is to ask subjects to produce sentences of a certain sort. Here, however, subjects will often do *only* as instructed, with very little naturalness and with much contrived elaboration. Given the difficulty of finding experimental methodologies to deal with language production, then, it is not surprising that a major emphasis on comprehension developed in experimental psycholinguistics.

Language acquisition. At the same time that some psycholinguists were exploring the derivational theory of complexity, others were asking how a transformational grammar might be acquired by the child. One of the most influential language acquisition groups was gathered around Roger Brown at Harvard. Brown and his associates adopted the view that the child is a kind of "little linguist" who analyses data and constructs and tests hypotheses as he builds up his mental grammar. According to this "cumulative theory of language acquisition" (Brown & Hanlon, 1970), the child first acquires the base structures of his grammar and then slowly augments this by the addition of transformational rules, with occasional restructuring taking place. An alternative view, and one espoused by McNeill (1970), is that the base structures are an innate part of the child's mental endowment. However, both views assume that the child constructs a mental transformational grammar by expanding his grammatical structures through the accretion of transformations.

One research strategy of those adopting this view was to examine the language of children over an extended period of time and chart grammatical development by constructing transformational grammars for successive developmental stages. Beginning in 1962, Brown and his colleagues undertook an extended longitudinal study of three children, whom they dubbed Adam, Eve, and Sarah. An enormous amount of data was collected from these three children and extensive analyses of their utterances were constructed. Brown (1973) reviewed much of that research in detail and provided one of the most readable and delightful accounts of a language acquisition project yet to be written.

One important contribution based on this material was Klima and Bellugi's (1966) study of the development of negative and question forms, They noted that at the earliest stages, negation in children's speech tends to be marked early in the utterance, as in "No singing song" and "No sit there," while later the child incorporates certain auxiliary verbs into negative structures, such as "We can't talk" and "I don't like him." However, at this second stage, only the auxiliaries *do* and *can* are cited. For other negatives, we find utterances without auxiliaries such as "That no Mommy" and

"He no bite you." At this stage, the auxiliaries occur only in negatives, and not in declaratives or questions.

Turning to questions, we find utterances represented both yes-no and *wh* questions at all stages. Some of these are exemplified in Table 4.2. At the earliest stage, children use intonation to signal both yes-no and *wh* questions, although the latter always have an initial *wh* word as well. At the second stage, the situation is relatively unchanged, but at the third stage, the child has begun to use *do, will,* and *can* in initial position to signal yes-no questions, although this inverted word order is not found in *wh* questions yet. That is, the child has not generalized a rule of inverted word order for all questions, contrary to that view of language acquisition in which the child is expected to overgeneralize. Indeed, as Klima and Bellugi point out, it is puzzling that the child seems to have *under*generalized a syntactic rule of inverted word order, limiting it only to yes-no questions. A second puzzling fact is that, if the child possesses base rules according to which *wh* forms originate in untransformed positions, we would expect to find utterances such as "The cowboy is doing what?" since in the deep structure, *what* originates in the direct object position. However, such structures do not occur in the data.

In summary, the child does not overgeneralize these forms, contrary to expectations and to his behaviour in other areas. Moreover, he does make the kinds of "mistakes" that the cumulative theory of language acquisition predicts, since he fails to produce sentences in the "basic" word order (e.g., "My spoon goed where?") before he "learns" the transformation of *wh* movement.

In addressing these problems, Prideaux (1976) argued that if a functional rather than transformational perspective is adopted, an obvious solution emerges. The inverted word order is not needed in the early *wh* questions since at that time the *wh* word itself serves as an indicator of a question. The child has no other *wh* structures in his repertory then, and in particular, no structures such as "I wonder where Mommy went" or "I know

TABLE 4.2 Yes-no and wh Questions from Three Successive Stages*

===

	yes-no Questions	wh Questions
Stage 1	See hole? Ball go? I ride train?	Who that? Where milk go? What cowboy doing?
Stage 2	See my doggie? You want eat? I have it?	Where me sleep? What the dollie have? Why you smiling?
Stage 3	Does lions walk? Did I saw that in my book? Will you help me?	What I did yesterday? Why Paul caught it? Where my spoon goed?

—————————————————————————

*After Klima & Bellugi, 1966

===

what he did." Later, however, as such forms emerge, the child comes to realize that his *wh* question forms such as "What I did yesterday?" are now functionally ambiguous: they are identical to embedded *wh* clauses, though he has earlier used them for questions. Once this functional ambiguity is encountered, the child apparently modifies his question forms to include inverted word order, thereby eliminating the ambiguity and leaving the earlier structure available for embedded clauses.

It can also be argued that the child never produces *wh* questions with the *wh* word in its deep structure position simply because his grammar does not involve movement rules at all; rather his rule is something like "Place the information-seeking *wh* word in a clause-prominent (initial) position." Even in the adult language, a non-initial *wh* word must occur under special stress and in such "echo" questions there is less a seeking of information than an indication of surprise, as in "You said he went *where?"*

While much of the research into the acquisition of syntax assumed the cumulative theory of language acquisition, it has become apparent that syntax alone is inadequate to explain the diverse phenomena encountered. Semantic and pragmatic factors seem intricately involved as well. Slobin (1966), for example, found that six-year-old children tended to confuse passive sentences like those in (7a) with actives such as (7b), although such confusion did not appear for pairs such as in (8).

7 a. The dog was chased by the cat.
  b. The dog chased the cat.

8 a. The girl was watered by the flowers.
  b. The girl watered the flowers.

The sentences in (7) are what Slobin called "reversibles" since the exchange of subject and object yield a perfectly acceptable and plausible sentence, while those in (8) are not reversible. Thus, the child appears to be attending to semantic and pragmatic factors in avoiding confusion in (8), but in (7) either reading is acceptable and he is falling back on word order to interpret the sentence.

Other evidence suggesting that pragmatic and semantic factors, along with others, led many researchers to broaden their perspectives to encompass others aspects than syntax. The cumulative theory of language acquisition seems to have gone the way of the derivational theory of complexity, at least in the minds of a great many researchers (cf. de Villiers & de Villiers, 1978, p. 115). Moreover, the notion that much of the child's linguistic knowledge is innate has, suggests Maratsos (1979), received little substantial support.

Summary. The early successes of the derivational theory of complexity and the cumulative theory of language acquistion came to be slowly eroded. Many of the early studies which purported to support both the psychological reality of transformations as mental operations and of abstract underlying levels of syntactic representation could not, in the long run, be maintained. The reasons for this development were, as we have seen, varied.

On the one hand, classical transformational theory was drastically altered in many ways. On the other, such varied linguistic factors as surface structure, sentence length, subject bias, semantic contributions, lexical choice, pragmatics, knowledge of the world, and the effect of context all appear to be involved in language processing. Moroever, a host of cognitive factors, including memory (both short- and long-term), recall, recognition, and on-line processing, are also involved. These varied factors often contributed in unexpected ways in the early studies. Indeed, even such committed transformationalists as Fodor, Bever, and Garrett (1974) were forced to conclude that the derivational theory of complexity was dead. The next question, of course, was what should be tried in its place?

4.3 Cognitive Strategies

Preliminaries. If any lesson was learned in dealing with the derivational theory of complexity, it was that there is far more to language processing than just syntax. This is not to say that syntax plays no role in processing, but rather that many other factors are operative as well. As Slobin (1979, p. 53) points out, the language user employs all the information he can as he produces and understands language, including his knowledge of the world, his knowledge of his language structure, meaning, rules of conversation, discourse, an assessment of the situation, and doubtless many other factors as well. From the realization that syntax is only one of the many components involved, and in concert with the demise of the derivational theory of complexity in the early 1970s, a new direction in language processing research evolved, and again Bever and his colleagues were instrumental in this development. In important papers Bever (1970a, 1970b), Slobin (1973), and others proposed early versions of what they called "perceptual strategies." According to this view, it was assumed that the speaker (or hearer or learner) employs a battery of heuristics or strategies to process language. Again we will focus

123

on comprehension and attempt to explicate the perceptual strategies paradigm briefly.

At the heart of this proposal is the assumption that in the process of comprehension, the hearer is actively engaged in constructing meaning representations for utterances through the use of various strategies which he applies to the input. It is assumed that he somehow parses the utterance, engages in a lexical search, constructs a syntactic representation, and, perhaps simultaneously, *constructs* rather than *extracts* the meaning. In this activity, he makes use of various language-specific factors, such as expectations based on his knowledge of the grammatical structure of his language. For example, upon hearing "the," the English speaker expects an adjective or a noun to follow since "the" signals the beginning of a NP. If the English speaker encounters a sentence-initial auxiliary, as in (9a), he expects that the sentence will be a question, although, as in (9b), this expectation might be incorrect.

9 a. Were all the boys all sent home?
   b. Were all the boys sent home, it would be a blessing to the principal.

It appears that structures like (9a) are far more common than those like (9b), and perhaps frequency alone can account for the expectation here. A basic assumption underlying this approach, is that the language user's expectations concerning structures, functions, and the like, guide him in making quick assessments in his parsing and therefore in his construction of semantic representations. In the earliest work on perceptual strategies, primary attention was directed toward language-specific proposals, and this is especially true in the pioneering work of Bever (1970a, 1970b). Accordingly, it is useful to examine some of his proposals. After examining some early proposals in the perceptual strategies domain, we shall suggest that a distinction be drawn between language-specific facts, such as the speaker's expectations built in part on his knowledge of his language structures, and language-independent and more general "cognitive strategies" which appear to interact with language-specific factors in processing.

Experimental Syntax

Early proposals. In his early work, Bever
(1970a; 1970b) formulated several strategies which,
he suggested, are operative in the comprehension
of English. Since these strategies typically depend
upon surface structural configurations, it is assumed
that the hearer constructs a (surface) syntactic
representation and then associates functional or
semantic information with certain aspects of that
representation. These pairings are neither
exceptionless nor necessarily purely deterministic.
Rather, the hearer makes a "best guess" as to the
grammatical functions and meanings of the
structures, presumably based on his expectations,
frequency of certain structures, structural cues,
semantic collocations, and the like. It is useful to
examine some of Bever's proposed strategies in
order to illustrate the general perceptual strategies
program as it was initially set out. Certain of
Bever's (1970a) proposed strategies are cited in
Table 4.3. Clearly, Strategies B and D depend on
English word order, while Strategies A and D
depend on the typical order of appearance of
semantic roles in an English clause. Therefore
Strategies A, B, and D are specific to English while
Strategy C is semantically based, but independent of
English word order. Finally, Strategy E" is highly
dependent on the facts of English noun phrase
structure and must therefore be language specific
as well.

An examination of these proposals reveals several
important aspects of the early perceptual strategies
program. It is assumed, for example, that the
hearer parses the incoming signal into at least
phrasal constituents with Strategy E" presumably
employed in recognizing the English NP structure,
although it says nothing about the meaning of the
elements within the NP identified by the strategy
nor about the function of that NP within a clause.
Strategy A, however, relates to the parsing of a
string of constituents, and suggests that they should
be grouped together as a single clause by virtue of
semantic cohesion. Strategy B suggests that for
(English) sentences containing more than one clause,
the first is expected to be the main clause unless
it is overtly marked with a subordinate function
word such as *because, after, before,* etc. Strategy
C seems to be a general "meta-strategy" requiring

TABLE 4.3 Some of Bever's (1970a) Perceptual Strategies

==

Strategy A. Segment together any sequence X . . . Y, in which the members could be related by primary internal structural relations "actor action object . . . modifier."

Strategy B. The first N ... V ... (N) ... clause (isolated by Strategy A) is the main clause, unless the verb is marked as subordinate.

Strategy C. Constituents are functionally related internally according to semantic constraints.

Strategy D. Any *Noun-Verb-Noun* (NVN) sequence within a potential internal unit in the surface structure corresponds to *"actor-action-object"*.

Strategy E". After "determiner . . ." the boundary of the head noun phrase is marked by (1) a set of morpheme classes that signal the end of a noun phrase (such as "s") or immediately subsequent morphemes that signify the beginning of a new noun phrase (such as "the," proper nouns) or a relative clause (such as "that") and (2) a subsequent lexical item that is less uniquely a noun.

Principle G. Sequences with constituents in which each subconstituent contributes information to the internal structure of the constituent are complex in proportion to the complexity of an intervening subsequence.

==

that semantic constraints bind constituents together into coherent units, clause-like in structure and propositional in semantic organization, such that verbs or adjectives serve as predicates with several associated NP arguments. Finally, Strategy D refers directly to the heads of potential constituents and states that the hearer will assign to certain syntactic sequences their "expected" semantic roles.

From these brief observations, it is clear that the notion of "strategy" as developed by Bever and his colleagues is rather loose. Some strategies are devoted to syntactic parsing (i.e., E"), some are very general constraints which suggest that certain constellations of elements (constituents?) are related semantically into coherent units (i.e., A, C), and others refer to grammatical facts peculiar to the specific language being processed in order to assign various constituents semantic functions (i.e., B, D). It is not clear from the early work whether the strategies are organized hierarchically or not, nor whether the distinction between language-specific and language-independent factors is crucial.

At this early point, the strategies approach was at best suggestive, although for each of his proposals, Bever (1970a) offered supporting empirical evidence. He noted, for example, that Strategy A was supported by the various click studies discussed above (e.g., Fodor & Bever, 1965; Bever, Lackner, & Stolz, 1969). Strategy B is supported by the work of Clark and Clark (1968), who showed that a sentence containing a subordinate clause is relatively harder to memorize if the subordinate clause precedes the main clause than if the order is reversed. Thus, a sentence like (10b) should be easier to memorize and therefore preferred over (10a).

10 a. Because the food was gone, the dog bit the cat.
   b. The dog bit the cat because the food was gone.

Strategy C is given support by the language acquisition study of Slobin (1966), who gave children sentences like those in (11), along with pictures. The children were required to verify the correctness of a particular picture when it was paired with a sentence.

11 a. The dog ate the cookie.
   b. The cow followed the horse.
   c. The cookie was eaten by the dog.
   d. The horse was followed by the cow.

The first two sentences are actives while the third

and forth are passives. However, (11a) differs from (11b) by virtue of the fact that the verb *eat* is not reversible, while *follow* is. That is, a horse may follow a cow or *vice versa*, but a cookie normally does not eat a dog. Slobin (1966) found that for passive sentences containing reversible verbs, as in (11d), picture verification was more difficult than if the sentence contained a non-reversible verb, as in (11c). Moreover, (11b) and (11d) were, for some children, equally difficult, although (11d) tended to be interpreted as "The horse followed the cow." Bever claims that Strategy C explains this result since the normal expectation is for the first NP to be an actor or agent when it occurs with an action verb.

Mehler and Carey (1968) presented subjects with sentences such as those in (12) (after Bever, 1970a, p. 297), and with each they showed subjects two pictures, one appropriate and one inappropriate.

12 a. They are fixing benches.
    b. They are performing monkeys.

Sentences like (12a) are in the progressive aspect, while those like (12b) contain a participial modifier, although the two types are superficially very similar since both contain *be* + *V-ing* followed by a NP. The subjects' task was to indicate which picture was the appropriate one, and the reaction times were measured. It was found that reaction times were relatively long for inappropriate pictures and also relatively long for the participial structures like (12b). This latter result was explained on the basis of the fact that participial structures are syntactically more complex than the progressive aspectuals. However, the same result would be predicted by the fact that the progressives are far more common, and the only place where participials conflict with the progressives is in structures like (12b). When a picture is both inappropriate and the stimulus is a participial, the reaction time was not twice either of the individual averages, but just the same as either. This suggests that the meaning and the syntax are processed in parallel, and the two types of complexity, semantic or syntactic, are processed independently.

The Mehler and Carey (1968) study also supports Strategy D, since the progressive structures like (12a), which preserve the "actor action object" roles, are processed faster than the participials, which do not maintain this functional structure. Indeed, Strategy D predicts just this result. The results reported in Slobin (1966) also support this strategy, since Slobin found that children more quickly verified pictures corresponding to active sentences, such as (11a, b), than pictures appropriate to the corresponding passives, such as (11c, d).

From the period of the earliest work on perceptual strategies, it was realized that sentences containing subordinate clauses constitute an important testing ground for proposals concerning language processing, simply because such sentences can vary in many ways. At the same time some structures with subordinate clauses appear to be more natural and relatively easier to understand than others. Similarly, some types appear earlier in language acquisition than others, suggesting that children employ certain strategies much like those apparently used by adults. For example, the fact that structures like (10b) tend to be judged as preferable, in isolation of course, to their putative paraphrased partners like (10a), indicates that there are important factors involved in processing complex sentences to be uncovered. For sentences containing relative clauses, such as those in (13), certain forms seem to be easier to process than others.

13 a. The guest expected to be late arrived.
   b. The guest who was expected to be late arrived.

In (13a), there is no internal marker to indicate that the verb *expected* is a passive participle within a relative clause, while in (13b) the presence of the relative pronoun *who* provides a clear indication that a relative clause is at hand. Here, Strategies A, B, C, and D conspire to lead the hearer to an analysis for (13a) in which the verb *expected* is treated as the main verb, and it is only with the appearance of the final verb *arrived* than the hearer is forced to reconsider his analysis.

A further property of complex sentences which might contribute to relative processing complexity concerns the nesting of one clause within another. It has long been recognized that for sets of paraphrases like (14), some members are intuitively easier to understand than others.

14 a. That for John to win the race was easy is obvious.
   b. It is obvious that for John to win the race was easy.
   c. It is obvious that it was easy for John to win the race.

It seems clear that (14c) is easier to understand than (14b), which in turn is easier than (14a). The reason appears to be simply that "center embedded" structures are in general more difficult to understand than "right branching" structures. But the fundamental question here is *why* center embeddings should be so hard to process. The answer is probably that when two constituents belong together in a unit (e.g., in a clause) but are separated by too many other units, the relative processing complexity increases. As Bever's (1970a, p. 330) Principle G (Table 4.3) suggests, the more intervening material between relevant constituents, the greater the processing complexity. This principle predicts that a sentence like (15a) is intuitively easier and more acceptable than (15b).

15 a. Sammy called up his friend who used to play on his baseball team but later moved to Hamburg.
   b. Sammy called his friend who used to play on his baseball team but later moved to Hamburg up.

The heart of Principle G is simply that a unit which contains semantically and syntactically cohesive constituents is easier to process if it is not internally interrupted.

The anti-interruption principle was perhaps best articulated by Slobin (1973), who attempted to formulate general "operating principles" which govern the processes involved in children's acquisition of their native language (see Table 4.4). The relevant

TABLE 4.4 Slobin's (1973) "Operating Principles"

===

Principle A. Pay attention to the ends of words.

Principle B. The phonological shape of words can be systematically modified.

Principle C. Pay attention to morpheme and word order.

Principle D. Avoid interrupting or rearranging linguistic units.

Principle E. Semantic relations should be overtly and clearly marked.

Principle F. Avoid exceptions.

Principle G. Grammatical markers should make semantic sense.

===

principle here is D, which actually encompasses two distinct principles. One states that the "normal order" of members of a unit should be preserved and the other states the preference for non-interrupted over interrupted structures.

Slobin's proposals herald a new perspective on the perceptual strategies issue. While Bever's early work and supporting empirical evidence served as a foundation for the strategies enterprise, it contained a complex of confounding factors. In particular, the distinctions between language-independent and language-specific factors was not clearly drawn, nor was the distinction between semantic and syntactic factors. Moreover, it was not clear just what kinds of roles the strategies played. Were they, for example, independent of grammar or was the grammar still somehow involved in language processing?

Fodor, Bever, and Garrett (1974) argued that while transformations were not viable as language processing steps, deep and surface structure were nevertheless still psychologically viable. The strategies were therefore viewed as heuristics the language user employs as he processes language. But a central question is then: What is a the purpose of a grammar if not to play a role in actual language use or acquisition? No answer to this question was ever forthcoming, other than the gratuitous one that a grammar was regarded as representing the implicit "competence" of the native speaker. Perhaps in response to this problem, some recent research, discussed below in Section 4.5, has reintroduced a competence grammar as that component providing representations which serve as the targets for the language parser as it constructs syntactic representations for sentences.

Recent proposals. If any single factor fueled the strategies approach to language processing, it was the demise of the derivational theory of complexity. However, some linguists went so far as to claim that a grammar is only a set of strategies. Slobin (1970, p. 175), for example, claimed to "... approach grammar as a set of linguistic strategies used to express various semantic relationships in spoken utterances." This view was apparently shared by Lakoff and Thompson (1975, p. 295), who stated:

> ...GRAMMARS ARE JUST COLLECTIONS OF STRATEGIES FOR UNDERSTANDING AND PRODUCING SENTENCES. From this point of view, abstract grammars do not have any separate mental reality; they are just convenient fictions for representing certain processing strategies (original emphasis).

Presumably, Lakoff and Thompson are inveighing against transformational grammmars when they speak of abstract grammars. Even if a transformational grammar has no separate reality, this does not mean that grammars and strategies are one and the same thing. In fact, the confounding between statements of grammatical structure and formulations of processing heuristics seriously confuses the entire strategies approach. Let us examine some of the problems briefly.

Experimental Syntax

Initially, the label "perceptual" seems misleading since the strategies are not so much perceptual in the usual sense of this term as they are cognitive. The process of language comprehension (or production or acquisition) seems to involve at least two separate components: (a) the structures to be (re)constructed, along with their meanings, and (b) the processing mechanisms (*strategies*) invoked to carry out that constructive act. Thus, the strategies deal with far more than just the "perception" of language. Rather, they are cognitive in nature and are potentially involved with various aspects of language use, including comprehension, production, and acquisition. Moreover, cognitive strategies appear to be fairly general information processing mechanisms which might be, and in certain cases clearly are, independent of language. For example, a strategy which treats interrupted units as more complex to process than non-interrupted units might well have application, for example, in visual perception or musical comprehension.

In what follows, we shall draw a sharp distinction between a statement of a grammatical rule or structure on the one hand and a cognitive strategy on the other. A grammatical rule may, for example, state that the subject of a clause is the first major NP to the left of the main verb, for English, or that a (non-topic) direct object is positioned to the right of the main verb. However, a particular strategy may well take advantage of such grammatical statements, which are typically language-specific, and thereby predict that one form should be relatively easier or more difficult to process than the other. Let us take a specific example to make clear the distinction between grammatical structure and a strategy. In the example sentences cited above in (15), the fact that (15a) is predicted to be more difficult than (15b) follows from two factors. The first is *grammatical* and simply states that, under well-defined circumstances, English syntax permits a verb-particle structure to interact with a following direct object NP in one of two ways: either the particle stands with the verb, and the two of them make up a single syntactic unit as well as a semantic unit as in (15a), or the particle may be placed after the direct object NP, as in (15b). The second factor, the anti-interruption strategy, states that an interrupted unit is more difficult to process than a non-interrupted one. Consequently, the prediction that (15b) is more complex to process is a function of the fact that English syntax allows the particle to be separated from its verb on the one hand, but such a separation is opposed by the non-interruption strategy. The prediction therefore follows from the general form of the strategy, but it is the grammar of English which presents the opportunity for the two structures of (15) to be considered. The facts relating to the particle separation are facts about English grammatical structure, but the cognitive strategy which favors non-interrupted structures is a general, language independent statement.

In an experiment designed to test the interaction of the strategy with the language-specific facts about English particle placement (Hunter, 1981; Hunter & Prideaux, 1983), subjects were given various sentences similar to those in (15) and were instructed to make judgements as to relative acceptability. The stimuli included sentences with the particle adjacent to the verb as well as with the particle moved to positions beyond a simple NP object, to a position after a NP+PP, and to a position after a NP followed by a relative clause. It was found that the further the particle is from the verb, the less acceptable the resulting sentence. However, the worst possible case is one in which the particle is moved across a direct object plus relative clause. The results of this study support the non-interruption hypothesis.

Sentence-based strategies. In the research carried out in the mid 1970s and later, attention came to be directed more and more to the formulation of general cognitive strategies, and testing the strategies was an important part of experimental psycholinguistic research. Since a fairly wide range of proposals has been offered, it is useful to attempt a synthesis of the more important ones. In particular, Bever's (1970a) Strategies A through D, coupled with Slobin's (1973) Operating Principle D, all point to the importance of the clause as a processing unit. It is useful to formulate some of the major cognitive strategies implicit in the early work. The CLOSURE, NORMAL

TABLE 4.5 Sentence Level Cognitive Strategies

===

CLOSURE. In processing a particular unit (clause, phrase, etc.), the hearer attempts to obtain closure on that unit at the earliest possible point.

NORMAL FORM. The hearer assumes that the unit being processed is in its "normal" or "canonical" form unless it is overtly marked to the contrary.

NON-AMBIGUITY. The hearer assumes that the unit being processed is not ambiguous.

BRACKETING. The hearer expects that when a new unit for processing is encountered, it will be marked as such.

===

FORM, BRACKETING, and NON-AMBIGUITY strategies are listed in Table 4.5 (cf. Kimball, 1973; Prideaux, 1982; Prideaux & Baker, 1982).

CLOSURE incorporates the non-interruption proposal implicit in both Bever's (1970a) Principle G and in Slobin's (1973) Operating Principle D, while NORMAL FORM restates Slobin's (1973) injunction against rearrangement of basic constituent ordering. CLOSURE predicts that in:

16 a. The thief who stole the briefcase saw the man.
   b. The man saw the thief who stole the briefcase.

sentence (16a) should be more difficult to process than (16b) since in (16a) the main clause is interrupted by a relative clause, while in (16b) the relative clause is non-interrupting. It is important to note that sentence length is held constant, and it is only the location of the subordinate clause which differs. By virtue of the position of English relative clauses following the head NP, a relative clause on a subject NP will always be interrupting. If we turn to a language like Japanese, however, which has the basic word order SOV, and which requires a relative clause to precede the head NP, we find structures like those in (17) (where OM = direct object marker, S = subject marker).

17 a. RC+S O V
hon o yonda sensei wa inu o mita
"book OM read teacher SM dog OM saw"
The teacher who read a book saw the dog.
b. S RC+O V
inu wa hon o yonda sensei o mita
"dog SM book OM read teacher OM saw"
The dog saw the teacher who read the book.

In this case, CLOSURE predicts that (17a) should be the easier to process, since its relative clause is non-interrupting. If only English data were considered, and if the predictions from CLOSURE for English are correct, one might be tempted to conclude that the reason (16b) was easier to process than (16a) had nothing to do with CLOSURE, but was rather because it is easier to attach a relative clause to an object NP than to a subject NP. Until a case like the Japanese examples is found, there is no immediate way to reject this second alternative. However, if the Japanese results come out as CLOSURE predicts, it can be concluded that CLOSURE rather than an object preference governs processing ease. In an experiment in which native speakers of Japanese judged the relative naturalness of Japanese sentences like those in (17), the results indicated a preference for non-interrupted sentences over interrupted ones, thereby supporting the operation of the CLOSURE strategy (Prideaux, 1980; 1982).

Further support for CLOSURE comes from a rather unexpected source: American Sign Language (ASL). Coulter (1983) notes that ASL relative clauses are more constrained in function than are English relative clauses, since the former must be definite descriptions of particular referents, and therefore cannot have generic heads. Structurally, however, ASL relatives almost have the appearance of being conjoined rather than subordinate, and they do not interrupt the main clause.

136

TABLE 4.6 Some English Relative Clause Structures

===

<u>Type</u>	<u>Structure</u> <u>and</u> <u>Example</u>
Subject/Subject (SS)	S+[RPs V O] V O The dog that bit the cat kicked the cow.
Subject/Object (SO)	S+[RPo S V] V O The dog that the cat bit kicked the cow.
Object/Subject (OS)	S V O+[RPs V O] The dog bit the cat that kicked the cow.
Object/Object (OO)	S V O+[RPo S V] The dog bit the cat that the cow kicked.

===

Both CLOSURE and NORMAL FORM are refinements of Bever's (1970) and Slobin's (1973) proposals, but formulated in language independent terms. An important challenge to Slobin's (1973) version of these proposals was offered by Sheldon (1974) and resulted from her work in language acquisition. Drawing upon a technique initially employed by Brown (1971), Sheldon attempted to test both the anti-interruption and anti-rearrangement aspects of Slobin's Operating Principle D in terms of children's comprehension of sentences containing relative clauses. She utilized a toy moving technique in which children acted out various sentences with toy animals. Following Brown (1971), she investigated four types of English sentences containing relative clauses. The four types are illustrated in Table 4.6.

In each of the sentences in Table 4.6, the relative clause contains a relative pronoun (RP) functioning either as the subject of the relative clause (RPs) or as the direct object (RPo). The coding for each type consists of two letters, the first of which (S or O) represents the grammatical function of the NP to which the relative clause is attached, and the second of which (again, S or O) represents the function of the relative pronoun within that relative clause. According to CLOSURE, types OS and OO should be easier to process than types SS or SO, since in the former there is no interruption. According to NORMAL FORM, however, types SS and OS should be easier to process than SO and OO, since in SS and OS the relative clause has the word order SVO just as a main clause, while types SO and OO contain relative clauses with word order of OSV, which is non-normal. Sheldon found that these predictions were not borne out in her data, but rather that types SS and OO were relatively easier than OS and SO. Accordingly, she proposed what she called the "parallel function" hypothesis, which states that if the relative pronoun plays the *same* role in the relative clause as the modified NP plays in the main clause, processing is easier.

Sheldon's parallel function proposal suffers from two weaknesses, however. First, it is *ad hoc* in the sense that it does not follow from other theoretical claims, but instead simply names the results. Second, and perhaps more important, however, is the manner in which Sheldon arrived at her results. Her 33 subjects were divided into three groups. The first group were between ages three years, eight months and four years, three months (3,8-4,3). Group II were of ages 4,6-4,11, and Group III were 5,0-5,5. Each group contained 11 children. When each group is examined individually, different results emerge. For Group I, the easiest structures are of type OO, with SS next, and SO the hardest. Group II shows the same pattern, but Group III indicates that SS is the easiest by far, with OO next, and again SO the hardest. Sheldon's results can be explained in terms other than those of the parallel function hypothesis once it is noticed that the youngest children model their interpretation of the compound sentences on the prototype of conjoined sentences. For example, if we ignore relative pronouns, as children often seem to do, we find that a conjoined structure like (18a) is similar to that of OO:

18 a. S V O (and) S V (O)
The dog bit the cat (and) the cat kicked (the cow).

b. S V (O) (and) V (O)
The dog bit (the cat) and kicked (the cow).

c. S and S V O
The dog and the cat bit the cow.

In (18b) we find a structure quite similar to SS, but without the relative pronoun. It is therefore possible that the child is initially utilizing prototypical structures of conjunction, which he already controls, in working out the relative clause analyses. If so, he is *expropriating* existing structures for new uses, rather than relying on some *ad hoc* principle of "parallel function." Detailed analyses and critiques of Sheldon's proposal are found in Prideaux (1979a) and Tavakolian (1981). An important point to be made here is that with any proposed strategy or hypothesis, it is crucial to demonstrate that the proposal is neither *ad hoc* nor implausible. Moreover, it is important to take into consideration the subject's perspective on the task. Along this line, it is surely plausible to expect that when confronted with novel structures, the child will make his first analyses based on structures he already knows.

Let us now turn to the last two strategies of Table 4.5. NON-AMBIGUITY simply states that the hearer expects things to be straightforward and in accord with canonical forms. While "ambiguity" normally refers to semantic matters, it can also refer to syntax. For example, the English sequence V+NP+NP is typically analyzed with the second NP as the direct object, as in (19a, b). However, the same sequence can, in some circumstances, be analyzed with the first NP as the direct object and the second NP as the object complement, as in (19c).

19 a. Sam brought Suzie a flower.
b. Sam called Suzie a taxi.
c. Sam called Suzie a dummy.

The NON-AMBIGUITY strategy suggests that a

sentence like (19b), which can potentially be analyzed two ways, should be more difficult to processs than one like (19a), which is amenable to only one analysis. Of course, this kind of ambiguity is also a source for (poor) puns and jokes. The results of MacKay's (1966) sentence completion experiment, discussed above in Section 4.2, also lend support to this strategy. In that experiment, MacKay's subjects found it harder to complete ambiguous sentences than non-ambiguous ones, suggesting that even potential ambiguity caused processing difficulty. The semantic aspect of the NON-AMBIGUITY strategy also finds support in the results of Slobin (1966), discussed above, in which children found reversible sentences more difficult to process than non-reversible ones.

The BRACKETING strategy is a general statement of several proposals, including Bever's (1970a) Strategy E", which deals with the onset of a NP in English. Another special case of BRACKETING might be called the "relative clause identification strategy", which states that "Whenever a clause begins with a relative pronoun, it is a relative clause modifying a noun" (Clark & Clark, 1977, p. 69). This strategy suggests that if a relative pronoun is present at the beginning of a relative clause, processing should be easier than if the relative pronoun is absent. Support for such a strategy lies in the reported difficulty of Bever's (1970a) "garden path" sentences like those in (20):

20 a. The horse raced past the barn fell.
   b. The guest expected to be late arrived.

There even exists diachronic evidence from the history of English for such a strategy (Bever & Langendoen, 1971).

Discourse strategies. In addition to strategies associated with sentence processing, others were proposed which are sensitive to certain aspects of discourse structure. One of the most important of these deals with the distribution of Given and New information. As Clark and Haviland (1974) proposed, following earlier suggestions of Halliday (1967 a, b; 1968) and Chafe (1970), sentences typically contain both information known to the speaker and hearer

("Given" information) and information known to the speaker but not to the hearer ("New" information). Moreover, it appears that languages tend to separate Given and New information systematically. In English, the tendency is for Given information to come before New in a sentence. Accordingly, the GIVEN-NEW strategy can be formulated as follows:

THE GIVEN-NEW STRATEGY. The hearer expects that Given information will normally be systematically separated from New information. Given information precedes New, although the order New-Given is possible if special grammatical devices are employed to signal the non-typical order.

Evidence for the GIVEN-NEW strategy is abundant. Let us first examine some intuitive evidence. Suppose the question in (21a) is asked, with the possible responses in (21b, c, d, e). (The capitalized words carry the main stress, which would normally be on the final content word of the sentence in a normal utterance.)

21 a. Who did Sam give the flowers to?
    b. He gave the flowers to SUE.
    c. He gave the FLOWERS to Sue.
    d. He gave Sue the FLOWERS.
    e. He gave SUE the flowers.

The form of the question in (21a) indicates that for the person responding to the question, the identity of the recipient is known. However, in response to (21a), only (21b) and (21e) are appropriate. The reason for this is simply that in (21b) *flowers* is Given information and precedes the New information *Sue*. However, in (21e), *Sue* is signalled as New by virtue of being uttered under stress. Thus, the normal order of Given-New can be violated only by appropriate use of, in this case, additional stress.

In an experimental context, Smyth, Prideaux, and Hogan (1979) set up passages in which some information was developed as Given and some as New. Subjects listened to the passages and later were instructed to indicate whether or not a particular sentence had occurred in the passage. The target sentences contained, among other things, direct and indirect objects, with both orders DO+IO and IO+DO. The objects also differed in terms of Given and New information. Subjects were found to be sensitive to the Given-New ordering, and this factor, rather than whether an object was direct or indirect, was crucial in determining the correctness of the subjects' responses. Subjects were very sensitive to changes in word order which violated the GIVEN-NEW strategy, but relatively insensitive to those which did not. Bock and Irwin (1980) also reported an experiment in which the GIVEN-NEW strategy was important in guiding subjects' selection of appropriate word orders in responses to questions.

Another important discourse based strategy discussed by Clark and Clark (1977) is the ORDER OF EVENTS strategy. This strategy states that if the relative order of two clauses in a complex sentence is the same as the order of the two events described by the sentence, it will be easier to process than if the order of clauses does not mirror the order of events. Consider the following sentences:

    22 a. After we see the movie, we'll get a pizza.
        b. We'll get a pizza after we see the movie.
        c. Before we get a pizza, we'll see the movie.
        d. We'll see the movie before we get a pizza.

The order of events is (1) see the movie then (2) get a pizza. Since (22a) and (22d) reflect this order, they should be easier to process than the other two. However, if we recall Bever's (1970a) strategy which suggests that the main clause usually comes first, then (22d) should be easier even than (22a). Clark and Clark (1977, p. 78) report that E. Clark (1971) found evidence that young children rely heavily on this strategy.

Summary. In this section we have discussed the cognitive strategies approach to language processing at considerable length. There are, however, many loose ends still unresolved. Perhaps the most important of these deals with the relationships among the various proposed strategies. While considerable evidence has been ámassed in support of individual strategies, and other proposals have been rejected, there is to this point still no coherent theoretical framework into which the strategies appear to fit. At this stage, then, we appear to have isolated various strategies but we have not yet determined how they interrelate nor what kind of general theoretical structure they fit into. The approach is promising, but much more research is needed before the theoretical structure emerges clearly.

A general assumption of the cognitive strategies program is that of "parallel processing," namely that several kinds of information are accessed and incorporated simultaneously. These include semantic, syntactic, discourse, and real-world factors. Such an assumption has been challenged, in particular, by proponents of a parsing approach to language comprehension. It is to this approach we now turn.

4.4 Parsing Strategies.

The types of sentence and discourse strategies discussed above have focused on a variety of considerations involved in language processing, including semantic, syntactic, discourse, and lexical factors. An assumption implicit in most of the proposals discussed above is that during sentence comprehension, the hearer uses as many resources as possible, often invoking parallel processing of syntactic, semantic, and lexical information. A second implicit assumption is that the hearer must construct a syntactic representation for the incoming sentence. The actual details of the construction and its attendant problems have served as the focus for that perspective on language processing which might be called the *parsing* approach.

The parsing approach shares with the cognitive stategies orientation an interest in those heuristics which the hearer employs in sentence comprehension. Here, however, attention is focused specifically on the steps and operations involved in the hearer's (or "parser's") construction of syntactic representations for sentences. In particular, this research attempts to specify those conditions which the human "parser" must meet in order that correct syntactic descriptions can be assigned to sentences. Furthermore, the parsing approach is much more closely tied to the formal representations of transformational theory than is the strategies enterprise, at least to the extent that considerable importance is attached to the detailed syntactic representations generated by a transformational grammar. Indeed, an implicit assumption of research in this area is that the (presumably transformational) grammar generates deep and surface structures for sentences, and the human parser's task is, in part, to construct the appropriate syntactic representation for a sentence as an early and crucial aspect of his comprehension enterprise.

Thus, within the parsing approach to language comprehension, major attention is directed to the construction of a set of principles and rules, along with appropriate constraints, which will permit the parser, as a psychological mechanism, to build up a syntactic representation for a sentence, where that representation takes as a target the representation provided by a transformational grammar. This approach, while more limited in scope and less ambitious than the more global aspirations of the cognitive strategies orientation, takes very seriously the assumption that a grammar is rather directly involved in a language comprehension, at least to the extent that it provides appropriate targets to which the parser must aspire in constructing syntactic representations. Another aspect of the parsing research strategy is its extensive utilization of the computer metaphor, in which the notion of programming languages and their parsing, along with other aspects of computer programming, provide a useful frame of reference in terms of which theories can be constructed

One of the more important early contributions in the parsing approach, and one from which a large number of studies later flowed, was Kimball's (1973) paper "Seven principles of surface structure parsing in natural language". Kimball noted that in the grammar of a natural language, one might find two rather distinct rules, such as A ---> X and B ---> X, where X is some string of elements. When the parser encounters the string X, how does it go about deciding which of the two rules applied? Put another way, how does the parser assign constituent structure to an incoming string? Kimball pointed out that there are two basic strategies possible in parsing: top-down and bottom-up. In the former case, a superordinate node at the top of the tree constitutes the starting place, and the substructure is developed downward, while in the bottom-up approach, structure is assigned to incoming elements and the tree is built up toward the top. Kimball opts for a top-down strategy, but with little supporting evidence. However, he did formulate seven specific parsing strategies to deal with complex structures (see Table 4.7). Moreover, he overtly recognized that limited short term memory poses real problems for the hearer, and he therefore attempted to design his parsing strategies to keep storage space relatively limited.

RIGHT ASSOCIATION predicts why a sentence like (23a) is normally interpreted with the *out* as part of the embedded clause, even though it could have originated in a position next to the verb, as in (23b), and have been moved to sentence-final position by particle movement.

23 a. Joe figured that Susan wanted to take the cat out.
   b. Joe figured out that Susan wanted to take the cat.

RIGHT ASSOCIATION simply predicts that as a constituent structure tree is being constructed, and as a new element comes into the purview of the parser, it is attached at the lowest possible node. In the case of (23a), the lowest node to which *out* can be attached is the S of the embedded clause, while, if it were a "moved particle," it would be attached to the higher node VP which contains the embedded clause. NEW NODES is motivated by the fact that sentences with function words are easier to process than when the function words are omitted, as Hakes (1972) demonstrated for sentences containing complementizers, such as (24).

24 a. Jack anticipated the answer would be difficult to uncover.
   b. Jack anticipated that the answer would be difficult to uncover.

TABLE 4.7 Kimball's (1973) Parsing Strategies

===

TOP-DOWN. Parsing proceeds top-down. However, English is a "look-ahead" language and can scan the next few words to avoid false starts.

RIGHT ASSOCIATION. Terminal symbols optimally associate to the lowest non-terminal node.

NEW NODES. The construction of a new node is signalled by the occurrence of a function word.

TWO SENTENCES. The constituents of no more than two sentences can be parsed at the same time.

CLOSURE. A phrase is closed out as soon as possible unless the next node is a constituent of that phrase.

FIXED STRUCTURE. When the last immediate constitutent of a phrase has been formed and the phrase closed, it is perceptually "costly" to back and reanalyze it.

PROCESSING. When a phrase is closed, it is pushed to down to syntactic or semantic processing and cleared from short term memory. Thus, once a parse is completed, go on the the next unit.

===

Sentences like (24b), while longer than their counterparts, are still comprehended faster. Unfortunately, Kimball regards NEW NODES as being a problem for those languages in which the function words follow the phrase rather than initiate it, as Japanese. And, as we saw in the previous section, this same evidence can be taken as supporting a more general cognitive strategy of BRACKETING.

The principle of TWO SENTENCES is a rather *ad hoc* condition formulated to account for the fact that double embeddings are typically hard to handle, as in (25).

    25 a. The cat the dog chased ran.
       b. The cat the dog the mouse saw chased ran.

CLOSURE, along with its supporting evidence, is familiar from our earlier discussions, and FIXED STRUCTURE is intended to deal with the difficulties attendant on a required reanalysis of such garden path sentences as (26).

    26 a. The boat floated on the water sank.
       b. The boat which was floated on the water sank.

The FIXED STRUCTURE strategy states that once a parse has been completed, it is shunted off to the next processing stage, presumably via PROCESSING, to a semantic analysis and is perceptually difficult to recover in syntactic form since the short term memory space has been cleared for the next material.

    Kimball's proposals were offered at about the time when the derivational theory of complexity was being severely eroded and serious doubt was being cast on the psychological viability of transformational theory. At about this time, Bever's (1970a) strategies were beginning to be examined in detail, again with the hint that a transformational grammar might have little to do with sentence processing. Consequently, Kimball's proposals, which did take into account detailed surface structures as generated by transformational grammar, were welcomed by those linguists committed to a transformationally oriented psycholinguistics. However, problems with the specifics of Kimball's proposals soon emerged and refinements were proposed.

    In her doctoral dissertation, Frazier (1978) assessed both Bever's (1970) and Kimball's (1973) proposals in some detail. She argued that Bever's view of language processing, which can access a variety of sources of cues simultaneously, is much too vague and unstructured, while Kimball's proposals are inadequate in certain details. In her discussion of specific parsing strategies, Frazier

TABLE 4.8 Frazier's (1978) Parsing Principles

===

LATE CLOSURE. When possible, attach material into the clause currently being processed.

MINIMAL ATTACHMENT. Attach incoming material into the phrase marker being constructed, using the fewest nodes consistent with the well-formedness rules of the language under consideration.

WEAK SEMANTIC PRINCIPLE. Constituent assignment decisions are not made in violation of lexical semantic constraints on the possible relations between words of a sentence, unless no other analysis of the sentence is possible.

===

assumes that the language processor (a) minimizes processing effort, (b) attempts to structure incoming material with material already analyzed, (c) assigns structure quickly, and does not remain neutral about a structure, (d) assigns only one structure to potentially ambiguous sentences, and (e) works in serial rather than parallel fashion. She also assumes that human memory capacity serves as a constraint on the parser's segmentation of stimuli. Frazier's proposals are found in Table 4.8.

Frazier argues that both LATE CLOSURE and MINIMAL ATTACHMENT need not be viewed as special parsing strategies, but are in fact properties of the parser itself, and are universal principles. Moreover, these follow from the nature of the two-stage parser proposed in Frazier and Fodor (1978).

Frazier's WEAK SEMANTIC PRINCIPLE follows from her view of serial processing, since she argues that syntactic parsing takes place independent of semantic guidance, but is carried out such that no semantic constraints are violated. A stronger semantic principle, which she rejects, is one in which the semantic constraints guide the parser's activity. Frazier's proposals represent an important extension and elaboration of some of Kimball's earlier proposals, and at the same time they focus attention rather directly on the detailed surface structure of a wide variety of sentence types in English.

Frazier and Fodor (1978) also adopt Kimball's orientation along with the view that a parser should address the detailed structural configurations provided by a transformational grammar. However, they argued that both top-down and bottom-up strategies are necessary, and that serious attention must be devoted to the parser's ability to "look ahead" a few words as it constructs a tree. In place of a single stage parser such as Kimball's, they proposed a two-stage parsing mechanism. The first stage, the "Preliminary Phrase Packager" (or PPP) serves to group words into phrases (NPs, VPs, PPs, Ss, etc.), while the second stage, the "Sentence Structure Supervisor" (or SSS) integrates the phrases created by the PPP into a full phrase marker or tree for the sentence.

In this model, the PPP is relatively "shortsighted," looking ahead only a little way. It organizes words into limited local constituents to be fed to the SSS, which is sensitive to such factors as the overall shape of a sentence, dependencies among words, structural requirements, and the like. It is the SSS which provides the final organization of the sentence. For example, in the two sentences of (27), the PPP organizes phrases in the same way.

27 a. Ann threw the book that Mary had been reading in the study.
   b. Ann put the book that Mary had been reading in the study.

Frazier and Fodor note that in (27a), *in the study* is naturally analysed as a part of the embedded relative clause, while in (27b) it is a part of the main clause. The reason is simply that *put* requires a locative phrase, but *throw* does not.

According to Frazier and Fodor's two-stage model, the PPP only organizes the constituents into phrases, but it is the job of the SSS to assemble these into a final phrase marker. Moreover, the

SSS stage can take into account selectional restrictions in order to provide a final structure in which the PP of (27b) goes with the main clause but the identical PP of (27a) fits into the embedded clause. The two-stage model therefore permits a kind of division of labor in parsing and, Frazier and Fodor claim, evidence such as that represented by the intuitive parsings of (27) support that model. Unaddressed by the model, however, is the issue of why English or any language should allow discontinuous constituent structures, especially when this possibility causes the parser such problems.

Frazier and Fodor suggest that several of Kimball's proposals, such as TWO SENTENCES, NEW NODES, and FIXED STRUCTURE actually follow from the combination of CLOSURE and RIGHT ASSOCIATION when these are properly represented in a two-stage parsing mechanism. They conclude that empirical evidence supports their model, and they suggest that the meanings of phrases are computed in the PPP before these structures are sent to the SSS for final assembly. Moreover, they claim that the final syntactic representation is a deep rather than a surface structure. In their proposal, the parser chunks phrases via operations of the PPP at the surface structure, but that the SSS assembles these into a deep structure configuration. This proposal, therefore, reinstitutes the deep/surface issue and its attendant grammatical theory as an important concern.

"Filler-gap dependency sentences" have provided valuable data for proposals as to the nature of the parser. In these structures, a particular constituent is not in its usual position but must be assigned a grammatical interpretation associated with that position. Such sentences result, in the transformational view of grammar, by the movement of NPs or *wh*-phrases out of their original deep structure positions. Examples of such sentences are those in (28), in which the presumed "gap" or place of origin of the displaced constituent is indicated by "_." The "moved" constituent or "filler" is underlined.

28 a. <u>What</u> do you want Mother to make _ for Mary?

    b. <u>Who</u> did you expect _ to make a potholder?

    c. <u>Who</u> did <u>you</u> expect _ to make a potholder for _?

Fodor (1978) addressed these structures. In (28a, b) there is only one gap-filler dependency, but in (28c) there are two. In (28c), *you* is associated with the first gap, the subject of *make*, while *who* is associated with the second, the object of the preposition *for* Fodor proposes a NESTED DEPENDENCY CONSTRAINT which states that in cases of two or more gap-filler dependencies, the two may not intersect, but one must always be nested within the other, as in (28c).

Fodor argues against the view that there is only a performance mechanism and no "competence" grammar of the familiar transformational sort. Rather, she argues that both a competence grammar and a parsing mechanism must exist psychologically, such that the competence grammar provides the target structures to which the parser aspires. She concludes that there are "gap-creating" rules (transformations) in natural languages because such rules are more highly valued in terms of innate mental structures than are alternatives which would make life easier for the parser. Once again, then, the autonomous grammar, independent of processing constraints, is espoused. Interestingly most of Fodor's data are her own intuitions about relative processing difficulty of particular sentences, and accordingly they might, at least in principle, suffer from the "N=1" problem discussed in Chapter One.

As one of the few theories which has paid more than lip service to psychological constraints, lexical functional grammar has been applied to the issue of syntactic closure. In particular, Ford, Bresnar, and Kaplan (1982) have argued that earlier accounts are all inadequate to account for the facts of closure. Instead they offer an explanation which directly incorporates a lexical functional grammar, along with various parsing principles, into a theory of processing.

Some of the proposals for natural language parsing systems have developed a strongly computing science orientation. One such is Marcus' (1980) PARSIFAL system in which a "grammar interpreter" is elaborated in some detail. This system is committed to the construction of those syntactic representations provided by recent versions of "trace theory" (Chomsky, 1982a, 1982b). Focus here is not on experimental evidence, but rather on a formal parsing system which will yield structures with formal properties decided in advance. Consequently, this work is one step removed for experimental considerations.

A similar tact is taken by Church (1982), although here the target structures are provided by the lexical functional grammar model proposed by Bresnan (1982) and Kaplan and Bresnan (1982), in which both constituent (surface) structures and functional representations are constructed. Church does evaluate in some detail earlier parsing proposals, but his real interest is similar to Marcus's. In short, many of the computer science oriented proposals for natural language parsing require a grammatical theory to produce structures which the proposed parsers can construct. The more psycholinguistically oriented proposals, on the other hand, attend to a variety of kinds of data, but still adopt the view that an independent grammar is needed in order to provide independently motivated structural descriptions for sentences. The issue of whether the human language user in fact constructs such representations, and if so what the external evidence for such a view might be, does not loom large in this enterprise.

While parsing strategies must no doubt exist in order to allow the hearer to construct grammatical representations for the incoming utterances he encounters, such strategies appear to reify the "parser" as a mechanism which is somehow independent, and yet a part of, the hearer's cognitive apparatus. Moreover, the strategies assume the correctness of the structural descriptions assigned by a (usually generative) grammar. While such an assumption is perhaps useful for purposes of an efficient research strategy, it must not be forgotten that independent evidence for such structures is also required. As we have discussed above, it is by no means clear that hearers actually assign the same kinds of constituent structures to sentences as a transformational grammar suggests (cf. Levelt, 1970).

4.5. Summary.

In this chapter we have taken a critical look at the derivational theory of complexity and have concluded that in spite of having gained a great deal of information about language processing from experiments undertaken within that paradigm, we are forced to conclude that the derivational theory of complexity is bankrupt. There is no real evidence at all that language users invoke a transformational grammar in any sort of step-by-step manner as they either produce or comprehend language.

However, a similar problem arises within the cognitive strategies approach. In particular, the question remains unanswered as to what kind of a grammar is actually used in language comprehension and production. There seems little support of any kind for transformational grammar in this respect, and although there is evidence in support of surface constituent structure, the question of the kind of grammar required is still far from resolved. Finally, we examined some recent proposals which bring the grammar back into the picture as an independent component providing structures which the human language user must also construct as he parses sentences.

Perhaps all that can be said at this point is that there is some evidence for a view of language processing which involves several independent and interacting components. One of these is presumably some sort of grammar, and another is the set of processing strategies used by humans regardless of the language they speak. Yet another component surely has to do with semantics, not only of the particular language under consideration, but of real world knowledge as well. In general, there seems to be evidence in support of a complex of interacting systems, all of which contribute significantly to language processing. One area in which there is still no consensus is whether processing takes place serially, or if there exists a set of parallel functions all operating at the same time. This issue divides the cognitive strategy proponants from the parsing advocates.

EXERCISES

4.1. In a chronometric study similar to that of Miller and McKean (1964), the PNQ sentence family was investigated to test for the derivational theory of complexity. Subjects heard 70 ADF sentences, one at a time. After each sentence was presented, a "cue" word or words of "Negative," "Question," "Passive," or some combination of these, was flashed on a screen. When the subject saw the cue, he was to carry out a mental transformation of the sentence into the target defined by the cue. As soon as he had the sentence in mind, he pressed a button. He then said his target sentence aloud. The reaction time, between the flashing of the cue and the button pressing, was measured and any errors made by the subject were counted. There were 10 replications for each of the target types, and 30 subjects participated in the experiment. The results were as follows:

Transformation	Average Response Time	Average Errors
NEG	.40 secs	1.1
QUES	.63	1.2
PAS	.94	3.1
N+P	1.61	2.9
N+Q	1.22	2.3
P+Q	1.97	5.1
P+N+Q	3.14	6.3

a. Do the response times support the derivational theory of complexity? Why (not)?

b. What are possible confounding variables associated with the independent variable?

c. What potential problems can you see in the use and measurement of the dependent variables?

d. Do the error scores support the derivational theory of complexity? Why (not)?

e. What other explanations can you offer for the results?

4.2. Language acquisition data from Jeff reveals the following developments over four stages:

Stage	Y/N Questions	WH-Questions
1	Mommy goed?	Where Mommy goed?
2	Did Mommy goed?	Where Mommy goed?
3	Did Mommy go?	Where Mommy went?
4	Did Mommy go?	Where did Mommy go?

a. It is often assumed that when a child first learns a rule, he tends to overgeneralize it. Comment on this claim with respect to (1) past tense formation, and (2) subject-auxiliary inverted word order.

b. At Stage 4, Jeff is beginning to produce and comprehend sentences like "I know where Mommy went". How does this shed light on the transition between Stages 3 and 4?

4.3. The basic word order of language P is SOV. However, when the direct object is a sentential NP, as in the English analogue "Jack understood that Edi would soon flee the country," P requires the word order SVO. When the object is a simple NP, SVO is never permitted. Explain, in terms of cognitive strategies, how this phenomenon might have arisen.

4.4. A language L has the basic word order VSO. In L, the relative clause (RC) follows the modified NP, and the relative pronoun (RP) is placed at the right of the relative clause. Parallel to the English structures in Table 4.6, we find for L:

Type	Structure
SS	V S+[V O RPs] O
SO	
OS	
OO	V S O+[V S RPo]

a. Fill out the other structures in the table above.

b. According to CLOSURE, which structures should be the easier to process? Why?

c. According to NORMAL FORM, which structures should be the easier to process? Why?

d. If NORMAL FORM and CLOSURE are equally weighted, what should be the order of relative ease of processing?

e. In L, the relative pronoun stem is *na*, while the coordinate conjunction "and" is *ana*. In conjoined constructions, the conjunction follows the second conjunct in L. Moreover, if two coordinated clauses share a NP, the second instance of that NP is deleted ("gapped"). This happens in English, for example, in sentences like "Jack went to town and _ bought a hat". In L, which of the four types of relative clause sentences should be most confused with a conjoined sentence in which the object is gapped? Why?

4.5. An English sentence like "A man who had been drinking beer staggered in" can be paraphrased (by "Extraposition") with "A man staggered in who had been drinking beer". However, a sentence like "A man who had been drinking beer introduced himself to the blond" does not permit a paraphrase of "A man introduced himself to the blond who had been drinking beer". Explain this phenomenon in terms of Kimball's (1973) RIGHT ASSOCIATION and CLOSURE strategies.

4.6. In what sense is a formal grammar required as a psychological "component" to accommodate the parsing approach of Fodor and Frazier? Why?

4.7. How can Kimball's parsing principles handle "garden path" sentences? Does Frazier's approach handle these any better (or worse)? Explain, with examples.

LABORATORIES

Chapter Five

EXPERIMENTAL SEMANTICS

5.1 Introduction

The study of semantics has a long and noble tradition, but one often shrouded in myth and misconception. For example, it is a commonly held view that words somehow "possess" meaning, independent of the speakers who used them or of the situations in which they are used. An extreme version of this view is that words even have "natural" meanings so that, for instance, *dog* somehow naturally and logically means what it does. While many people would probably reject such an extreme view as silly or unenlightened, perhaps because it represents an unfashionable cultural ethnocentricity, a weaker version is often vigorously maintained, namely that a word should possess a fixed and unchanging meaning, again independent of how the form is used by speakers of the language. Those holding this view delight in "correcting" others, often claiming that unprincipled culprits are corrupting the language.

One major component of this myth is the belief that the meaning of a word should properly reflect and maintain its etymology. Besides an implicit rejection of the obvious fact that languages constantly change over time, this prejudice extols the historical meaning of a word as the only appropriate one. For example, since the word *auditor* presumably derives from the Latin *audire* "to hear," it is properly used to refer to a student who sits in a class but who is not registered in it,

159

since he is only there to listen. However, it is more difficult to associate the meaning of "hear" with that use of *auditor* referring to those accounting specialists who inspect our financial records. And what about the actress who *auditions* for a part? She is not hearing at all, but rather allowing others to see and hear her.

A classic example of this ' prejudice is the perfectly common word *silly*, which in earlier English meant, as its modern German cognate *selig* still does, "blessed" or "holy." Yet if etymology determines meaning completely, then we would have to deny that *silly* could possibly mean what it does.

These two admittedly simple examples highlight the fact that we all seem to have special ideas and opinions about our language. In fact, every speaker of the language, whether he realizes it or not, is an expert about the way his language works. An unfortunate aspect of this fact is that some attitudes and prejudices have become institutionalized as "true," with little understanding of the real nature of language and its various interacting subsystems. This is not to say that in all styles and situations, "anything goes." Indeed, our culture does recognize norms and standards of usage, just as other cultures do. But the point is that these are socially established standards, not *a priori* true or transcendentally given.

From an empirical perspective, we acknowledge that language changes over time, that uses for particular words change, often very quickly, and that we often exploit such natural aspects of language use as simile and metaphor. Indeed, it has even been argued that it is through the metaphoric functions of language that we extend our creativity to encompass new and unusual situations, recasting them into more familiar and therefore more comfortable and tractable conceptual constellations (cf. Lakoff & Johnson, 1980).

—Accordingly, we can reject the prejudices that meaning equals etymology and that meaning resides in words rather than in speakers. Instead, we adopt the view that it is people who mean, and who

TABLE 5.1 Some Types of Meaning

===

Type	Characteristics
lexical	words, morphemes, core meaning, features, fields, connotation, denotation, prototypes
sentential	propositions, predicates, arguments, semantic roles, discourse factors, speech act functions, inference, presuppositions
discourse	scripts, schemata, story grammar, cohesion devices

===

convey their meanings through the medium of a shared code, namely language. It is therefore incumbant upon those holding these views, including most linguists, to specify what they understand meaning to be or, to put the issue more squarely, to specify just what specific factors are involved in the study of meaning. In this chapter, we first attempt to delineate some general types of meaning and then examine each in some detail. The present approach, like virtually any other attempt at an overview of semantics, will necessarily leave some loose ends. For example, we shall ignore here issues of truth-conditional semantics. Rather, our goal is to investigate those aspects of semantics which have been dealt with from an empirical point of view.

A number of alternative approaches can be taken to the study of meaning. It is possible, for example, to discuss various kinds of semantic functions, such as reference or association, and then evaluate the relevant research in each such area. Alternatively, it is possible to focus primary attention on the meanings of words, to the exclusion of those other aspects of meaning which are equally, or perhaps even more centrally, important. Many other approaches are also conceivable, but the relatively straightforward one chosen here is first to enumerate what we consider to be the more important aspects of meaning and then to examine these in some detail in light of the conceptual issues and empirical studies associated with each. Any serious attempt to examine the multi-faceted notion of meaning must address at least those aspects listed in Table 5.1. In the following sections, each of these types will be discussed.

5.2 Lexical Semantics

Traditional views. The study of the meaning of words is as old as the history of philosophical inquiry. Although there are units of meaning smaller than that of the word, lexical semantics has nevertheless typically focused on word meaning. Most approaches to the study of the meaning of words at least tacitly assumes that all speakers within a given linguistic community know and share a common "core" meaning for most words. This view reflects the commonplace observation that in order for us to communicate with each other, we must share a linguistic code, one essential part of which is the set of meaningful elements which we arrange into sentences.

Perhaps the oldest view of lexical semantics is the referential theory of meaning, which claims that the meaning of a word is some real world object, event, or state of affairs specified or referred to by that word. In this view, the referential function of language is central: we use words to refer to things in the real world. Of course, a clear knowledge of a situation is crucial for the referring act to succeed. We must know, for example, that in a particular situation, *John* is being used to refer to a particular individual. Moreover, two or more expressions can have the same reference. For example, *John* and *my cousin* may both refer to the same individual. Such coreferential information does not reside in the forms themselves, but in their use in a given situation. Coreference may be expressed in a given language by various means. The English reflexive forms in "John cut himself" and "All the members of the squad like each other," for example, are systematic devices used to indicate coreference.

One problem with the referential theory of meaning is that although it permits two linguistic expressions to refer to the same object, we may know full well that the two forms do not mean the same thing. For example, *John*, a proper noun, is a personal name, while *my cousin* conveys information about a kinship relation and not a name. Even though both may refer to the same individual, the sentence "John is my cousin" is informative in a way that "John is John" is not.

A second problem with the referential theory of meaning is that a particular word can be perfectly meaningful in ordinary discourse and have no real world referent at all. This observation applies not only to such abstract nouns as *justice* and *truth*, which seem to be mental concepts rather than real world objects or events, but also to such expressions as *the present king of France* and *unicorn*. According to a strict application of the referential theory of meaning, a sentence like "Susan wanted to find a unicorn" should be as meaningless as "Susan wanted to find a glurph." But we know that the former is meaningful in a sense that the latter is not.

These examples suggest that there is more to word meanings than reference, and while we cannot deny the importance of referential functions to words, we must admit that other factors are also involved in word meaning. The denotative theory of word meaning is an approach designed to address some of these problems. This theory claims that a word refers not to real objects but rather to abstract classes of objects of events, namely to our mental concepts. In such a view, for example, *cat* refers not to a particular object but instead to our mental concept of cats. This approach shifts the referential function away from language proper and onto concepts: it is concepts and not words which refer to, or correspond to, or are tied to, real world objects.

Association theory. Both the referential and denotative theories of word meaning are philosophical in origin, as is a third view, the associative theory of meaning. According to this view, which can be traced back to Aristotle, the associative meaning of a word is the sum total of all the things a person thinks of when he hears the word (Deese, 1970, p. 109). A considerable body of experimental work in psychology has been predicated on this view, which locates a given word within a complex mental network and relates it to other words via association links of varying strengths.

One classic methodology employed in this research is the free association test, in which a subject is given a word and asked to respond with the first thing which comes into his mind. Alternatively, the subject may be asked to cite in a given period of time as many words as he can think of associated with the stimulus word. The associate meaning of a word might then be defined as the sum of those words offered by subjects, perhaps weighted in terms of varying degrees of importance (cf. Deese, 1965). One remarkable facet of this approach is that there is so much consistency across subjects. For example, Woodworth and Schlosberg (1954) noted that when one thousand subjects were given the stimulus word *needle*, 160 of them responded with *thread*, 158 with *pin(s)*, 152 with *sharp*, 135 with *sew(s)*, and 107 with *sewing*. Only four responded with *darning* or *cloth*, and only one with *tailor*.

An interesting aspect of associative responses is the ways in which they can be classified. Some responses are typically either synonyms or antonyms. These responses, which reside in the same general category as the stimulus word, are called paradigmatic responses, while those which refer to the function of the stimulus word, such as *sew(ing)*, are called syntagmatic responses. Other responses types include subordinate (*dog-poodle*), superordinate (*dog-animal*), and rhyming ("klang") responses (*needle-beedle*).

In spite of the apparent strength of certain associates, however, it is clear that there is more to the meaning of *needle* than a list of somewhat related words. Part of its meaning may be related to its function, to its shape and size, to how it is used in a given context, and probably to a host of other factors as well.

Semantic differential. Another attempt to formulate an objective measure of meaning was that of Osgood (1954) and his associates (e.g., Osgood, Suci, & Tannenbaum, 1957), who attempted to quantify meaning in terms of what they called the semantic differential. This is a technique in which subjects are asked to locate various stimulus words on a seven-point scale anchored at either end by a pair of bipolar terms such as *strong-weak, good-bad*, etc. With hundreds of subjects tested on many words, rated on a variety of scales and in several languages, an important result emerged, namely that the several scales employed could all be reduced to the three dimensions of evaluation (good-bad), activity (active-passive), and potency (strong-weak). Thus a particular word, such as *red* or *love* might be located at one point in the three dimensional space represented by the three axes of evaluation, activity, and potency. If, however, both forms are found to lie at the same point, this does not mean that they have the same meaning. What is suggested, however, is that subjects' attitudes or affective feelings toward the two words is similar. The semantic differential does not provide a measure of the denotative meaning of words at all, but it does allow for a measure of connotative aspects.

Feature theory. The idea that the core meanings of words can be broken down into separate components or features has dominated a great deal of the theoretical and experimental work in lexical semantics. The central idea here is that the basic meaning of particular lexical items can be specified at least partially, and perhaps exhaustively, in terms of an independent set of semantic features. This decompositional approach is familiar in phonology, where phonological segments are described in terms of a set of distinctive features such as "voiced," "stop," etc.

The importation of the distinctive feature methodology into anthropology led to the evolution of componential analysis for such lexical classes as kinship terms in a host of languages. It was found, however, that kinship components may differ across languages, while in phonology it is assumed that there exists a universal set of phonetic features

Experimental Semantics

from which all languages draw. Componential analysis can also be applied to other domains of human behavior, such as the description of particular cultural activities such as religious rituals and puberty rites.

The feature theory orientation in lexical semantics was inspired in large part by Katz and Fodor (1963), Katz and Postal (1964), and Chomsky (1965), who treated words as bundles of distinctive features. Some features are semantic while others are grammatical and yet others are selectional. For example, the English word *boy* can be analyzed in terms of such features as *animate, human, male, young, common, countable, noun,* etc. In this list, the inherent semantic components of animacy, humanness, relative age, and sex would appear to be universal to the core meaning of the word in the sense that the meaning of *boy* in any language would presumably involve these features. Certain other features, such as countable and commonness, tend to be more language-specific, since all languages do not observe these distinctions in their grammars.

Analogous to phonological distinctive features, the proposed features for lexical classes came to be treated as binary, so that a form is marked with either + or - for a given feature. Thus, *boy* would be specified as [+human], [+animate], etc. while *dog* would be marked as [-human], [+animate]. thereby distinguishing the classes of human and non-human animate nouns. While the feature approach indicates the core or basic meaning of a lexical item in terms of a set of presumably universal semantic features, any special or idiosyncratic properties of a word must be indicated by idiosyncratic features. For example, the fact that *foot* and *man* have irregular plurals can be indicated lexically by some idiosyncratic marker of irregular plural formation. With a relatively small set of semantic features, classes of words can be established. Thus, *boy, man, girl, student, plumber, George Washington,* and *secretary* all share the feature [+human]. The more features shared by a set of words, the more closely related they are semantically, while the fewer features used to define a set, the larger "natural class" that set represents.

166

Experimental Semantics

It is clear in a feature analysis of lexical items
that different kinds of features are needed for
different parts of speech. Thus, while the feature
human is important for nouns, it bears little
relevance for adjectives or verbs. Similarly, the
distinction between action and state verbs, as found
for example in *buy* versus *own*, can be specified in
terms of a feature of *stativity* which is has little
relevance to nouns. Thus, *buy*, as an action verb,
is [-stative], while *own* is [+stative]. Diagnostic tests
have been offered to determine stativity. Lakoff
(1966) suggested that [+stative] verbs are typically
not found in the progressive aspect on in the
imperative form. Thus, the examples in (1) support
the analysis of *buy* as [-stative] and those in (2)
support *own* as [+stative].

1 a. He is buying a boat.
   b. Buy a bottle of wine for dinner.

2 a. *He is owning a boat.
   b. *Own a new car right away.

If the feature approach to core meaning is on
the right track, there should be a universal set of
semantic features which participate in the statement
of possible cooccurrences of lexical items across
languages. If this is true, then the fact that a verb
like *smile* requires a [+human] agent as in (3)
should be a fact about the meaning of the verb
rather than a fact about English grammar.

3 a. The electrician was smiling when he gave
      Fred the bill.

   b. *The earthworm was smiling as it crawled
      along.

One obvious problem for a theory of semantic
features is that of the exhaustiveness of meaning.
If the core meaning is defined in terms of a
universal set of semantic features, this will permit
the formation of natural classes, such as all the
[+animate, -human] nouns (*dog, cat, worm*, etc.). One
obvious advantage of such natural classes is that
they permit easy statement of selectional
restrictions. For example, certain verbs and
adjectives select only animate agents (*eat, walk,*

167

etc.) while others require [+abstract] subjects (*obvious, apparent,* etc.). But the detailed differentiation among members of certain classes remains unspecified by such general features. For example, the nouns in (4) are defined as [-human, +animate].

4. dog, cat, mouse, snake, louse, robin, whale

All these nouns can fit into a sentence frame such as "The __ all ate well," but it is clear that they are not synonyms and, more importantly, they differ along a variety of dimensions. Snakes slither, while mice scurry. Reptiles such as lizards run but others may waddle every bit as much as sloths. Consequently, if we wish to differentiate among members of a class in terms of features, we are forced into having as many distinctive features as the zoologist needs in his highly specialized taxonomy. Moreover, even if we focus on the class of *dog*, there are a great many distinct kinds, sizes, and colors. Thus, pushed to its logical extreme, the feature theory requires a unique feature for each specific member of each class. We quickly run into the problem of diminishing returns in such an enterprise.

In practice, however, linguists usually do not push the feature analysis so far. The usual gambit is to employ just those features which allow us to identify general classes and state selectional restrictions, with the fine tuning of subclasses left unaddressed.

The feature theory of lexical semantics invites the possibility that some hierarchical structure exists among certain sets of features and that cross-classification can occur. A partial hierarchy of features is illustrated by the fact that the set of [+human] nouns constitutes a subset of [+animate] nouns, since presumably all humans are animate. One way to represent this is in terms of redundancy rules such as:

[+human] ---> [+animate].

Of course, the converse is not true since there are many [+animate] nouns such as *dog, chicken, perch,* etc. which are [-human], just as many [-human] nouns like *table, tree, ring,* etc. are [-animate].

The possibility of cross-classification, in which independent features intersect to define classes, can be illustrated by the four possible combinations in (5).

5 a. [+animate, +common]: dog, child, plumber
   b. [+animate, -common]: John, Sally, Fido
   c. [-animate, +common]: rock, house, pin
   d. [-animate, -common]: London, Japan.

The cross-classification potentialities afforded by a set of independent features provides the means for specifying natural classes along independent dimensions. Thus, one can talk about all [+common] nouns just as readily as about all [-animate] nouns, even though some lexical items may belong to both classes.

One theoretically important aspect of feature theory is what has been called the "marked/unmarked" distinction, according to which an unmarked item is the usual or normal case while the marked one is somehow special or unusual. In phonology, for example, back vowels such as /u/ and /o/ are normally rounded, and accordingly the unmarked case for back vowels is that they have the feature [+round]. The markedness distinction has been exploited in grammatical and semantic feature theory as well. For example, an English verb may be in the present or past tense, the progressive or perfect aspect, or be marked for tense but no aspect. The examples in (6) indicate the possibilities for a verb like *smile*.

6. a. Sammy smiles. (PRESENT)
   b. Sammy smiled. (PAST)
   c. Sammy has smiled. (PRESENT, PERFECTIVE)
   d. Sammy had smiled. (PAST, PERFECTIVE)
   e. Sammy is smiling. (PRESENT, PROGRESSIVE)
   f. Sammy was smiling. (PAST, PROGRESSIVE)
   g. Sammy has been smiling. (PRESENT, PROGRESSIVE, PERFECTIVE)
   h. Sammy had been smiling. (PAST, PROGRESSIVE, PERFECTIVE)

In order to assess the feature theory for English verbs, Clark and Stafford (1969) presented subjects with sentences varying in aspect and tense, much like those in (6). Error scores in a recall task indicated that subjects tended to recall progressive forms as non-progressive, perfective forms as non-perfective, and present tense as past. They interpreted the results as supporting a feature system, with the tendency to loose the features of [+perfective] and [+progressive]. However, since features are binary, a sentence in the non-progressive aspect is nevertheless marked for that feature, namely as [-progressive], and similarly for the perfective. An alternative interpretation, and one which accords with the markedness notion, is that the unmarked aspects are [-progressive, -perfective] and the unmarked tense is [-past]. If this is the case, then in recall tasks in which there is no motivation from context to focus on the special qualities of a marked tense or aspect, such sentences tend to be stored and recalled in their unmarked forms. The results of this study can therefore be interpreted as support for a markedness theory.

Another place where markedness theory applies is in such adjective pairs as *high*/*low*, *long*/*short* and *deep*/*shallow*. Clark and Clark (1968) suggest that in such pairs the unmarked member is more basic both semantically and morphologically. In these pairs, the unmarked members are *high*, *long*, and *deep*. The unmarked members typically form the basis of the dimension name which the pair designates. For example, one normally asks about the *height* of a building rather than its *shortness*, the *length* of a table, and the *depth* of a lake. According to the markedness theory, the unmarked members should be easier to process, recall, and learn. In examining pairs of comparative adjectives, Clark and Card (1969) used stimuli such as "X is happier (narrower, etc.) than Y" and found that subjects tend to recall the unmarked comparative better than the marked ones.

E. Clark has argued that the feature theory of lexical meaning predicts that children should learn the unmarked members before the marked ones, and the more general features associated with a word should be acquired before the more specific ones. In a series of studies, E. Clark (1971; 1973; 1974) explored and offered extensive evidence for the semantic feature theory. For example, in E. Clark (1971), it was reported that the unmarked member *before* of the *before/after* pair was learned first. In an earlier study, Donaldson and Balfour (1968) found that children not only learn the form *more* before *less,* but they also often treat *less* as if it meant *more,* a result replicated for example in Palermo (1974).

As appealing and intuitive as a feature theory of lexical semantics may seem, it is not without problems. One already mentioned above is that of exhaustiveness of a word meaning in terms of features. While it may be methodologically convenient to incorporate only the major features relevant to classes of lexical items, the question still remains as to how the native speaker makes distinctions among members of classes. Does he have a large set of mental features which serve to distinguish members of a given class down to the most minute difference, or are the differences best represented in some other system? For example, does the mental distinction between a *poodle* and a *spaniel* involve such features as size, hair length, temperment, and the like, or do we make *ad hoc* distinctions based on only "dog" features?

A second problem, and one highlighted by Palermo (1978), is that a feature theory of word meaning involves the abstraction of features from a whole concept. According to the feature theory, in order to know a concept we must extract the relevant feature(s). But, in order to recognize what features are relevant, we must already know the concept. One unsatisfactory escape from this dilemma can be found by assuming that the relevant and necessary abstract features are genetically provided and innate. Yet little evidence for this exists, and it can even be asked what would constitute empirical evidence for the innateness of such features as animacy, stativity, and the like. Another alternative is that some general organizing principles of cognition and perception are innate, from which we derive the relevant features as we learn words. Some concepts and categories seem

171

constant across languages, perhaps because of the basic make-up of human biology and society. For example, E. Clark (1973) suggests that the earlier semantic features acquired by children follow from the development of their perceptual categories. The viability of a feature theory of lexical semantics is by no means settled, and alternative positions have been proposed.

Semantic fields. Another approach to lexical semantics which also holds that the core meaning of a word is at least in part a function of the properties it shares with other, related words, is the semantic field theory. This approach, which has much in common with both the feature and association theories, assumes that related words participate in a semantic field whose properties and dimensions are defined to a great extent by the members of the set themselves. This view assumes that "... the meaning of a lexical item is a function of the meaning relations obtaining between that item and other items in the same domain" (Fillenbaum & Rapoport, 1971, p. vii).

While the development of the notion of a semantic field has been influenced both by theoretical work in linguistics (e.g., Fillmore, 1969; Katz, 1972) and by experimental work in psychology (e.g., Deese, 1962; Fillenbaum & Rapoport, 1971). The theoretical aspects of field theory lend themselves readily to feature analysis, although the specific features suggested in field theory tend to be derivative from the set of items under investigation. Moreover, field theory tends to examine the differences among members of a class, while feature theory primarily invokes general features to distinguish among the classes themselves. Accordingly, field theory attends to finer differences then does feature theory. The experimental methodologies used to explore semantic fields are similar to those used in the semantic differential and in word association studies.

In their extensive research on the nature of the "subjective lexicon," Fillenbaum and Rapoport (1971) asked what kind of mental organization speakers impose "related" words. They examined nine semantic domains: color terms, kinship terms, pronouns, emotion names, propositions, conjunctions, verbs of possession, verbs of judging, and evaluation terms. Some of these, such as the verbs of judging, had already been investigated from both a psychological and a linguistic perspective. In their research, Fillenbaum and Rapoport used two distinct tasks, both of which involved having subjects make judgements of relative similarity among members of a given set. In one method, subjects were presented with an alphabetic list of terms and asked to construct a graph with linkages among members determined by perceived closeness of meaning. In the other task, subjects were presented with all possible pairs of words in the set and asked to select the pair most similar in meaning. This pair was given a score of "1." Then the next most similar pair was found, given a score of "2," and so on until all pairs had been rated. The techniques of multidimensional scaling and hierarchical cluster analysis were were used to analyze the data.

It is usually assumed in field theory studies that subjects' judgements of relative similarity among members of a set are based on the underlying dimensions or factors which they employ to define the organization of the set. Unlike feature theory, however, the semantic field approach does not require binary features. Rather it seeks to discover the basic dimensions in terms of which the members of a set are organized, and it recognizes the possibility, again unlike feature theory, that the dimensions are likely to have differential importance or salience. The determination of the relevant dimensions permits the construction of an n-dimensional semantic space in which each term can be located. The relative proximity of words in the space gives an indication of their perceived similarities.

The color terms provide an important test case for the techniques involved in the empirical study of semantic space since it is known that colors can be located within a three-dimensional perceptual space whose dimensions correspond to the physical properties of hue, brightness, and saturation. Fillenbaum and Rapoport's analysis of data collected on 24 color terms indicated that hue was the most important dimension, with little importance accorded to either brightness or saturation. This result could be due to the selection of the color terms used or, more likely, to the fact that hue is more salient cognitively than the other two. Fillenbaum and Rapoport note that some semantic fields may involve certain core concepts, such as possession and transfer of possession for the *have* verbs, with subsets differing internally in terms of the relevant dimensions needed.

One problem with the semantic field approach is that the particular set of items to be studied is selected *a priori* by the experimenter. Yet if his selection is somehow skewed with respect to the major dimensions involved, the results may not reflect the complete mental organization. A second problem is that the structural relations among a set of lexical items may be as much a function of the particular experimental task as of the subject's perception of the items being related. Moreover, it is not at all clear that the semantic space derived in a particular experiment necessarily represents the subject's mental organization, since it could also be possible that the subjects are creating a structure by virtue of being asked to relate and assess several terms. In short, it is premature to regard structural representations arising from such experiments as a kind of fixed mental map of the relationships among the items. Such a conclusion would need to be buttressed by far more information and data, as Magnera (1982) has argued in her extensive analysis of the research in this area. Finally, it is important to note that the semantic field approach permits some features or dimensions to be more salient than others. This can be readily illustrated by the set of words in (7).

7. cow, horse, dog, lion, fox, mouse

If *tigress* is added to (7), then the entire list might be mentally restructured by the presence of the feature *female*, but if *rock* is added, the relevant additional feature would be something like *living*. Thus, the relative salience of some features is at least potentially a function of the particular set of items being investigated, and if the set is altered by additions or deletions, this might alter the perceived salience of the relevant features.

Prototype theory. One additional approach to lexical semantics must also be discussed, especially since it differs so much from those in which features loom large. This is the prototype approach to word meaning championed by Rosch (1973; 1975; 1977), who maintains that a feature theory is simply inadequate as a psychological representation for concepts. She argues that some defining properties are more salient than others, so that, for example, some birds are typically conceived of as more "bird-like" than others. This observation supports the results of Henley (1969), who found that subjects tend to categorize animals according to such defining properties as varying degrees of size and ferocity rather than in terms of logical or zoological taxonomic features. According to the prototype theory, a given semantic category is mentally structured in terms of shared attributes. Some members of a category are judged to be closer to the prototypic member and therefore better representatives of that category than others.

Rosch and Mervis (1975) hypothesized that the most prototypic members of a category are those with the most attributes in common with other members and with the least in common with members of other categories. In a series of six experiments, they adduced considerable evidence for this view. In one study, for example, subjects were given six categories (furniture, vehicle, fruit, weapon, vegetable, and clothing) and were instructed to write down typical members for each within a space of 90 seconds. Subjects treated apples and oranges as highly representative of the fruit category, for example, while tomatos and olives were far less representative. Similarly, *chair, sofa,* and *table* were prototypic pieces of furniture, while *vase* and *telephone* were among the least prototypic.

Rosch and her colleagues argue that the use of distinctive features for the specification of categories does not provide an accurate picture of how such categories are mentally represented. Instead, they propose that a notion of "family resemblance" is a far more accurate and realistic characterization of the mental representation of such categories. Thus a robin is more prototypically a bird than, for example, a penguin, since a robin shares more defining characteristics (has feathers, flies, is medium sized, etc.) with other members than the penguin does. Similarly, there is a greater family resemblance between a robin and a sparrow than between either of these and a penguin. Such an approach involves both functional and physical attributes, so that a robin is a typical bird not only because of its size and feathers, but because it, unlike the penguin, can fly. The whale, although biologically a mammal, is often viewed as more similar to a shark than to a dog since both the whale and shark live in the water, swim, have fins, etc. The concept of prototypes has a strongly intuitive appeal which underscores the importance of the physical and functional factors. Moreover, it emphasizes that all category defining attributes are not equally important of salient in our mental representations for members of categories.

Presumably, the notion of prototypes could be readily extended to other domains as well. For example, *have* and *own* seem to be more prototypically possession verbs than *borrow* or *lose*. Palermo (1978) has proposed that some prototypical concepts are innate (i.e., color, geometric shape) while others are acquired.

To this point we have examined a variety of approaches to the study of lexical semantics and we have seen several factors emerge as important to the analysis of word meaning. One is that humans typically conceive of meanings in terms of core versus peripheral aspects, where the core is to some extent defined in terms of shared properties, features, and/or attributes. However, all defining attributes are not equally salient, and the ones which dominate in salience may well come to have that position as a function of the task or situation in which members of a given set are evaluated. A second point is that the denotation of a word does not exhaust its meaning: connotative, emotive, and affective aspects are also important in our assignment of meaning to words, although there appears to be considerable individual differences among speakers in certain denotative areas. Thirdly, it is clear that meaning does not reside in words, but in the language users who imbue words with meanings. Finally, from a conceptual point of view, we have noticed that a feature theory of meaning is more useful in defining classes of lexical items, while the semantic field and prototype approaches seem more appropriate for treating the distinctions among members of a given set.

5.3 Sentential Semantics

Approaches to the study of the meanings of sentences are somewhat more limited than those addressing the meaning of words. It is useful to partition the meaning of a sentence into at least three parts: the propositional "core," the illocutionary force (Searle, 1969) or speech act function, and those variations associated with discourse properties. At the outset we must distinguish between metaphorical and figurative uses on the one hand and the more literal and directly informative uses on the other, much along the lines we suggested in our discussion of the distinction in lexical semantics between core denotational meaning and the more connotative aspects. For example, if we were to hear the sentence "He is really quite a dog," we might interpret it in a rather direct sense as expressing praise for a particular animal or, in other circumstances, we might interpret it as an ironic or humorous expression for one's displeasure or amusement at some bit of canine behaviour. It might even be used in an adolescent sense to refer to someone's behaviour or appearance. From a denotational point of view, only the first, more literal, meaning would be up for discussion, and the fact that so much attention is normally directed to literal meanings is possibly because this is the easiest aspect to deal with.

Propositions. As we noted in Chapter One, a clear distinction must be maintained between the form of a sentence and the content or message that form is intended to convey, although for the native speaker, this distinction is often difficult to recognize since the coding system itself, the grammar, is so habitualized and well established. As we also noted there, one way to represent the meaning of a sentence is in terms of its propositional content. Both linguists, such as Fillmore (1968) and Chafe (1970), and psychologists, such as Carpenter and Just (1975), Kintsch (1974), Kintsch and Keenan (1973), and Bransford and Franks (1971), have presented arguments for the desirability of representing core meaning propositionally.

It is generally argued that the meaning of each clause in a sentence can be represented by a proposition, although some simple clauses might require more than one proposition. In addition, various forms of sentence which differ either in terms of the speech act function or in some "stylistic" way as, for example, by differences in indirect object position, may share the same core propositional content. Let us consider the sentences in (8).

8 a. John gave the flowers to Sue.
   b. John gave Sue the flowers.
   c. Did John give the flowers to Sue?
   d. Did John give Sue the flowers?

The relative positions of the direct object *the flowers* and the indirect object *Sue* differ in these examples, but that difference alone, it might be argued, does not reflect a difference in the propositional content of the sentences. However, the first pair differs from the second in terms of form and also in terms of function. It is possible to factor out the differences among the sentences much as was done in the earlier work in transformational grammar (e.g., Chomsky, 1957) in order to isolate a kind of semantic kernel. In this instance, the core proposition of all members of (8) might be represented as in (9).

9 a. *give (John, the flowers, Sue)*
   b. *give* (AGT, GOAL, RECIPIENT)

In (9a), the verb *give* is the predicate and the three NPs are its arguments. From our knowledge of the meaning of *give*, as partially represented in (9b), we can associate the first argument with the semantic agent, the second with the semantic goal, and the third with the recipient. While the form of the sentence changes in (8), the propositional content remains unchanged.

Of course, there is much more to the meaning of the sentence than just its propositional content, and it might even be argued that the rough and ready rule of thumb which pairs one proposition with one clause is both too rough and not ready enough. Lakoff (1970), McCawley (1971), and others of the so-called "generative semantics" movement argued for rather extensive lexical decomposition, such that an often apparently simple sentence was decomposed into an elaborate complex of nested propositions. The generative semanticists argued, for example, that a sentence like (l0):

10. John broke the vase.

should be decomposed semantically into a set of embedded propositions which were represented as syntactic trees. In (10) we have the two basic ideas that (a) John caused something to happen, and (b) what he caused was the breaking of the vase. That is, the propositional content of (10) should be along the lines of (11b) rather than (11a).

11 a. *break (John, the vase)*
   b. *cause (John, break (the vase))*

In such an analysis, an entire proposition, such as *break (the vase)* can itself be embedded as an argument in another proposition.

Apparently, the propositional representations for sentences can be elaborated in several directions. One question which must be dealt with at some point is just what defines the nature of the semantic roles played by NPs. Are these roles small in number? What criteria are used to establish them and differentiate among them? Another direction which must be explored is just how far lexical and propostional decomposition should be taken. For example, although we might prefer (11b) to (11a) on analytic grounds, the empirical question is whether or not the native speaker represents the propositional meaning as one or the other or neither. This brings us to the fundamental question in terms of the propositional representation of meaning: to what extent is there empirical evidence that speakers and hearers actually employ propositional representations.

Experimental evidence. Considerable experimental evidence has accrued to support the claim that at least a part of the semantic representations of sentences can be accounted for in terms of propositional representations. This evidence often hinges on the fact that such representations play a direct role in cognition and memory. One important study along these lines is that of Carpenter and Just (1975), who presented subjects with pictures of either four red or four black dots. With the presentation of each picture, they presented a sentence such as one of those in (11).

11 a. The dots are red.
   b. The dots are not red.
   c. The dots are black.
   d. The dots are not black.

When shown a particular picture and presented with a given sentence, the subject's task was to verify whether or not the picture was true with respect to the sentence. The results were as follows: (a) affirmative sentences were verified faster than negative ones; (b) true affirmatives were verified faster than false affirmatives; (c) false negatives were verified faster than false affirmatives. Carpenter and Just explained these results by claiming that the mental representations for both the sentences and the pictures are propositional, with the verification task being one of matching. To see how this follows, we can consider the case in which the picture presented is one of black dots. Accordingly, the propositional representation is *black* (*dots*), where the predicate is *black*, and its single argument is *dots*. The propositional representations corresponding to the four sentences in (11) are those in (12).

12 a. *red* (*dots*)
   b. *not* (*red* (*dots*))
   c. *black* (*dots*)
   d. *not* (*black* (*dots*))

If we examine the propositional representations in (12), we notice that the positive sentences always have simpler forms than the negatives, thereby accounting for the fact that the affirmatives are faster to process than the negatives. Of the four sentences, two (11b and 11c) are true with respect to the picture of black dots and two are false (11a and 11d). For the true sentences, (11c) has the same propositional representation as the picture, and should therefore be the fastest to verify, while (11b), although true, requires the additional operation that *not (red (dots))* is equivalent in these circumstances to *black (dots)*. Accordingly, the affirmative true sentence is closer in propositional representation to the picture than the negative true sentence. For the false sentences, however, (11d) contains the propositional representation for the picture while (11a) does not. Therefore the false negative sentence should be easier to match with the picture representation than the false affirmative, and it was. Thus, the notion of matching, along with the assumption that both the sentences and pictures are mentally represented as propositions, neatly accounts for the empirical results.

While it is tempting to conclude from this study that all sentences are mentally represented as propositions, such an extrapolation is unwarranted. For example, all the sentences in this experiment are simple declaratives, and this study provides no information as to the appropriate mental representation of the speech act function. Moreover, the verification task might be argued to be quite unnatural, since much of our use of language does not involve verification, but rather other aspects of communication. What is needed here is supporting evidence from other sources.

Other approaches to propositional representation have been explored by Kintsch and his associates. Kintsch and Keenan (1973) found that reading time increases as a linear function of the number of propositions within a text. Moreover, even when the number of words is held constant and the number of propositions is increased, reading time increases. This suggests that in reading, the encoding of the content is a function of the number of propositions.

In attempting to establish a method for establishing the propositional representation for a text, Kintsch (1974) treated a "text" as a set of sentences and a "text base" as that set of propositions associated with the text. The number of propositions is typically larger than the number of sentences in the text. The methodological problem is to formulate a coherent protocol both for establishing propositions and then for empirical testing of the effects of a given propositional representation. Kintsch and Glass (1974) used recall as a dependent variable and, when the number of words is held constant but the number of propositions increases, asked if recall is in terms of the text sentences or of the text base propositions. Sentence (13a), for example, has a single associated proposition, while (13b) has three.

13 a. The settler built the cabin by hand.
   b. The crowded passengers squirmed uncomfortably.

Kintsch and Glass (1974) found that for unipropositional sentences like (13a), 91% of their subjects tended to recall the sentence in its surface form, but for sentences like (13b), only 74% of the subjects recalled the surface form. In this latter case, there was a marked tendency to recall the content in terms of the propositions.

We have so far used the notion of "memory" rather freely, so some attention should be given to this term before going on. Psychologists often distinguish short term memory from other types in that short term memory is that in which "exact wording is stored for brief periods of time" (Clark & Clark, 1977, p. 135). Short term memory has quite a limited capacity and information is either quickly moved into long term memory in some distilled form, or it is discarded. Long term memory is often treated as consisting of at least two distinct components. One, *episodic memory*, is concerned with memory for particular episodes or events which we have experienced, while the second, *semantic memory*, deals with what we know about the real world and how that information is represented mentally. For example, we may recall some episodic particulars of a party we attended, but we may also recall things that happened at the party as a function of our semantic memory.

Inference. When we recall sentences, we normally tend to recall the gist or the meaning rather than the exact wording. Just as we may be able to provide a brief account of a movie we have seen or a book we have read, we do not present that summary in terms of the actual sentences heard or read, but rather we extract what we consider to be the essential elements, organize them, and construct sentences to represent them. Sachs (1967) provided experimental evidence in support of this view. In recall tests for specific sentences in passages, her subjects quickly lost the syntax but did recall paraphrases so long as the original meaning was preserved.

Not only do we recall meaning with little attention to the original form, but we also seem to recall more than we actually hear. That is, we apparently constuct a meaning representation not only for a sentence, but also for various inferences or deductions we might draw from that sentence. For example, upon hearing the sentence (14a), we might readily conclude that (14b) is also the case.

14 a. Stan didn't forget to bring the book.
   b. Stan brought the book.

Of course, the second sentence is not necessarily true since Stan might have failed to bring the book on purpose and not because of his absentmindedness. If we assume the truth of (14b) from (14a), this suggests that we are engaging in what Glucksberg and Danks (1975) called "constructive comprehension," which involves an integration of various pieces of meaning, some directly from sentences encountered and some constructed as inferences, whether logical or not, from those sentences. That is, we seem to fill in blanks in comprehension in order to integrate meanings into coherent and complete pictures.

This aspect of semantic integration was dramatically demonstrated in the work of Bransford and Franks (1971), who showed that when subjects were presented with related ideas, they integrated these into a single scenario. In their pioneering study, Bransford and Franks constructed four complex sentences, each consisting of four "ideas." Each idea corresponds roughly to a simple sentence or, semantically, a single proposition. The four scenarios, with their composite members, are represented in Table 5.2. Each simple idea from each story can be combined with one or more others to make up relatively complex sentences. A sentence with two "ideas" might be "The ants in the kitchen ate the jelly." Bransford and Franks took each set of simple ideas and constructed sentences made up of one, two, or three ideas (but none with all four ideas combined in the same sentence). They then selected a set of 24 sentences, some with one, some with two, and some with three ideas from the four stories, scrambled these and read them to the subjects. The subjects then heard a set of 28 sentences, some from the original set and some not. Their task was to decide whether or not each sentence had been in the original set and to indicate their confidence in each judgement.

The results showed that the more complex a sentence was, the more certain subjects were that it had been in the original set. In fact no sentence containing all four ideas was in the original set, though some were in the test set, and for these subjects felt quite strongly that they had been in the original set. Bransford and Franks concluded from this that subjects did not attend to the surface syntax of the sentences but rather integrated related sentences into single complex representations. In recall, subjects seemed to feel that the syntactic form most coherently representing the integrated form was a part of the original set. In short, subjects tended to integrate the materials into a single representation and store this in memory.

Although considerable experimental evidence has accrued to support the integrative notion of meaning representation, it is too facile to dismiss entirely the importance of syntax in arriving at the meaning representation. Upon examining the sentences in Table 5.2, we notice several important factors. First, the simple "ideas" associated with the

TABLE 5.2 Four Complex Sentences*

===

1. The ants in the kitchen ate the sweet jelly which was on the table.

   a. The ants were in the kitchen.
   b. The ants ate the jelly.
   c. The jelly was sweet.
   d. The jelly was on the table.

2. The warm breeze blowing from the sea stirred the heavy evening air.

   a. The breeze was warm.
   b. The breeze stirred the evening air.
   c. The evening air was heavy.
   d. The breezing was blowing from the sea.

3. The rock which rolled down the mountain crushed the tiny hut at the edge of the woods.

   a. The rock crushed the hut.
   b. The rock rolled down the mountain.
   c. The hut was tiny.
   d. The hut was at the edge of the woods.

4. The old man resting on the couch read the story in the newspaper.

   a. The man read the story.
   b. The man was old.
   c. The man was resting on the couch.
   d. The story was in the newspaper.

---

*From Bransford & Franks, 1971

===

four stories vary considerably in form. Some are very simple indeed and can be represented propositionally as a single predicate plus one argument, such as WARM (BREEZE). Others are relatively more complex, such as CRUSH (ROCK, HUT). Moreover, some of the presumably simple ideas are not so simple as might be thought. For example, "The hut was at the edge of the woods" can conceivably be represented as two propositions. Finally, there seems to be considerably more internal semantic coherence within certain of the stories than in others. The story about ants is considerably more internally coherent than the breeze story. In summary, while a notion of semantic integration seems quite reasonable, it is premature to dismiss entirely the role of syntax in the construction of the meaning representation.

Further experimental evidence suggests that not only is sentence meaning represented mentally in an integrated form, but also that inferences constitute part of that representation. Bransford, Barclay, and Franks (1972) presented subjects with sentences like those in (15).

15 a. Three turtles rested beside a floating log, and a fish swam beneath them.
   b. Three turtles rested on a floating log, and a fish swam beneath them.

Subjects were then given a recognition task in which they were to indicate if particular sentences were in the original set or not. For the pair in (15), the test sentences in (16) constitute crucial examples in the recognition set.

16 a. Three turtles rested beside a floating log, and a fish swam beneath it.
   b. Three turtles rested on a floating log, and a fish swam beneath it.

Subjects who heard (15a) correctly rejected both (16a) and (16b), but those who heard (15b) rejected (16a) but not (16b), presumably because (16b) constitutes an inference drawn from (15b). That is, since the turtles rested on the log and the fish swam beneath the turtles in (15b), then the fish necessarily swam beneath the log. These results suggest that the semantic memory for sentences is made up in part of inferences, and these are in fact not distinguishable from that part of the meaning representation formed from the original sentences, once they are all placed in memory.

Speech act functions. While there appears to be considerable evidence that sentences are processed and stored in some sort of propositional representation and that inferences are also drawn and stored, the question still remains as to the speech act functions associated with sentences. For example, it is possible to use a variety of syntactic forms to convey a single speech act function, all of which might be appropriate in different contexts to involve the notion of command. An example of such variety is found in (17).

17 a. Would you please close the door?
   b. Close the door.
   c. It is too hot in here.
   d. Are you are warm as I am?
   e. I wonder if you would mind closing the door.

Of course, the list in (17) could be extended greatly. One aspect of our control of our language is our sensitivity to the appropriateness of certain constructions in different social situations. For example, while (17a) is syntactically a yes-no question in form and would be appropriate in certain situations where (17b), structurally an imperative, would seem brusque.

In an attempt to assess both direct and indirect speech act functions, Clark and Lucy (1975) had subjects deal with pairs of positive and negative requests such as those in (18) through (20).

18 a. Can you open the door?
   b. Must you open the door?

19 a. Why not open the door?
   b. Why open the door?

20 a. I would love to see the door opened.
   b. I would hate to see the door opened.

The (a) members of these pairs are all positive requests while the (b) members are negatives, in spite of the syntax. Thus, (19a) is syntactically negative but positive in its function. Clark and Lucy found that subjects appear to compute the direct meanings first, and then the indirect speech act, and moreover, negative indirect speech acts, such as the (b) members, take longer to process than positive ones regardless of the presence or absence of syntactic negation. Apparently, then, speech act functions are dealt with differentially in terms of their force and directness.

Contextual factors. Sentences can also vary in form as as a result of contextual factors. In Chapter Four we saw that the GIVEN-NEW strategy governs how various NPs are ordered, with the normal case having the Given NPs prior to the New ones. In examining issues like this, it is essential to recognize that although we are speaking of variations within sentences, the sources of those variations are external to the sentence. Once a particular form is selected, however, the hearer uses his knowledge of how context influences sentence form to reconstruct an appropriate interpretation. Upon hearing a sentence like "John gave SUE the flowers," the hearer can at least guess with some confidence that *Sue* is New information.

Other syntactic phenomena which are triggered by context factors include such variations as clefts and pseudoclefts, which may also be associated with information distribution (cf. Prince, 1978).

Pronominal anaphora may also be governed by context. In an isolated sentence like "John knew that she loved parties," we immediately know that *she* refers to someone other than *John* by virtue of the distinct genders of the two forms. But if *she* is replaced by *he*, then *he* could refer to *John* or someone else. In such instances, the hearer's assignment of a referent for the pronoun depends crucially on the context.

Other areas in which the forms of a sentence is influenced by context include the selection of a particular NP as subject. Kuno and Kaburaki (1975), for example, have proposed an "empathy" hierarchy according to which the hearer is more empathetic to certain grammatical roles and certains kinds of nouns than others. Similarly, Itagaki (1982) and Itagaki and Prideaux (1983) investigated the role of perspective or point of view on the selection of grammatical subjects and semantic agents and experiencers. Subjects were given modified versions of fables and told to rewrite them from the point of view of one or another of the characters. It was found that the character defining the point of view appears significantly more often both as grammatical subject and semantic agent or experiencer than any other character. Thus, perspective itself contributes to the form sentences take.

In summary, the meaning representation of a sentence can be characterized in terms of an often complex propositional representation plus speech act information. Moreover, context factors enter into the representations, perhaps as a kind of "overlay" on certain semantic arguments to mark them as topics, focused constituents, Given, New, or signalling perspective. Once this information is semantically relevant, it contributes to the form of sentences.

5.4 Discourse Semantics

If we turn away from the representation of particular sentences, we can ask just how longer stretches of language--texts and discourse--are organized. Two important notions of relevance here are *schema* and *script*.

Schemata. In discussing memory for texts, Bartlett (1932) argued that remembering is more than the reproduction of the input; it is a reconstructive process. He promoted the notion of "schemata theory" and the role that schemata play in memory. A schema, or in Minsky's (1975) terms, a "frame," is "an organizational representation of a person's knowledge about some concept, action, or event, or a larger unit of knowledge" (Kintsch, 1977, p. 374). That is, a schema or frame is a kind of standardized representation of some event or action. As Kintsch (1977) points out, a very simple example is a verb frame, namely a specification of a verb and its argument structure. Thus for a sentence like (21a) we could have an associated verb frame like (21b) in our memory.

21 a. John smiled.
    b. *smile* (AGENT)

In this particular instance, we would associate the semantic role of agent with *John*. In discourse, however, larger schemata can be discerned, in which a set of events is organized into a kind of stylized episode. Kintsch (1977, p. 376) offers the example of the "Boulder airport bus" schema, which can be sketched as a series of ordered steps much as in (22).

22 a. go to the station
    b. buy a ticket
    c. enter bus
    d. ride bus
    e. leave bus at airport.

In this schema, the basic steps are spelled out, but obviously the details can vary with each trip.

Rummelhart (1977) has developed what he calls a story schema in which a particular story can be decomposed into individual parts, along the lines of (23).

23. Story =   Setting + Episode
    Setting =   State + State + State + ...
    Episode =   Event + Reaction
    Event =   Episode, Change of State, Action, Event,...
    Reaction =   Internal Response + External Response

Rummelhart is trying to characterize what it means for a set of sentences to constitute a story, and to formulate a "story grammar." Of course, the attempt to formulate the structure of a story or narrative is an ancient undertaking. In certain kinds of literature, there exist quite strict constraints on order, events, and the like. Similarly, in one form of modern oral literature, the joke, constraints and requirements are fairly strict. For example, in telling a joke, one must be certain to preserve relevant salient features in order that the punch line goes through properly.

TABLE 5.3 The Restaurant Script

===

1. enter: go in
                  sit where?
                  sit down

2. order: examine menu
                  decide
                  tell waiter

3. eat: receive food
                  consume food

4. exit: ask for check
                  receive check
                  tip
                  pay cashier (waiter)
                  leave

===

Scripts. Another approach to the organization of discourse, and more importantly, to the organization of knowledge in memory is the notion of "script" (Schank & Abelson, 1977). A script is a set of ordered components which serve as a prototype or scenario for a class of events. Schank and Abelson argue that we learn scripts which in turn aid us in representing mentally certain coherent sets of events. One such is the famous "restaurant script" illustrated in Table 5.3. The restaurant script is appropriate for a "normal" restaurant, but it would not work for a fast-food outlet such as McDonalds, where one pays before eating. Moreover, additional components might also be added, such as a drink-ordering step or a dessert step. Some variations appear to fall within the domain of the restaurant script with little difficulty, while others seem bizarre. For example, it would stretch the script considerably to move from one table to another with each course consumed, or to wear one's raincoat at the table.

There is a host of possible scripts. A familiar one is the "Hi, how are you?" script which we often play out with friends before we enter into more intimate conversation. Since this script serves to inititate the social interaction, without it we feel awkward about plunging into personal discussions. Other scripts include the birthday party script for children, the airline trip script, the formal lecture script, the sermon script, and a myriad of others. Scripts are learned and provide an organizational structure for the representation of knowledge. Many are largely specific to certain cultures, so that what constitutes a child's birthday celebration in one culture might differ drastically from that in another.

Other factors which enter into the organization of discourse include such grammatical devices as tense sequences, pronoun selections and anaphora, as well as such semantic factors as serial order of events, perspective, coherence maintenance devices specific to certain genres, and the like. Finally, we should mention some general observations concerning constraints on discourse. Grice (1975) has suggested four important maxims or "conversational postulates" which appear to govern the way we interact with each other in conversations. These are cited in Table 5.4. We all know people who in the course of conversation violate one or another of these maxims. We know, for example, people who engage in information overkill, telling us far more about some particular item than we are interested in knowing, or those who have trouble focusing their comments on the topic at hand. We also have different ways of dealing with such people. With some, we might violate the normal "turn taking" associated with conversations and attempt to cut off or redirect our addressee's train of thought. Rarely, however, do we simply tell him that he is being verbose or irrelevant.

These examples suggest that we have just begun to scratch the surface in our understanding of the semantics of discourse. and its organization seem remains largely hidden from us, even though significant starts have been made in numerous areas.

5.5 Summary

In this chapter, we have examined in considerable detail, perhaps in violation of the maxim of quantity, numerous topics in semantics. We have

TABLE 5.4 Grice's Conversational Maxims

```
============================================
```

Quantity: Provide as much information as
            needed, but no more;

Quality: Information must be of a
            sufficiently high quality;

Relevance: Information must bear directly on
            the issue;

Manner: Information must be expressed
            clearly and concisely.

```
============================================
```

found that lexical semantics can be approached in many ways, including the analysis of features, semantic fields, prototype theory, and in terms of denotation versus connotation. Again, we notice that one theoretical approach might account for certain aspects of meaning, but ignore others, leading us to conclude that there is at this juncture no "right" way to treat lexical semantics, but rather that many sub-theories exist, each of which seems to be more or less adequate for certains aspects of meaning.

In the domain of sentential semantics, we have focused on propositional representations for the core meaning of sentences, and we have examined empirical evidence in support of the psychological viability of such representations. We have also examined the speech act aspects of sentence meaning and have noted the importance of context in the shape of particular sentences. Finally, in a brief overview of discourse organization, we have mentioned schemata and scripts as useful concepts for handling some aspects of larger chunks of language. All these notions seem useful and suggest that a more eclectic approach to meaning is required than we might wish. But at this stage, which seems to be a kind of Ptolemaic stage in linguistic theorizing, we can probably require no more. Semantics is both the heart of language and its most elusive aspect.

EXERCISES

5.1. For each of the following words, first write out your own definition. When you have finished, look up each word in the *OED* and determine if and how that word has changed in meaning over time.

attend, bungalow, conspire, copacetic, decimate, gadget, gossip, noon, ohm, parachute, register

5.2. In a word association experiment in which the stimulus item was *chair*, subjects gave the following as responses: *table, leg, furniture, sitting, cushion, bear.* What type of associate is each?

5.3. For each of the following sets of words, determine which semantic features are involved in (a) uniting and (b) distinguishing them. For each set, fill out any remaining members on the basis of gaps uncovered by your features.

a. pup, bitch, dog, kitten, bull, calf

b. criticize, reproach, chide, reject, blame

c. mother, daughter, son, grandfather, uncle

d. frost, pumpkin, leaves, cool, moon

e. believe, doubt, know, understand, suppose

5.4. Rank order each of the following words as relatively closer or further from your prototypic notion of "dog." Then explain what dimensions you feel are relevant for your own prototypic notion.

poodle, cocker spaniel, German shepherd, black lab, Doberman, greyhound, terrier.

5.5. Characterize as clearly as you can the major similarities and crucial differences among the feature, semantic field, and prototype theories of lexical semantics.

194

5.6. Construct a propositional representation for each of the following sentences:

a.   Sam thought that Fred was writing a novel.

b.   Who did Marilyn marry?

c.   That Turner became a painter upset Malcolm.

d.   It was decided that the party would start at nine.

e.   James is not a good electrician.

5.7. Provide propositional representations for the four basic "ideas" of Bransford and Franks (1971) "rock-hut" story, as found in Table 5.2.

5.8. A given syntactic form such as a yes-no question structure can serve a variety of speech act functions (e.g., question, command, etc.), and likewise, a given speech act function can be encoded by different syntactic structures. For the speech act function of "command," associated with "bringing a book to class," construct several different syntactic forms, and comment on the situations in which each would or would not be appropriate.

5.9. Specify the basic components of the "going to a movie" script. Now, which additional, optional components might typically be allowed? What degree of freedom exists in the ordering of such optional components with respect to the obligatory ones. Cite examples to illustrate.

LABORATORY

Laboratory 10. Semantic Fields

Chapter Six

CONCLUSIONS

6.1 Introduction

It is always a difficult, if not downright dangerous, endeavor to attempt a summary of the state of affairs in a rapidly developing and changing field of inquiry. This is all the more true in an area like psycholinguistics, where a host of distinct and often divergent research programs are being carried out under the auspices of frequently contending sets of assumptions and theoretical orientations. Indeed, one of the most difficult problems here is to decide on which theoretical framework, assumptions, and methodological perspective to adopt. Consequently, rather than attempting a gratuitous summary of what has been dealt with in the preceeding chapters, it will be of more use to focus some attention on more fundamental issues, such as (a) how well our methodological assumptions and research strategies have paid off, (b) what we have learned about the interaction of theory and experimentation, and (c) what kinds of linguistic descriptions (grammars) are the most useful for psycholinguistics. It is to such matters as these that this final, brief chapter is devoted.

6.2 Language Subsystems

One of the most important research strategies associated with much recent work in experimental psycholinguistics seems to be that of the adoption of a "modular" or "component" view of language.

Conclusions

This view, popularized within theoretical linguistics by Chomsky's (1980, 1982a, 1982b) approach, which partitions a grammar into a variety of independent components, seems to have been implicitly adopted by a large number of psycholinguists. Within psycholinguistics, however, a rather different view of modularity seems to have evolved, one in which several different language *subsystems* or *components* can be isolated and investigated (cf. Hatch, 1983). These include, among others, such components as the *grammar, lexicon, pragmatics, discourse constraints,* and *phonology.*

In the preceding chapters, we have examined a wide variety of linguistic phenomena within a number of distinct components or subsystems. In Chapter Four, for example, a variety of syntactic factors was explored, some of which appeared to deal with the forms of sentences, while others dealt with the effect various processing strategies might have as the hearer undertakes to comprehend language. The role of the lexicon, and our knowledge of lexical representations, showed up in a number of places, including in our discussion of morphology and in our explorations of the propositional representations of sentences. Pragmatic factors were shown to play important roles in semantics, while contextual and discourse factors are involved in both syntactic and semantic aspects of processing. In short, the modular approach as a research strategy seems extremely useful and productive.

An important aspect of this approach to language is that while each component can be isolated and studied independently, the interactions among components must also be borne in mind. Failure to countenance the interaction among various systems can lead the incautious researcher astray. A useful illustration of just this failure to attend to interactions among components is that of the old, and now hopefully moribund, doctrine of "stylistic variation" as represented by optional transformations. At one time in the not-too-distant past, optional transformations, such as PARTICLE MOVEMENT or DATIVE MOVEMENT, were said to represent pairs of "stylistic variants," with no real meaning difference associated with the differences in form.

According to that view, sentences like "Algernon sent Suzie a pig" and "Algernon sent a pig to Suzie" are merely stylistic variants, although just what the notion "stylistic variant" is supposed to mean remained unaddressed. However, with the realization that discourse factors such as the distribution of Given and New information can determine the relative order of constituents within a sentence, the free variation assumed to exist between such stylistically varying pairs as these at least partially disappears, as we saw in the discussion of processing strategies in Chapter Four. The recognition of a distinction between sentence-level syntax and discourse factors, and the interaction between these two components, has eliminated much of the syntactic "free variation" found in earlier descriptions.

The separation of the lexicon from the grammar has also constituted an important step in the modularization of language subsystems. Much of the impetus for treating the lexicon as an independent and highly structured component has of course come from theoretical studies (e.g., Bresnan, 1981; Chomsky, 1982a). At the same time, however, considerable evidence has accrued in support of the notion that the language user knows a great deal about the nature of a lexical item, including its "argument structure." Moreover, this knowledge has been shown to be utilized by hearers as they process language. For example, the hearer knows that *put* requires a locative phrase as an obligatory argument, while *lose* does not, thereby accounting for the differences in speakers' judgements as to where the PP *in the bedroom* should be attached in sentences such as the following:

1 a. Mary lost the book that Sue had been reading in the bedroom.
   b. Mary put the book that Sue had been reading in the bedroom.

Examples such as these provide strong support for the psychological viability of speakers' extensive knowledge of not only the meanings of lexical items, but their structures as well, thereby highlighting once again the distinction between the components of grammar, lexicon, and parsing strategies.

The evidence discussed in Chapter Five dealing with the propositional representation of the core meaning of sentences constitutes further evidence for the modularity of language. The fact that sentences seem to be processed at least in part in terms of their propositional cores, plus the fact that subjects tend to integrate the meanings of sentences and draw inferences from them, supports the distinction between grammar on the one hand and syntax on the other.

One important aspect of the modular view of language subsystems which has emerged in psycholinguistics, but which is generally absent in purely theoretical treatments, involves the role of processing strategies interacting with the syntactic, lexical, discourse, or pragmatic components of language. According to this view, a hearer has access not only to his linguistic knowledge, including knowledge about the structure of his language, his lexicon, the pragmatics of the situation, and the like, but also to general cognitive strategies (such as CLOSURE, NORMAL FORM, etc.) as he constructs a mental representation of the meaning.

The success of such a modular approach to linguistic description is reflected in the success that has accrued in support of particular processing strategies as well as that associated with particular proposals for the nature of representation of syntactic, lexical, and pragmatic information. One of the hallmarks of psycholinguistic research over the past two decades has been the continual reaffirmation of the success of a modular view of interacting language subsystems.

6.3 Theory and Experimentation

In the early days of experimental psycholinguistics, it was generally assumed that the linguist's job was to construct theories about the "nature of language," that is, about just how language worked The psycholinguist's task was somewhat derivative, namely to take the linguist's theories about the nature and structure of language and determine just how these were incorporated into the language processing system. An important part of this division of labor was the implicit assumption that the linguist could contribute his theoretical share to the joint task from a position quite immune to empirical issues. Indeed, one basic assumption of theoretical linguistics during the halycon days of transformational grammar was that of the "ideal speaker-hearer" whose competence was virtually identical with his performance in that he was not subject to false starts, short term memory problems, and the like. It is not surprising that with the adoption of the ideal speaker-hearer as focus of theoretical attention, there was little ground for interaction between the linguistic theorist and his psycholinguist tag-along.

With the demise of the derivational theory of complexity, however, many psychologists and psycholinguists seemed to feel that the linguists had somehow let them down. This attitude sometimes led psychologists to disassociate themselves entirely from the linguists' theorizing, with the result that the linguistic knowledge and insights gained over many years about the structure of language tended to be ignored by psycholinguists.

Such a tendency is not at all surprising if all the theoretical input to the study of language processes is a one-way street from the linguist to the psychologist. However, much recent research in psycholinguistics seems to highlight not only the need for two-way traffic, but also the fact that the linguist and the psycholinguist can profit by the other's research (cf. Kess, 1976b). Indeed, the inductive-deductive spiral discussed in Chapter One takes place once the blinders are removed and the mind is opened to the suggestions and results of others working in related areas. The advent of much interdisciplinary research in the cognitive sciences over the past few years seems, in this light, to be a very promising sign of interaction among relatively diverse groups.

It has been the central premise of this book that experimental research can and must have an important role to play in linguistics. Without the interaction of theory and experiment, linguistics can easily reduce to armchair speculation, a charge still

Conclusions

often heard from a variety of directions.

Even today, some linguists cling to the view that linguistics should be treated as an autonomous discipline, and one which in principle must not be contaminated by influences from other disciplines such as psychology (cf. Kac, 1980; Newmeyer, 1983).

It should nevertheless be clear from much of the more recent research, especially in syntax and semantics, that a two-way flow of information is emerging. Much of the work in semantics, following Sachs (1967) and Bransford and Franks (1971), for example, suggests that linguists must seriously attend to such notions as semantic integration and storage, much as Kimball (1973) and Frazier and Fodor (1979) have attempted. Work in lexical semantics, including research in both prototype theory and lexical fields, constitute an important challenge to feature theory and the kind of componential analysis held so dear by linguists for such a long time.

In short, there is interaction emerging, although proponents of both, or all, positions still seem reluctant in many cases to take challenges seriously. To this extent, then, the "armchair" label attached to much of linguistics may still have something to recommend it.

6.4 What Kind of Grammar?

Within the domain of linguistic theory itself, it may be asked just how research and results in psycholinguistics has affected the way linguists construct their grammatical theories. There clearly has been some influence in a variety of places. For example, Dik (1978) has explictly stated that his theory of functional grammar should be responsible to a variety of adequacy conditions, one of which is that of "psychological adequacy."

Nevertheless, within linguistics a formal grammar has typically been conceived of as a description of linguistic forms, while the relationship between such descriptions and the mechanisms of language production and comprehension has remained quite obscure. Indeed, the failure of the derivational theory of complexity, with its assumption of the direct incorporation of a transformational grammar into a processing system, perhaps best illustrates the incompatability of such a grammar with psycholinguistic requirements of language processing. At the heart of the problem, from the psycholinguistic point of view, is the kind of rule adopted within formal grammars.

The classical notion of "rule" in formal grammars is one which relates one *structure* to another. The entire notion of "deriving" one structure from another, more abstract structure, albeit under the constraint of meaning preservation or some other equally arbitrary condition, lends itself very naturally to an interpretation in which the language user is viewed as carrying out such structural rearrangements mentally as he produces or comprehends sentences. This interpretation is precisely the one underlying the entire derivational theory of complexity research paradigm. And, as we have seen, such a formulation of grammatical rule is quite incompatable with what has been learned about language processing.

However, a more *functionally* oriented notion of grammar seems considerably more compatible with psycholinguistic requirements. In particular, a notion of grammar in which functional information is paired with syntactic structure via specific linguistic devices seems more directly useful to the psycholinguist. If a particular grammar contained a "rule" which stated, for example, that a questioned *wh-* word is positioned in clause initial position, regardless of its grammatical role, while a non-*wh-* word is positioned according to its grammatical function, this grammar would never involve a "transformation" by which a *wh-* phrase is moved from one position to another. Such a notion of rule, which involves the pairing of function with structure, constitutes a significant departure from the more traditional grammatical view of rule.

To illustrate this functional notion of grammatical rule briefly, let us consider the following sentences as data, with the aim of constructing some potential functional rules.

2 a. Sammy sent a rose to his girlfriend.
   b. Sammy sent his girlfriend a rose.
   c. Did Sammy send a rose to his girlfriend?
   d. Who did Sammy send a rose (to)?
   e. What did Sammy send (to) his girlfriend?

This list of sentences, with numerous other variants, could readily be expanded. However, for our purpose, the issue is just what kinds of functional rules are needed? In particular, just what kinds of rules relate functional information to grammatical structure?

First, we need a rule which states that an indirect object NP, which is not a *wh-* phrase or a topic, is realized to the right of the main verb, and a similar rule for a direct object NP. Such rules could be crudely represented as in (3), where the "<===>" notation indicates a pairing of the functional information on the left side with syntactic (constituent) structure on the right, and the square brackets mark clause boundaries.

3 a. NP = DO <===> [X V X NP X]

   b. NP = IO <===> [X V X (to) NP X]

The rules would, of course, need to be constrainted by the condition that the NPs under consideration are not topics or *wh-* phrases, for under those conditions the NP is placed at the left of the clause, as in (3).

3 c. NP = WH <===> [NP X]

An important aspect of these rules is that they do not derive the two alternative orderings of the direct and indirect object from a single syntactic source. Rather the rules, including the variables, permit the linearization of the direct object either before or after the indirect object. Neither of these structures is viewed as more basic than the other, at least to the extent that one serves as a syntactic source for the other.

To this point, however, all we have is the free variation in the word orders of the two objects. Yet experimental research involving discourse constraints such as the GIVEN-NEW strategy, provide evidence that there is a discourse condition on the relative order of the NPs. Thus, a further rule, one which derives it values from the context, is needed, namely one along the following lines:

4.   NPa = GIVEN <===> [X NPa X NPb X]
     NPb = NEW

This rule simply states that if, in a pair of NPs, one is Given and the other is New, the Given NP precedes in the clause. Of course, as we know, the order New-Given can occur if special stress is used, and such a further rule is also required. What is crucial in this brief example is the fact that the rules are formulated in order to represent empirically established facts governing the forms of sentences.

In his discussion of a "performance grammar," Carroll (1973) offered similar kinds of rules which pair "I-markers" with surface constituent structure. These rules, which construct sentences from left to right, are sensitive to grammatical functional relations such as "deep subject," "deep object," etc. as well as to such other relations as constituent emphasis, theme, and sentence mode (declarative, interrogative, etc.). A rule for assigning English word order in a yes-no question is roughly the following (after Schlesinger, 1977, p. 37):

5.   If the sentence mode is "interrogative" and no single constituent of the sentence in questioned, the left-most consitutent is the first auxiliary constituent.

Rules like these require functional specifications in terms of grammatical relations such as subject and direct object. Indeed, many versions of functional grammar being proposed today seem, in varying degrees, to adopt a perspective in which functions and structures are somehow paired (cf. Carroll, 1973; Dik, 1978; Kac, 1978, Kaplan & Bresnan, 1982; Prideaux, 1979b). Many psycholinguistic findings appear to be much more compatible with this perspective of grammar than one which does no more than relate one structure to another.

Conclusions

The recent and still developing lexical functional theory of grammar (Bresnan, 1981) is another which seems potentially quite compatible with real language processing. In this theory, too, grammatical structure is paired with functional information, and no transformations are allowed in the theory. The theory has seem some preliminary success in terms of the parsing proposals found in Ford, Bresnan, and Kaplan (1982), in the sentence production suggestions of Ford (1982), and in the language acquisition proposals of Pinker (1982). This theory, unlike some other functional theories, makes an overt claim that a competence grammar of the lexical functional sort is directly incorporated into a language processing model and is also directly involved in language acquisition. The theory employs both grammatical functions and semantic ("thematic") roles, much Dik's functional grammar does.

An alternative to the view that the functional information should be represented in terms of grammatical functions has been advanced by Schlesinger (1971; 1977), who argues for semantic rather than functional representations. In particular, he proposes that "Input-markers" ("I-markers") be constructed in terms of semantic relations such as AGENT, GOAL, ACTION, ATTRIBUTE, and the like. Thus, for a sentence such as (6):

6. Alice kicked the poor lizards.

the I-marker would be a structure roughly like (7), where the sentence mode (or speech act functions) are for the moment ignored.

7. (AGENT-ACTION   Alice,   (GOAL-ACTION (ATTRIBUTE poor, lizards), kick)

Such I-markers are hierarchically organized, but their linear order has no significance. I-markers are mapped into constituent structures by various *realization rules*. These include: (a) *relation rules*, which specify how the I-marker relations are expressed in a particular language in terms of word order, affixes, etc.; (b) the *lexicon*, which translates the "protoverbal" elements of the I-markers into words and phrases, while at the same time assigning them lexical categories (N, V, etc.); (c) *concord rules*, which account for inflections and the like; (d) *intonation rules*, which assign phonological contours; and (e) *phonological rules*, which assign phonological shapes.

Schlesinger's approach, unlike most other functionally oriented perspectives, opts for semantic constituents in the I-markers. He argues that grammatical functional notions like subject and object, while permitting certain rules and relations to be stated in simple and elegant forms, at the same time complicate the language acquisition process. He argues in support of a "semantic assimilation hypothesis" which states that semantic roles such as AGENT tend to assimilate others such as INSTRUMENT or GOAL in certain positions. Thus, Schlesinger's view of agent is a broader one than, for example, Fillmore's (1968).

While many, and perhaps most, of the grammatical proposals adopted by psycholinguists have originated primarily within linguistics and have been developed by linguists using the familiar linguistic arguments of distribution of forms, syntactic relatedness, etc., Schlesinger's proposals spring primarily from the perspective of the language user, in terms of which economy and ease of learning and representation count for more than the linguistic criterion of capturing significant generalizations. Indeed, Schlesinger's proposals are extremely plausible from the perspective of the language user, and his evidence in support of them is impressive.

It should perhaps be pointed out at this point, however, that the notion of the "correctness" of one grammatical theory over another is not being argued. Rather it is the *usefulness* or *compatibility* of a grammatical system that is of importance. For psycholinguistic research, it appears that a functionally oriented grammar, and one which focuses primarily on the surface in its constituent structure component, is far more useful than a grammar which ignores functional factors. Of course, a reasonable question can then be posed: why bother with some version of grammar which is of no use for addressing real language processing? There are a variety of answers to this, not the least important of which is that some grammars may have other important uses, such as pedagogical or historical grammars. Another answer, however, is that only those grammars which have relevance to language processing and which are constrained by processing factors can have any claim on the label of "psychological reality."

In the final analysis, as we discussed in Chapter One, a grammatical theory is only as good as its compatibility with empirical facts, and within psycholinguistics this imposes a variety of severe constraints on what an acceptable rule of grammar can be.

6.5 Summary

Although we we have examined in these chapters a host of issues from a wide variety of areas, it is abundantly clear that there are a great many more areas which we have not mentioned at all. There is, for example, an enormous amount of research dealing with such areas as language pathology, reading, second language acquistion, sociolinguistics, and numerous other areas. Indeed, each of these areas is so important that major research journals and many books are being devoted to each. Rather than try to cover all these areas in the present work, or to cover them only superficially, the decision was made to address them not at all. This choice, while deliberate, unfortunately excludes most of "applied" linguistics, areas in which there is an enormous amount of interest today.

Our orientation was however different: we wanted to provide an overview of some of the more central research in experimental linguistics in light of the discipline's historical context. At the same time, we wanted to provide the student with both exercises and laboratories so that he or she could at least get a hint of the kinds of research being carried out in psycholinguistics. The decision to exclude so much was prompted, therefore, not by the view that the excluded areas are of little interest or importance, but rather by the limitations of size and scope.

It is clear that a great deal has been learned about language processing and acquisition during the past few decades, while at the same time a variety of new and innovative techniques have been designed to test a host of new hypotheses. It is nevertheless clear that there is a very long way to go, and that experimental psycholinguistics is just beginning to scratch the surface in our study of language processing. Perhaps that is one of the delights of the field: there is no end in sight.

LABORATORIES

These laboratories are designed to introduce the student to research in experimental linguistics. Their primary aim is to highlight the importance of empirical research, with attention directed away from an "armchair" view of linguistics and toward a scientific treatment of empirical data.

One fact which quickly becomes clear when dealing with experimental data is that people differ considerably in their treatment of linguistic materials. Some of these differences reflect those "individual differences" about which our psychologist colleagues have so often spoken. However, some differences found among subjects are the product of systematic group differences which might be attributed to a host of factors, including age, educational level, dialect, and background, among others. While these laboratories do not focus on the particulars of such differences, they are nevertheless intended to give the student an appreciation of the kinds of variation found among speakers and which must be addressed in any serious empirical study of language.

While extensive and often highly technical statistical methods are of crucial importance for advanced work in experimental linguistics, elaborate statistical tools are not employed in these laboratories. The two sections following the labs serve to introduce some basic statistical notions and provide a short introduction to both t-tests and X^2 tests, the only statistical tests needed for the labs. The appendices contain tables for critical values of t and X^2.

LABORATORY NOTEBOOK

A laboratory notebook is an essential component of a laboratory research project. It is a journal or scientific diary to keep track of what you did, why you did it, etc., so that someone else (or even you yourself) can extract this information later on. It is *not* meant to be published, so the exact format is not crucial. What does matter is that it be:

(a) accurate
(b) reasonably organized
(c) original (*never* copies from scrap pieces of paper)
(d) comprehensive.

Be as brief as you can, but record ALL relevant information. Do not worry about trying to record too much. If you have any doubts, write it down.

Be reasonably neat, but do not spend all day trying to improve your penmanship. NEVER, NEVER TEAR ANY PAGES OUT. If you decide that you made an error in recording numbers, etc., simply stroke them out and rewrite them. Always leave the "wrong" numbers visible. Very often, they turn out to be "right" in the end.

Set up your lab notebook as follows:

(a) Page 1: NAME, ADDRESS, PHONE, COURSE, TITLE

(b) Leave several blank pages for a TABLE OF CONTENTS which will be filled in as you complete the laboratories.

Each of your labs should be written up in your lab notebook in accordance with the following format (adopted from *Publication Manual* of the American Psychological Association).

1. TITLE. Use the title given for that lab.

2. ABSTRACT. This is a brief summary of what was done, why it was done, and what was found.

3. INTRODUCTION. Discuss the assigned references, and provide your reader with the rationale and purpose of the study.

4. METHOD. Specify your subjects (number, type, etc.), any apparatus you might have used, and your procedure. It is important that you indicate here not only what you were supposed to do, but what you actually DID. For this purpose, good lab notes are essential.

5. RESULTS. This is where you record your data (tables, figures, etc.). You should also provide a brief verbal description of your numerical results.

6. DISCUSSION. Here you discuss your results, offer pertinent observations about the data, specify any possible confounding variables, indicate your conclusions (backed up with evidence), answer any questions asked in the lab, and state how this study has addressed the issues discussed in the INTRODUCTION.

LABORATORY 1.   VARIATION IN ACCEPTABILITY JUDGEMENTS

REFERENCE

Spencer (1973)

INTRODUCTION

Linguistic descriptions (grammars) are often constructed on the assumption that all the forms (phrases, sentences, etc.) being described are uniformly and equally acceptable to all speakers.

A form is said to be *grammatical* with respect to a particular grammar if that form is described (generated) by the grammar. Consequently, a form is either grammatical or ungrammatical with respect to a particular grammar. Grammaticality is a binary (yes/no) function.

Acceptability, on the other hand, refers not to a particular grammar, but rather to judgements of forms made by native speakers. A given form may be judged relatively acceptable or relatively unacceptable. Accordingly, acceptability is not a binary function, but rather constitutes a spectrum ranging from "completely acceptable" to "completely unacceptable."

A wide range of factors govern judgements of acceptabilty. Some of these are: (a) dialect differences, (b) the appropriateness of a particular form for a particular context, (c) semantic compatability of lexical items, and (d) syntactic form.

PURPOSE

The purpose of this laboratory is to demonstrate variation in acceptability judgements when (a) several subjects independently evaluate the same sentences, and (b) several tokens of the same sentence type are evaluated.

Laboratories

PROCEDURE

Students will act as subjects for the experiment, which will be conducted and analyzed during the laboratory session. Read the instructions carefully. Follow the instructions and carry out the experimental task.

DATA

The data will be tabulated in several ways and will be entered into three tables in your lab notebook.

In conjunction with the other students in the laboratory, calculate the mean and standard deviation for each item.

Construct "TABLE 1. Acceptability Scores" in your lab notebook. This table should contain three columns, the first labelled "Item," the second labelled "Mean," and the third labelled "Standard Deviation." Under "Item" list the item numbers from 1 through 35, and enter beside each its mean and standard deviation.

There are 18 items in the data which contain Verb-Particle constructions. These sentences each contain a verb (V) and a particle (PRT). In some cases, the PRT is immediately after the V, while in other cases it has been positioned after either a NP, a PP, or a RC (relative clause). The following syntactic structures are each represented by three token sentences in the data.

        A.   NP V PRT NP PP
        B.   NP V NP PRT PP
        C.   NP V NP PP PRT
        D.   NP V PRT NP RC
        E.   NP V NP PRT RC
        F.   NP V NP RC PRT

Construct in your lab notebook "TABLE 2. Acceptability Scores for the V-PRT Structures." Calculate the mean for each of the six different structures and enter these into Table 2. Then calculate the standard deviation for each and enter these values into Table 2. Finally, rank order the six structures from most to least natural and enter these values in Table 2 under a column labelled "Rank Order." Thus, Table 2 should contain four columns. The first should be labelled "Structure," and under it should be listed the six structural types. The other three columns are simply the mean, standard deviation, and rank order columns.

Finally, there are six items in the experiment (items 2, 6, 10, 14, 18, and 22) about which one linguist has offered his own judgements (Postal, 1970). In your lab notebook construct Table 3 and enter the mean score for the six sentences in the apppropriate places. Use the following format (Postal's judgements are provided here for you):

==
TABLE 3. A Comparison with Postal's Data

Item	Mean Score	S.D.	Postal's Judgement
2			1
6			1
10			5
14			3
18			5
22			1
==

RESULTS

The summary of results found in Table 1 will not be interpreted here since that table contains a tabulation of the raw data only. Focus your attention on Tables 2 and 3.

1. Interpret Table 2 in terms of the syntactic forms of structures with the PRT placed in different positions.

2. Interpret Table 3 in terms of the semantics of the sentences.

CONCLUSIONS

1. What reasons can be given for the results represented in Table 2? What factors contribute to these results?

2. A NP can contain either a PP or a RC within it, according to the following rule:

$$NP \longrightarrow NP \left(\begin{Bmatrix} PP \\ RC \end{Bmatrix} \right).$$

Some transformational grammarians have postulated the following optional rule of Particle Movement:

```
T. PARTICLE MOVEMENT (OPTIONAL)
SD:        V    PRT NP
SC:        1     2 3      --->
           1     0 3+2
```

From the results of this experiment, offer a criticism of the validity of this rule.

3. Given the results in Table 3, how seriously can acceptability judgements of a single speaker be taken? Justify your conclusion by reference to the results of this experiment.

ACCEPTABILITY EXPERIMENT INSTRUCTIONS

Some sentences are relatively more acceptable than others. In this experiment you will be given a list of 35 sentences, in written form, and below each you will find a scale of numbers from 1 (completely unacceptable) to 5 (completely acceptable). Your task is to make a judgement as to the relative acceptability of each sentence.

First, read through the entire list of sentences to familiarize yourself with the range of stimuli. Now, read through the list again, and pick out the *least acceptable* (worst) sentence. Circle "1" for that sentence. Once again, read through the list, but this time find the *most acceptable* (best) sentence, and circle "5" for it. You have now *anchored* your acceptability scale at either end.

Finally, read each sentence, beginning with the first, and make a judgement as to its relative acceptability. Indicate your judgement by circling one of the numbers from "1" to "5" inclusive.
The scale of acceptability is to be understood as follows:

5 - completely acceptable and natural; no problem at all;
4 - relatively acceptable, but not as good as (5);
3 - uncertain as to acceptability; cannot decide;
2 - relatively unacceptable, but not completely;
1 - completely unacceptable; sounds strange and non-English.

Judge each sentence independently. Do not go back and change your previous judgements.

ACCEPTABILITY EXPERIMENT STIMULI

1 = LEAST ACCEPTABLE   5 = MOST ACCEPTABLE

1. Sam sliced up the steak which he had carefully cooked.
   1 2 3 4 5

2. To whom was it obvious that Max was a Hungarian?
   1 2 3 4 5

3. Fred paid the mortgage on his lakefront cottage off.
   1 2 3 4 5

4. To visit relatives is a lot of fun.
   1 2 3 4 5

5. Stan took all the trash out from the party.
   1 2 3 4 5

6. To whom was it most disgusting that Max quit?
   1 2 3 4 5

7. The rancher sold the cattle off which he had raised from calves.
   1 2 3 4 5

8. That for Fred to win the race is easy is obvious.
   1 2 3 4 5

9. Fred called his cousin who used to live in Halifax up.
   1 2 3 4 5

10. That Betty was like Bill struck Jack.
    1 2 3 4 5

11. Jack turned on the lamp near the door.
    1 2 3 4 5

12. That Sam loved pancakes became obvious to Mary.
    1 2 3 4 5

13. Tom broke the door which was heavily reinforced down.
    1 2 3 4 5

14. This onion soup reminds me of 1943.
    1 2 3 4 5

15. Mary handed her quiz in on phonological theory.
    1 2 3 4 5

16. It pleased Mary that Joe accepted the gift.
    1 2 3 4 5

17. Bob woke his guest up who was sleeping on the sofa.
    1 2 3 4 5

18. Jack struck Betty to be like Bill.
    1 2 3 4 5

19. Marilyn threw the letter from her boyfriend away.
    1 2 3 4 5

20. It is apparent that Pete will win the election.
    1 2 3 4 5

21. Jason tired the fish out which he had hooked an hour earlier.
    1 2 3 4 5

22. Who did Max impress as being honest?
    1 2 3 4 5

23. June left the question about Swahili out.
    1 2 3 4 5

24. It is certain that for Sue to drive a tractor is a problem.
    1 2 3 4 5

25. Ann brought in the laundry which was drying outside.
    1 2 3 4 5

26. That Fred arrived late upset Sue.
    1 2 3 4 5

27. They talked the exam which they had both failed over.
    1 2 3 4 5

28. It is uncertain that it is impossible for an ostrich to fly.
    1 2 3 4 5

29. Jim put the bill away from the gas company.
    1 2 3 4 5

30. That Sue can leave before Joe has been approved.
    1 2 3 4 5

31. Peter looked over the results which the computer had provided.
    1 2 3 4 5

32. Megan expects that Susan cannot prepare dessert.
    1 2 3 4 5

33. Jeff wrote down all the capitals of South American countries.
    1 2 3 4 5

34. It is a chore to cut the lawn.
    1 2 3 4 5

35. Sarah tied up the dog with the brown tail.
    1 2 3 4 5

LABORATORY 2. INTERFERENCE PHENOMENA

REFERENCE

Weinreich (1968, Sections 2.1-2.2)

INTRODUCTION

When an adult is learning a second language, he typically makes several types of errors in speaking the target (T) language. Some of the errors result from the student's incomplete control of the syntactic or morphological structures of T, or from his lack of adequate vocabulary. Others result from various learning strategies which he employs incorrectly, such as overgeneralizing a particular rule or incorrectly extending an analogy. Still other errors, often called "transfer" or "interference" errors, may result from the influence of his native (N) language. Transfer errors are perhaps most notable in phonology, where the phonological structure of N influences the student's pronunciation in T, especially early in his language learning.

PURPOSE

The purpose of this laboratory is to investigate transfer errors in phonology, using data from a single subject whose native language is Japanese and who is beginning to learn English. Attention will focus on segmental phonology and on phonotactics.

PROCEDURE

Data will be provided and analyzed in the laboratory. You will be given a list of English words, along with their "mispronunciations" (in phonetic transcription) by a native speaker of Japanese just beginning to learn English. Transcribe each English word phonemically according to your own pronunciation of the word.

You will then compare the "correct" (native) pronunciation of each word with the Japanese "mispronunciation" of it and attempt to discover the factors from Japanese phonology which account for the mispronunciations.

The following facts about Japanese phonology are crucial to this laboratory exercise. Pay close attention to them.

(a) The phonemes of Japanese are the following:

```
p   t   k         i           u
b   d   g             e   o
m   n                   a
h   s
    z
    r
w   y
```

(b) Japanese exhibits several palatalization phenomena, among which are:

$$/t/ \longrightarrow \begin{cases} [\check{c}] & / \!\!-\!\!/i,y/ \\ [c] & / \!\!-\!\!/u/ \\ [t] & / \text{ elsewhere} \end{cases} \qquad /d/ \longrightarrow \begin{cases} [\mathfrak{p}] & / \!\!-\!\!/i,y/ \\ [\mathfrak{z}] & / \!\!-\!\!/u/ \\ [d] & / \text{ elsewhere} \end{cases}$$

$$/s/ \longrightarrow \begin{cases} [\check{s}] & / \!\!\rightarrow\!\!/i,y/ \\ [s] & / \text{ elsewhere} \end{cases} \qquad /h/ \longrightarrow \begin{cases} [\varsigma] & / \!\!-\!\!/i,y/ \\ [\phi] & / \!\!-\!\!/u/ \\ [h] & / \text{ elsewhere} \end{cases}$$

(c) Japanese may optionally devoice high vowels between voiceless consonants or in word-final position following a voiceless consonant.

(d) Some important phonotactic constraints of Japanese are:

1. All words must end in either a vowel or /n/.
2. The only permitted consonant clusters are geminate consonants (e.g., /tt/, /bb/, /ss/, etc.) or a sequence of a nasal plus a consonant (e.g., /mb/, /nt/, etc.).
3. Words are generally of the form CVCVCV... and the typical syllable is (C)V.
4. Vowels may be short or long (e.g., /a/, /u/, /aa/, /uu/, etc.).

DATA

The data will be organized into three tables of English-Japanese pronunciation correspondences. In your lab notebook create a separate table for each of the following:

1. Table 1. English initial consonants of the form / sC /

2. Table 2. English initial consonant clusters of the form stop plus / l / or / r /.

3. Table 3. English final consonants.

RESULTS

1. Interpret Table 1. Explain what aspects of Japanese phonology account for the "errors." Be as general as possible in your explanation.

2. Interpret Table 2. Again, explain as generally as you can what aspects of Japanese phonology account for these "errors."

3. Interpret Table 3. Explain why different English consonants seem to require different final vowels in the Japanese versions.

4. When English speakers are learning Japanese, they too often make pronunciation errors. Explain the reasons for the following "mispronunciations:"

===
ENGLISH MISPRONUNCIATIONS

Gloss	Japanese	English Mispronunciation
boat	[øune]	[fuunei]
was	[atta]	[at ə]
cutting	[kitte]	[kitei]

===

Laboratories

CONCLUSIONS

1. What is meant by a "foreign accent"? Why are all "foreign accents" not alike?

2. Some people have claimed that an adult's learning of a second language is no different in principle from a child's learning of his first language. Comment on this claim, in light of this laboratory exercise.

INTERFERENCE DATA

English	Japanese
grow	[guřoo]
laugh	[řaɸu̥]
spin	[su̥pin]
stick	[su̥tiku̥]
foot	[ɸuuto]
swim	[su̥wimu]
frog	[ɸu̥řagu]
sweep	[su̥wipu̥]
Alfred	[ařuɸu̥ředo]
truck	[tořaku̥]
tender	[tendaa]
roughly	[řaɸu̥řii]
mother	[mazaa]
lovely	[řabaři]
author	[oosaa]
rubber	[řabaa]
scotch	[su̥kočị]
match	[mačị]
fled	[ɸu̥ředo]
nice	[naisu̥]
bridge	[buřiʝi]
jury	[ǰiuřii]

skid	[su̥kido]
table	[tebuřu]
sway	[su̥wee]
spot	[su̥pooto]
feed	[ɸuido]
cheat	[čiito]
bride	[buřaido]
train	[tořen]
tred	[toředo]
cry	[kuřai]
dried	[dořaido]
grain	[guřen]
grasp	[gu̥řasu̥pu̥]
bleed	[buřiido]
glow	[guřoo]

LABORATORY 3. PHONOLOGICAL STAGES IN LANGUAGE ACQUISITION

REFERENCE

Menn (1971)

INTRODUCTION

The acquisition of phonology, like other aspects of language acquisition, can be investigated longitudinally. According to this method, data gathered over an extended period of time, as the child or children mature linguistically, can be treated as representing sequential stages of language development. Since language development is a more or less continuous process, the segmentation of the developmental process into discrete stages is actually somewhat artificial. Nevertheless, analysis of longitudinal data in terms of stages can facilitate the discovery of developmental patterns in phonology, morphology, or syntax.

Stages can be defined in a variety of ways. For example, chronological age, utterance length, utterance complexity, and even the child's control of certain phonological segments are all criteria which have been employed in the definition of stages.

As a child begins to learn his language, his models are those speakers whom he encounters daily. He obviously attempts to imitate the pronunciation of his parents, siblings, playmates, etc., but his earliest attempts are notably distant from the "correct" adult forms. For example, he tends to "simplify" polysyllabic forms to monosyllables, and he attends primarily to stressed syllables. Moreover, he may reduce consonant clusters, substitute one phone for another, and in numerous ways produce forms which are far from the adult targets.

PURPOSE

The purpose of this laboratory is to investigate the acquisition of the early segmental phonology of a single child, Daniel, from his earliest speech up

229

to the age of about 26 months. Attention will be directed toward the acquisition of initial consonants and final sibilants.

PROCEDURE

Data are from a single child, Daniel, and are organized into three successive stages. Stage 1 covers the period from the onset of speech to the age of 22.5 months; Stage 2 covers the period of 22.5 to 24 months; and Stage 3 covers the period of 24 to 25.5 months.

Your first task is to transcribe each word phonemically, thus providing the "correct" adult model. Daniel's data are already transcribed phonemically.

You will next focus attention on initial consonants or consonant clusters and on final consonants, as defined by the adult model, and chart the development of each of these classes of phonemes.

DATA

The data will be organized into three tables as follows:

1. Table 1. Word-initial Single Consonants. List each word-initial single consonant (no consonant clusters), as defined by the adult model, in column 1. In columns 2, 3, and 4 list the child's treatment of each of these consonants at Stages 1, 2, and 3. Label each column properly.

2. Table 2. Word-initial Consonant Clusters. List here all the initial consonant clusters, and the child's treatment of each of them at each stage, much as in Table 1.

3. Table 3. Word-final Sibilants. In this table, list all the word-final sibilants of the adult data, and indicate the child's rendition of each for each stage.

If, in any of the tables, you find that the child is not producing any analog (e.g., no consonant) to any segment, enter a dash in the appropriate place in the table.

RESULTS

1. Interpret Table 1. State your interpretation in terms of classes of segments rather than in terms of individual phonemes. Attempt to generalize as to the developmental patterns found in the table.

2. Interpret Table 2. Be as general as you can in your analysis of how the child develops in his treatment of initial clusters.

3. Interpret Table 3. Again, make general statements about his developmental pattern through the three stages.

CONCLUSIONS

1. What are the simplest initial consonants for the child to produce? Speculate as to why these are the simplest.

2. How would you expect the child to pronounce "peas" at each of the three stages? Give reasons.

3. Why do you think the child pronounces / str / as / d / but / skw / as / g / ?

LANGUAGE ACQUISITION DATA FROM DANIEL

Gloss	Adult	Stage 1	Stage 2	Stage 3
nose		no	nof	noz
boot		bu	bu	but
car		ga	gar	kar
cheese		ʒi	ʒif	giz
kiss		gl	glf	kls
mouth		mæw	mæwf	mæwf
bottle		ba	baw	baw
bread		be	be	beb
gate		gə	ge	get
carry		gæ	gæ	kæwi
cracker		gæ	gæk	gæk
squirrel		gæ	gæ	gew
Steve		i	if	iv
tea		di	di	ti
snake		ne	nek	nek
squeeze		gi	gif	giz
hose		o	of	oz
blow		bo	bo	bwo
plane		e	e	en
light		ay	ay	ayt
glasses		gæ	gæs	gæs
juice		u	uf	gus
dog		da	da	dag
clay		ge	ge	ge
fish		l	lf	fls
toast		do	dos	tos
bath		bæ	bæf	bæf
street		di	dit	dit

LABORATORY 4. MORPHOLOGICAL RELATEDNESS

REFERENCES

Derwing (1979), Wheeler & Schumsky (1980)

INTRODUCTION

What is meant by "morphological relatedness?" Within inflectional morphology, this question is simple to answer since for a given pair of forms we can usually determine whether or not there is a common stem, systematic suffixes, and the like. For example, we can assert that *walking* and *walked* are morphologically related since we can establish a common stem *walk*, with a consistant semantic content, and we can establish the suffixes *-ing* and *-ed* on the basis of verb paradigms.

Within derivational morphology, however, the issue is frequently more complex. Morphological relatedness is usually established in terms of semantic and phonetic similarity. But if we consider the following pairs of forms, we notice that there exist degrees of *both* semantic and phonetic similarity:

a. read - reed
b. dog - hound
c. refuse - refusal
d. opaque - opacity

.

The first pair are phonetically identical but semantically unrelated, while the second pair are semantically similar but phonetically very distant. The third and fourth pairs constitute an interesting problem since both pairs are semantically similar, although in (c) there is a constant stem ([rəfyúz]), while in (d) there is a vowel change in the stem ([e] - [æ]). Linguists often assert that two forms either *are* or *are not* morphologically related, but the above discussion suggests that both phonetic and semantic relatedness are matters of degree.

PURPOSE

The purpose of this laboratory is to demonstrate the degree of semantic and phonetic relatedness among a set of 50 pairs of words. It will be shown that native speakers can systematically determine degrees of phonetic and semantic relatedness among pairs of words.

PROCEDURE

Students will serve as subjects. Students should complete the two experiments below *before* the laboratory period so that the laboratory session can be used for the analysis of the results.

In this experiment, subjects have two separate tasks, although both tasks involve making judgements on the same set of 50 pairs of words. The subjects' tasks are to evaluate the 50 pairs of words in terms of semantic and phonetic relatedness.

Task 1. Semantic Similarity. Read the instructions on the page entitled "Semantic Similarity Test Instructions" and then turn to the list of 50 words on the page labelled "Semantic Similarity Test." Follow the instructions, circling one number from 0 through 4 for each pair. Refer to the instructions as often as necessary.

Task 2. Phonetic Similarity. Read the instructions on the page labelled "Phonetic Similarity Test Instructions" and then turn to the page labelled "Phonetic Similarity Test." Follow the instructions, circling a number from 0 through 6 for each pair of words. Refer to the instructions as often as necessary.

DATA

In the laboratory, combine your data with that of the other students and calculate the mean semantic similarity score and the mean phonetic similarity score for each item.

1. In your lab notebook, construct "TABLE 1. Mean Similarity Scores" for the 50 pairs of words.

In one column list the numbers from 1 through 50 (corresponding to the pairs). In the second column enter the semantic similarity scores for each item, and in the third column enter the phonetic similarity scores for each item. Use the mean scores for each entry. Label each column appropriately.

2. In your lab notebook, construct "FIGURE 1. Mean Semantic and Phonetic Similarity for Each Pair." This figure has its abscissa (x-axis) labelled "Phonetic Similarity" and should be graduated in intervals of .5, from 0 at the origin to 6.0 at the right. Each interval should be about 1 cm. The ordinate (y-axis) is labelled "Semantic Similarity" and should be graduated in intervals from 0 at the origin to 4.0 at the top, with each .5 interval about 1 cm. Plot the position of each pair (by number) on the figure, using the mean values in Table 1 to provide the x and y values for each pair.

RESULTS

1. From the data in Table 1 and Figure 1, select the three pairs of words which are:

(a) most similar both phonetically and semantically;
(b) most dissimilar both phonetically and semantically;
(c) most similar semantically and most dissimilar phonetically;
(d) most similar phonetically and most dissimilar semantically.

2. In your lab notebook create "TABLE 2. Extremes in Similarity." Into appropriately labelled columns enter these four triples of words (by words, not numbers).

3. Interpret Table 2, focusing attention on groups (a) and (c). What are the features which characterize each of these two groups?

4. If you were constructing a descriptive grammar of English, which pairs of forms from the list would you feel comfortable in relating morphologically? Explain your reasons.

CONCLUSIONS

The two English words *galaxy* and *lactic* are etymologically related, as are the pair *shirt* and *skirt*. Should either (or both) of these pairs be related morphologically in a synchronic descriptive grammar of English? Why (not)? What status does etymological relatedness have in the construction of a synchronic grammar? Give reasons.

SEMANTIC SIMILARITY TEST INSTRUCTIONS

There are 50 pairs of English words on the following two pages. Consider each pair from the point of view of the degree of similarity in *meaning,* not sound, which you judge to exist between them. Rank this similarity on a scale from 0 to 4, using the descriptions below as a guide. Circle the appropriate number beside each word.

4 - a clear and unmistakable connection in meaning between the two words;
3 - probably a connection in meaning between the two words;
2 - unable to decide whether there is a connection in meaning or not;
1 - probably not a connection in meaning between the two words;
0 - no connection whatsoever in meaning between the two words.

NOTE: Treat all words as *English words only.*

SEMANTIC SIMILARITY TEST

1. gypsy - Egyptian 0 1 2 3 4
2. handkerchief - hand 0 1 2 3 4
3. halloween - holy 0 1 2 3 4
4. eraser - erase 0 1 2 3 4
5. numerous - number 0 1 2 3 4
6. kitty - cat 0 1 2 3 4
7. cookie - cook 0 1 2 3 4
8. heavy - heave 0 1 2 3 4
9. slipper - slip 0 1 2 3 4
10. strawberry - berry 0 1 2 3 4

11. cupboard - cup 0 1 2 3 4
12. muggy - mist 0 1 2 3 4
13. barber - beard 0 1 2 3 4
14. hideous - hide 0 1 2 3 4
15. birdhouse - bird 0 1 2 3 4
16. spider - spin 0 1 2 3 4
17. feather - fly 0 1 2 3 4
18. dirty - dirt 0 1 2 3 4
19. eerie - ear 0 1 2 3 4
20. awful - awe 0 1 2 3 4

21. teacher - teach 0 1 2 3 4
22. weather - wind 0 1 2 3 4
23. Friday - fry 0 1 2 3 4
24. bashful - bash 0 1 2 3 4
25. fabulous - fable 0 1 2 3 4
26. lawyer - law 0 1 2 3 4
27. ladder - lean 0 1 2 3 4
28. necklace - lace 0 1 2 3 4
29. month - moon 0 1 2 3 4
30. liver - live 0 1 2 3 4

31. quietly - quiet 0 1 2 3 4
32. lousy - louse 0 1 2 3 4
33. cranberry - crane 0 1 2 3 4
34. messenger - message 0 1 2 3 4
35. wonderful - wonder 0 1 2 3 4
36. buggy - bug 0 1 2 3 4
37. puppy - dog 0 1 2 3 4
38. precious - price 0 1 2 3 4
39. holiday - holy 0 1 2 3 4
40. shepherd - sheep 0 1 2 3 4

41. hungry - hunger 0 1 2 3 4
42. breakfast - break 0 1 2 3 4
43. carpenter - wagon 0 1 2 3 4
44. handle - hand 0 1 2 3 4
45. sweater - sweat 0 1 2 3 4
46. doggie - dog 0 1 2 3 4
47. timid - tame 0 1 2 3 4
48. wilderness - wild 0 1 2 3 4
49. skinny - skin 0 1 2 3 4
50. rubber - rub 0 1 2 3 4

PHONETIC SIMILARITY TEST INSTRUCTIONS

There are 50 pairs of English words in the list on the following two pages. Consider each pair from the point of view of the degree of similarity in *sound,* not meaning, which you judge to exist between them. Rank this similarity on a scale from 0 to 6, using the descriptions below as a guide. Circle the appropriate number beside each pair.

6 - both words sound exactly the same;
5 - (closer to 6 than to 3);
4 - (closer to 3 than to 6);
3 - the two words sound about half the same;
2 - (closer to 3 than to 0);
1 - (closer to 0 than to 3);
0 - there is no similarity whatsoever in sound between the two words.

NOTE: Treat all words as *English words only.*

PHONETIC SIMILARITY TEST

		0	1	2	3	4	5	6
1.	gypsy - Egyptian	0	1	2	3	4	5	6
2.	handkerchief - hand	0	1	2	3	4	5	6
3.	halloween - holy	0	1	2	3	4	5	6
4.	eraser - erase	0	1	2	3	4	5	6
5.	numerous - number	0	1	2	3	4	5	6
6.	kitty - cat	0	1	2	3	4	5	6
7.	cookie - cook	0	1	2	3	4	5	6
8.	heavy - heave	0	1	2	3	4	5	6
9.	slipper - slip	0	1	2	3	4	5	6
10.	strawberry - berry	0	1	2	3	4	5	6
11.	cupboard - cup	0	1	2	3	4	5	6
12.	muggy - mist	0	1	2	3	4	5	6
13.	barber - beard	0	1	2	3	4	5	6
14.	hideous - hide	0	1	2	3	4	5	6
15.	birdhouse - bird	0	1	2	3	4	5	6
16.	spider - spin	0	1	2	3	4	5	6
17.	feather - fly	0	1	2	3	4	5	6
18.	dirty - dirt	0	1	2	3	4	5	6
19.	eerie - ear	0	1	2	3	4	5	6
20.	awful - awe	0	1	2	3	4	5	6
21.	teacher - teach	0	1	2	3	4	5	6
22.	weather - wind	0	1	2	3	4	5	6
23.	Friday - fry	0	1	2	3	4	5	6
24.	bashful - bash	0	1	2	3	4	5	6
25.	fabulous - fable	0	1	2	3	4	5	6
26.	lawyer - law	0	1	2	3	4	5	6
27.	ladder - lean	0	1	2	3	4	5	6
28.	necklace - lace	0	1	2	3	4	5	6
29.	month - moon	0	1	2	3	4	5	6
30.	liver - live	0	1	2	3	4	5	6
31.	quietly - quiet	0	1	2	3	4	5	6
32.	lousy - louse	0	1	2	3	4	5	6
33.	cranberry - crane	0	1	2	3	4	5	6
34.	messenger - message	0	1	2	3	4	5	6
35.	wonderful - wonder	0	1	2	3	4	5	6
36.	buggy - bug	0	1	2	3	4	5	6
37.	puppy - dog	0	1	2	3	4	5	6
38.	precious - price	0	1	2	3	4	5	6
39.	holiday - holy	0	1	2	3	4	5	6
40.	shepherd - sheep	0	1	2	3	4	5	6

41.	hungry - hunger	0	1	2	3	4	5	6
42.	breakfast - break	0	1	2	3	4	5	6
43.	carpenter - wagon	0	1	2	3	4	5	6
44.	handle - hand	0	1	2	3	4	5	6
45.	sweater - sweat	0	1	2	3	4	5	6
46.	doggie - dog	0	1	2	3	4	5	6
47.	timid - tame	0	1	2	3	4	5	6
48.	wilderness - wild	0	1	2	3	4	5	6
49.	skinny - skin	0	1	2	3	4	5	6
50.	rubber - rub	0	1	2	3	4	5	6

LABORATORY 5. THE ACQUISITION OF THE ENGLISH PAST TENSE

REFERENCES

Berko (1958); Derwing (1980); Derwing & Baker (1980)

INTRODUCTION

One reason language acquisition is so important is because of the notion of "overgeneralization." As they pass through various stages in the acquisition of their native language, children attempt to formulate generalizations and rules for such persistent grammatical properties as verb tense, noun plural, and the like. However, at different stages of their development, the children's production of certain forms may well be quite distinct from that of the adult "correct" form, and such errors in child speech provide valuable clues into the kinds of rules and generalizations that the children are attempting.

For example, if a child is learning the English diminutive with its associated /-i/ suffix on nouns, he will likely base his pronunciation on forms such as *doggie* and *horsie*. Accordingly, if he overgeneralizes, or more correctly, simply generalizes, the suffixes to all nouns, he will produce forms like *catty* rather than the correct *kitty*. The form *catty* therefore provides evidence that the child has generalized, since he likely has not heard that form from an adult, at least as a diminutive. Later, of course, the child learns to sort out the regularities from the irregularities. The "incorrect" production of irregular forms therefore constitutes evidence for the rule the child has learned at a particular stage.

PURPOSE

The purpose of this laboratory is to examine and analyze four stages in the acquisition of English past tense morphology, with special attention directed to certain classes of irregular verbs.

DATA

The data represent a somewhat idealized but basically accurate picture of the sequence of development of certain English past tense forms from Stage 1, the earliest stage of speech, through Stage 4, a pre-adolescent stage which, for our purposes, corresponds to the adult norm.

1. In your lab notebook, construct "TABLE 1. Data" in which you represent the data as given, but in phonemic representation. All your analyses will be based on the morphophonemic behavior of the verbs and consequently a phonemic representation for each is crucial.

2. Next, inspect each of the verb stems and classify all the verbs into distinct classes, depending on how they pattern developmentally. One such class will be the "regular" forms and will include such items as *walk*, etc. Once you have classified the verbs, with each class assigned a number or label, construct in your lab notebook "TABLE 2. Verb Types." Label one column in Table 2 as "Type" and the second column as "Tokens." In the first column list each verb class, and in the second column, the verb tokens from the data belonging to that type.

RESULTS

1. Analyze each of the verb classes represented in Table 2. Trace the development of each type through all four stages.

2. Explain why *bring* is treated like *sing*, and why at Stage 3 certain verbs appear to have no distinguishing past tense suffix.

3. Notice that the past tense forms for Stage I, the earliest stage, are identical to those of Stage 4. Does the child forget the rules of past tense formation during Stages 2 and 3? Offer an explanation for this apparently bizarre situation.

CONCLUSIONS

1. How would you expect the child to pronounce the past tense of each of the following words at each stage? Why?

(a) bloom
(b) sit
(c) shrink
(d) slide

2. In what other areas of English morphology would you expect to find overgeneralizations? Cite some examples you would expect to find.

ENGLISH PAST TENSE ACQUISITION DATA

Stem	Stage 1	Stage 2	Stage 3	Stage 4
walk	walked	walked	walked	walked
talk	talked	talked	talked	talked
laugh	laughed	laughed	laughed	laughed
float	floated	floated	float	floated
pet	petted	petted	pet	petted
go	went	goed	went	went
get	got	getted	get	got
have	had	haved	had	had
take	took	taked	took	took
write	wrote	writed	write	wrote
steal	stole	stealed	stole	stole
sing	sang	singed	sang	sang
swing	swang	swinged	swang	swang
sink	sank	sinked	sank	sank
bring	brought	bringed	brang	brought
grow	grew	growed	grew	grew

LABORATORY 6. SENTENCE RELATEDNESS

REFERENCES

Baker, Prideaux, & Derwing (1973); Fletcher (1980); Prideaux & Baker (1974)

INTRODUCTION

Much experimental research has been devoted to the syntactic and semantic properties of grammatically related sentences which all belong to a given "sentence family." A sentence family is a set of sentences all sharing the same basic lexical items but differing in terms of such grammatical properties as *voice* (active or passive), *mood* (declarative or interrogative), and *modality* (affirmative or negative). The "PNQ sentence family" has received a great deal of attention. It consists of eight sentences, each differing from the others by at least one of the three parameter of voice, mood, or modality. An example of this sentence family is the following:

The cat isn't stalking the bird.	ADN	N
Isn't the bird being stalked by the cat?	PIN	PQN
Is the cat stalking the bird?	AIF	Q
The bird is being stalked by the cat.	PDF	P
Isn't the cat stalking the bird?	AIN	QN
Is the bird being stalked by the cat?	PIF	PQ
The cat is stalking the bird.	ADF	--
The bird isn't being stalked by the cat.	PDN	PN

To the right of each sentence, in the first column, is a specification of the grammatical properties of each sentence. The first letter (A or P) represents the voice of the sentence, the second letter (D or I) represents the mood, and the third letter represents the modality (F for affirmative or N). In the final column is a specification of the marked grammatical properties of the sentence, in terms of the "grammatical transformations" each sentence would have undergone in a transformational derivation. Such "housekeeping" rules as subject-verb agreement and affix hopping are ignored here.

PURPOSE

The purpose of this laboratory is (a) to establish the perceived semantic relationships among the various members of the PNQ sentence family, and (b) to determine whether the grammatical properties of the sentence relate to or contribute to the semantic similarities.

PROCEDURE

Students will serve as subjects and should complete the experiment below *before* the laboratory period so the laboratory time can be spent in the compilation and analysis of the data.

In this experiment, subjects are to compare pairs of sentences and make judgements as to the degree of semantic similarity they find in each pair.

Read the instructions and carry out the experiment, making an entry in each cell of the matrix for each pair.

DATA

Combine your data with that of your fellow students and compute the mean similarity score and the standard deviation for each of the 28 pairs.

In your lab notebook, construct "TABLE 1. Sentence Relatedness Data" with five columns. In the first column list the 28 pairs of sentences (e.g., AB, AC, ... , GH). In the second column enter the mean similarity score for each pair. In the third column enter the standard deviation for each pair. In the fourth column enter the shared grammatical properties of each pair, in terms of the parameters P, N, and Q. For example, pair AB share N, since both are negatives. If a particular pair has no shared grammatical properties, enter a dash in the column. In the fifth column enter the non-shared grammatical properties, again in terms of P, N, and Q. For example, pair AB differ in PQ since one is an active sentence and the other is a passive, and one is a declarative and the other a question. Be sure to label each column properly, both here and in the later tables.

RESULTS

1. Construct in your lab notebook "TABLE 2. Voice Differences." In the first column list the four pairs of sentences which differ only by voice (e.g., only by P). In the second column list the shared grammatical properties for each pair. In the third column enter the mean similarity score for each pair. In the fourth column enter the standard deviation for each pair.

From the results in Table 2, comment on the way the similarity scores vary as a function of the shared grammatical properties. Which pairs exhibit the most variation? Why?

2. Construct in your lab notebook "TABLE 3. Active-Active Comparisons." In the first column list the six pairs which share the active voice. In the second column list the shared grammatical properties of each pair, and in the third column list the non-shared properties for each pair, as in Table 1. In the fourth column enter the mean similarity scores for each pair and in the fifth column the standard deviations.

From the results in Table 3, comment on how the similarity scores vary with respect to shared and non-shared grammatical properties. Which items show the greatest variation? Speculate as to why.

3. In your lab notebook construct "TABLE 4. Passive-Passive Comparisons." In the first column list the six pairs which share the passive voice. Construct four other columns exactly as in Table 3.

From the results in Table 4, comment on the way that the similarity scores vary with respect to shared and non-shared grammatical properties. Which pairs show the greatest variation in scores? Why?

CONCLUSIONS

1. Discuss the ways in which Tables 3 and 4 differ, and explain the reasons for the similarities and differences.

2. Pairs of sentences like DH and AG are frequently perceived as being quite different in meaning, while pairs like BF and CE are generally viewed are being rather similar in meaning. To what can you attribute these different perceptions?

SENTENCE RELATEDNESS EXPERIMENT

1. Read the following sentences:

```
                          B   C   D   E   F   G   H
```

A. The cat isn't stalking
    the bird. . . . . —   —   — — —   — —

B. Isn't the bird being
    stalked by the cat? . . . . —   — — — —   — —

C. Is the cat stalking
    the bird?. . . . . —   — — — —

D. The bird is being
    stalked by the cat.. . . . . — —   — —

E. Isn't the cat stalking
    the bird?. . . . . —   — —

F. Is the bird being
    stalked by the .cat? . . . . —   —

G. The cat is stalking
    the bird. . . . . —

H. The bird isn't being
    stalked by the cat.

2. Read through the list again and pick that pair of sentences which you consider to be the *most similar* in meaning. In the "upper triangular matrix," place a "1" in that cell corresponding to the pair you have just picked.

3. Again read through the list and pick that pair of sentences which you consider to be the *least similar* in meaning. In the "upper triangular matrix," place a "9" in that cell corresponding to the pair you have just picked.

4. You have now provided "anchor points" for the use of the scale from "1" to "9." For each of the remaining cells, compare each pair of sentences in terms of similarity of meaning. In each cell place a number from "1" to "9" inclusive, where the lower numbers correspond to relative nearness in

251

meaning and the higher numbers to relative distance or dissimilarity in meaning.

LABORATORY 7. THE DERIVATIONAL THEORY OF COMPLEXITY

REFERENCES

Baker & Prideaux (1980); Miller & McKean (1964); Palermo (1978, Ch. 4)

INTRODUCTION

Some sentences seem to be easier to process and understand than others, quite independent of their lexical items. In fact, even for pairs of sentences which are virtually synonymous ("paraphrases"), one member is often considerably more natural and easier to understand than the other. For example, the following two sentences are paraphrases, although sentence (b) is far more natural and far easier to understand than sentence (a).

a. Was for Jason to win the race easy?
b. Was it easy for Jason to win the race?

Examples such as this suggest that the grammatical form of a sentence contributes greatly toward its relative ease of comprehension.

One specific proposal to account for such differences in ease of comprehension is the so-called "Derivational Theory of Complexity" or DTC. This proposal, which is based on transformational grammar, hypothesizes that the formal, transformational complexity of a sentence determines its cognitive complexity. In particular, the DTC claims that the psychological complexity of a sentence is a monotonic function of the transformational complexity of that sentence. A sentence which has undergone more transformations in its formal derivation should, according to the DTC, be more difficult to comprehend and less natural than a sentence which has undergone fewer transformations.

The DTC is clearly an empirical hypothesis which can and must be subjected to empirical test.

253

PURPOSE

The purpose of this laboratory is to test the DTC experimentally.

PROCEDURE

Students will act as subjects for the experiment. Read the instructions carefully, then turn to the stimulus sentences and carry out the experiment.

DATA

The stimuli consist of four types of pairs, with four replications of each type. These types are:

1. A/RC (pairs 1, 7, 10, 13). One member of this pair contains a NP with a prenominal adjective, while the other member contains a relative clause with an adjective. In transformational terms, these two forms differ by two grammatical transformations, RELATIVE CLAUSE REDUCTION, which deletes the relative pronoun plus a form of *be*, and ADJECTIVE PREPOSING, which moves the stranded adjective to a prenominal position.

2. P/A (pairs 2, 5, 9, 15). One member of this pair is a passive sentence while the other is an active. Transformationally, the passive form is derived from the active by the PASSIVE transformation.

3. EX/nEX (pairs 3, 6, 12, 16). One member of this pair has a sentential subject which remains in the subject ("non-extraposed") position, while the other has the sentential subject moved ("extraposed") to the end of the sentence, leaving *it* in the subject slot. Transformationally, this movement is accounted for by a rule of EXTRAPOSITION.

4. TP/FP (pairs 4, 8, 11, 14). One member of this pair is a full passive (FP), while the other member is a "truncated" passive (TP). The truncated passive is derived from the full passive by a rule of AGENT DELETION which deletes *by* + *someone/everyone*.

In these four types, the first member of each pair (A, P, EX, TP) is, in formal transformational terms, the more complex since it has undergone more transformations in its derivation than the second member.

When you have completed the experiment, tabulate your results in "TABLE 1. Preference and Naturalness Judgements" in your lab notebook. This table should contain four columns. In the first column list the four types of structures mentioned above (A/RC, P/A, EX/nEX, and TP/FP). In the second column enter the number of times you chose the first member of each pair. In the third column enter for each type the proportion of times the first member of each pair was chosen as the more natural. For example, for type A/RC, if you chose the A member as the more natural once, and the RC member as the more natural three times, you should enter opposite A/RC the value .25 (=1/4). In each case, use the first member of each pair as the numerator and 4 as the denominator. In the fourth column enter your mean naturalness difference score for each of the four types. Be sure to label each column appropriately.

RESULTS

1. Pool your data in Table 1 with that of the other students in the laboratory. Compute the mean preference for each of the four types and the mean naturalness difference for each of the four types. Enter these results into "TABLE 2. Mean Preference and Naturalness Judgements." This table should contain four columns. The first contains the types, while the second and third contain the mean preferences and naturalness judgements for each of the types. In the fourth column, enter the number of transformations by which the two members of each pair differ. Be sure to label each column appropriately.

2. Construct "TABLE 3. Chi-square Tests." Here you will calculate the chi-square value for each of the types. Set up this table as follows:

Laboratories

```
==========================================
             TABLE 3.  X² Tests
```

Type	O	E	(O-E)	(O-E)²	X²	p
A/RC						
P/A						
EX/nEX						
TP/FP						

```
==========================================
```

In the O column enter the total number of times the first member of each pair was actually chosen. This value is obtained by summing, for each separate pair, the entries from Table 1, column 2. The expected (E) value for each type is predicated on the assumption that the two members of each pair are "paraphrases" and are equally expected. Thus, for each type, there are four tokens per subject, and n subjects, so the expected value is $1/2 \times 4 \times n = 2n$. From the values for O and E, you can calculate the values of (O-E) and (O-E)², thereby having the values to calculate chi-square value for each type. After the chi-square for each type has been calculated, check this value against the values listed in Table B, where df=1. Which chi-square values are significant, and at what level?

CONCLUSIONS

Examine Tables 2 and 3 and address each of the following questions:

1. Does either the Mean Preference score or the Mean Naturalness Judgement correspond to the transformational complexity?

2. In general, what does increased transformational complexity contribute toward sentence length?

3. In the cases in which transformational complexity does not appear to contribute to or determine relative naturalness, can you suggest other factors which might determine that one member of a given pair is more natural than the other? Do not hesitate to construct tentative explanations for each type separately.

256

4. What do the chi-square values in Table 3 suggest about theoretical claims of "paraphrase" and "synonymy" for the four pairs?

5. What are your general conclusions as to the empirical status of the DTC?

DTC EXPERIMENT INSTRUCTIONS

On the following page is a set of sixteen pairs of sentences. Read through all the sentences. Try not to place contrastive stress on any particular words, but rather read the sentences with a "normal" intonation.

You will notice that for each pair, one sentence is usually more natural and easier to understand than the other. The differences in naturalness within the various pairs is not always the same, however. In some pairs the two sentences seem almost equally natural, while in other pairs one sentence is far more natural than the other.

For each pair of sentences you have two tasks. First you must decide which member of the pair is the more natural and easier to comprehend. Indicate your choice by circling the letter of the more natural sentence (circle "a" or "b"). Second, for the same pair, estimate how far apart the two sentences are in naturalness. Indicate your judgement of the differences in naturalness on the five-point scale to the right of each pair. If you judge the two sentences to be very near to each other in naturalness, circle "1," but if you feel that they are very far apart in naturalness, circle "5." Use the following guidelines for the five-point scale:

1 - very close in naturalness;
2 - close in naturalness, but not as close as 1;
3 - midway between 1 and 5;
4 - far apart in naturalness, but not quite 5;
5 - very far apart in naturalness.

Complete both tasks for one pair before going on to the next pair. Remember, for each pair you should:

a. circle the letter of the more natural member;
b. indicate your perception of the difference in naturalness between the two sentences on the five-point scale.

258

DTC EXPERIMENT STIMULI

1. a. The dog which was big annoyed me.
    b. The big dog annoyed me.
       1 2 3 4 5

2. a. Sam sent the flowers to Marilyn.
    b. The flowers were sent to Marilyn by Sam.
       1 2 3 4 5

3. a. That George left the meeting early amazed
       us.
    b. It amazed us that George left the meeting
       early.
       1 2 3 4 5

4. a. The actor was applauded for his fine
       performance.
    b. The actor was applauded for his fine
       performance by everyone.
       1 2 3 4 5

5. a. Fred was amused by the clown.
    b. The clown amused Fred.
       1 2 3 4 5

6. a. That Jeff could solve the problem was
       interesting.
    b. It was interesting that Jeff could solve the
       problem.
       1 2 3 4 5

7. a. Janice gave the child the yellow toy.
    b. Janice gave the child the toy which was
       yellow.
       1 2 3 4 5

8. a. John was chased around the corner by
       someone.
    b. John was chased around the corner.
       1 2 3 4 5

9. a. Sally broke three plates.
    b. Three plates were broken by Sally.
       1 2 3 4 5

10. a. The police stopped a driver who was drunk on our street.
    b. The police stopped a drunk driver on our street.
       1 2 3 4 5

11. a. Susan's toe was stepped on at the dance by someone.
    b. Susan's toe was stepped on at the dance.
       1 2 3 4 5

12. a. It was apparent that Lucy enjoyed the card.
    b. That Lucy enjoyed the card was apparent.
       1 2 3 4 5

13. a. The judge sentenced the unhappy thief to thirty days.
    b. The judge sentenced the thief who was unhappy to thirty days.
       1 2 3 4 5

14. a. The dog was hit at the intersection.
    b. The dog was hit at the intersection by someone.
       1 2 3 4 5

15. a. Unfortunately, the child bit the dentist.
    b. Unfortunately, the dentist was bitten by the child.
       1 2 3 4 5

16 a. For Quebec to separate might be disasterous.
   b. It might be disasterous for Quebec to separate.
       1 2 3 4 5

LABORATORY 8. THE PRODUCTION OF RELATIVE CLAUSES

REFERENCE

Wardhaugh (1977, Ch. 8).

INTRODUCTION

In sentences like:

a. The dog [which chased Sam] belongs to Sue.
b. My cousin watched the program [which Bill recommended].
c. Suzie gave Fred the cake [which she had baked earlier].
d. Marilyn eagerly read the new book [Sally had bought for her].
e. James bought his running shoes at the store [where Fred works].
f. The dog [barking under the window] frightened Janet.

the clauses enclosed in brackets are relative clauses. A relative clause (RC) is one which modifies a particular noun by providing further information about that noun. Each RC normally contains a relative pronoun (RP) such as *who, which, that, where*, etc., which refers back to the modified noun (its *antecendent*). The relative pronoun is said to be coreferential with its antecendent.

English permits RCs to be formed on nouns playing almost any grammatical role. An RC can be attached to a subject, direct object, indirect object, etc. Furthermore, the RP must itself play a grammatical role within the RC. For example, the RP *which* is the subject of the RC in (a), while it is the direct object of the RC in (b). Under certain conditions, the RP can be omitted, as in (d) and (f).

In ordinary language use, just how often, and where in sentences, are RCs used? Are more found on subjects or on objects? Do most RCs have overt RPs or are RPs generally omitted if they can be? Is the RP *that*, which is neutral with respect to the semantic class of the modified noun, used more or less often than the other RPs?

Answers to these questions are needed in order to establish a secure basis for any positional tendencies which might occur for RCs in English.

PURPOSE

The purpose of this laboratory is to examine the types of RCs which are produced in normal language.

PROCEDURE

An individual was instructed to describe the game of baseball as if he were speaking to someone who knew nothing about the game. He was told to avoid any technical terms (base, pitcher, etc.) until he had defined them. His verbal description was taped. Our data for this experiment consist of the following transcript of the tape. All pauses and hesitation forms are included, and there is no attempt to "regularize" or "sanitize" the data.

DATA

"A favorite sport of many people ... is the game of baseball, which involves ... uh ... nine positions. Therefore, ... uh ... we have ... a diamond-shaped field ... which is called the infield. And then there is the outfield ... which surrounds ... one-half of the diamond. ... uh ... You have home ... and you have, at one point, of the diamond ... you have first base, second base, third base ... at other points of the diamond. All these stops a runner has to make ... are called bases. And once he reaches home, which is the main base, ... he scores a run ... or a point for his team. ... uh ... In order to score a run, he's got to ... come to bat. uh ... The bat is a stick ... uh ... a wooden stick that is used to hit the ball ... uh ... which is thrown at him uh by the pitcher of the other team. ... The team in the field has a pitcher and a catcher behind home base who catches the ball ... uh ... that is tossed by the pitcher. There is a man at first base, at second base, at third base, and a man in between third and second base ... uh ... and three men ... in the outfield and ... their purpose is to catch ... the ball that is hit by the player at bat. ... uh ... If they catch the ball before the ball hits the ground, then the player is out ... and ... another person comes to bat. If the ball hits the ground before ... uh ... one of the players in the field catches it, ... uh ... then they have to try and throw the ball to the base that the player is closest to ... in order to put him out. If the player gets to a base before the ball ... gets to the base, then he's safe and can remain there until he gets to advance ... uh ... by the same means. ... uh ... The object of the game for the fielders is to put three players out ... from the other team. Therefore the ... the team at bat can have ... uh ... stay at bat and keep batting until three of their men are put out and then they'll change sides. The batting team that ... which is the people not out on the field ... will go out into the field and the team in the field will come to bat and ... uh ... Each change of this nature is called an inning. ... And there are nine innings in the game. ... If the score is tied at the end of nine innings, ... uh ... they'll play extra innings ... until there is a tie-breaking score which somebody scores. ... Then the game is finished up."

RESULTS

1. In your lab notebook, construct "TABLE 1. Relative Clauses." In this table, number and list each sentence from the text which contains an RC. Do *not* count prenominal adjectives or postnominal prepositional phrases as RCs. In each sentence containing an RC, count the number of NPs which could have had an RC attached. Beside each sentence, enter this number. This table should have three columns: one for the sentence number, one for the sentence, and one for the number of potential NP hosts per sentence. Label each column accordingly.

2. For each of the sentences in Table 1, determine for the main clause (a) the grammatical function (subject, direct object, object of a preposition, etc.) of the NP on which the RC is formed, and (b) whether or not the RC interrupts

the main clause. For each relative clause, determine (a) the relative pronoun, and (b) the grammatical function of the relative pronoun. Construct "TABLE 2. Relative Clause Data" and enter in it the information you have just tabulated.

3. Let N be the total number of possible host NPs from Table 1. Let $N = a + b$, where a is the number of sentence-final potential host NPs and b is the number of sentence-internal potential host NPs. Let R be the total number of RCs. Let $R = i + n$, where i is the number of *interrupting* RCs in the text and n is the number of *non-interrupting* RCs.

If an RC can occur on any NP, the expected number on an internal (interrupting) NP is $Ei = R(b/N)$, while the expected number on a final (non-interrupting) NP is $En = R(a/N)$. Let Oi be the number of actually occuring interrupting RCs and On be the number of actual non-interrupting RCs. Create "TABLE 3. Chi-square for Relative Clause Position" and enter into this table Ei, En, Oi, and On. Also enter into the table $(Oi-Ei)^2$ and $(On-En)^2$. From these values, calculate the X^2 value, with df=1, according to the formula:

$$X^2 = (Oi-Ei)^2/Ei + (On-En)^2/En.$$

At what level is the X^2 significant? What do you conclude about a position effect for RCs for this speaker's English?

4. Is there a tendency for relative clauses to appear more frequently on one grammatical relation than on another? Which is preferred?

CONCLUSIONS

1. Why do you think speakers would prefer to place a relative clause on the last NP in a sentence rather than on an internal NP?

2. If the relative pronoun *that* is found to have a higher frequency of occurrence than other RPs throughout the language in general, what would account for such a preference?

LABORATORY 9. COGNITIVE STRATEGIES

REFERENCES

Bever (1970); Clark & Clark (1977, Ch. 2); Prideaux (1982); Prideaux & Baker (1983); Slobin (1973)

INTRODUCTION

In rejecting transformational grammar as a model for actual language production or comprehension processes, many scholars have suggested that hearers employ a set of "perceptual," "mental," or "cognitive" strategies to extract the meaning of sentences rather directly from surface structures. Throughout the psycholinguistic literature, numerous such strategies have been proposed, some of which are semantic in nature and others of which are syntactically based. Similarly, some of the strategies seem to be language-specific while others are language independent. Attention here will be focused on the following two language independent strategies:

> THE CLOSURE STRATEGY. A non-interrupted clause is easier to comprehend than an interrupted clause.

> THE NORMAL FORM STRATEGY. A clause in normal word order is easier to comprehend than one in non-normal word order.

If these strategies are applied to sentences containing relative clauses, specific predictions can be made concerning the relative difficulty of different sentence types. Consider the following four English structures containing relative clauses (where RP is a relative pronoun):

SS: NP[RP V NP] V NP
The boy [that chased the dog] saw the man.

SO: NP[RP NP V] V NP
The boy [that the dog chased] saw the man.

OS: NP V NP[RP V NP]
The boy saw the man [that chased the dog].

OO: NP V NP[RP NP V]
The boy saw the man [that the dog chased].

In the coding to the left of each sentence, the first letter represents the grammatical role (subject or object) of the NP on which the relative clause is formed, while the second letter represented the grammatical role (again, S or O) of the relative pronoun within the relative clause.

According to the CLOSURE strategy, types OS and OO should be easier to comprehend than the other two types (e.g., OS, OO > SS, SO), since the former are not interrupted by relative clauses. According to the NORMAL FORM strategy, types SS and OS should be easier to comprehend than the other two types (e.g., SS, OS > SO, OO) since the relative clauses in SS and OS have the "normal" word order SVO.

The two strategies can be combined to establish a prediction of the rank order of relative ease, according to the following analysis:

Type	CL Violated?	NF Violated?
SS	yes	no
SO	yes	yes
OS	no	no
OO	no	yes

When taken together, the strategies predict that the relative ease of the four structures should be as follows: OS > SS, OO > SO.

PURPOSE

The purpose of this experiment is to test empirically the CLOSURE and NORMAL FORM strategies.

PROCEDURE

Students will act as subjects. Read the instructions carefully and carry out the experiment, judging each sentence in terms of your own intuitions of relative naturalness. The data will be pooled and analyzed during the laboratory.

DATA

There are four replications of each of the four sentence types in the experiment. You will first tabulate your own data, calculating the mean naturalness score for each of the four sentence types, and then you will pool your data with that of the other students and calculate the mean naturalness scores for the pooled data. Finally, you will conduct t-tests on each pair of types to determine which are significantly different from each other.

1. Construct "TABLE 1. Relative Naturalness" in your lab notebook. This table should contain two columns, one for the sentence types and one for the mean naturalness score for each type. In Table 1 enter only your own data. Since there are four replications for each type, simply sum the four naturalness scores for each type and divide by four to obtain the mean scores for each type.

2. Construct "TABLE 2. Pooled Naturalness Scores" in your lab notebook. Pool the data in Table 1 with that of the other students and calculate the mean naturalness scores and standard deviations for each of the four types. Use the following format for Table 2:

```
=========================================
     TABLE  2.  Pooled  Naturalness  Scores

  Subject      SS      SO      OS      OO

      1
      2
      .
      .
      .
      n


      sum
      mean
      sd
=========================================
```

Under the "Subjects" column list the subjects (students) from 1 to n. In each of the other columns, enter each student's mean score for that type. Finally, sum the scores for each type and calculate the mean and standard deviation for each.

RESULTS

1. Examine Tables 1 and 2. What is the rank ordering of sentence types in terms of increasing difficulty? What is the rank ordering of types in terms of increasing variation?

2. Consider each pair of types. Carry out a *t*-test for correlated samples for each pair. Calculate the value of *t* for each pair, and from Table A find the significance level for each pair. Which pairs differ significantly at the .05 level?

CONCLUSIONS

1. Do the results from either Table 1 or Table 2 conform to the predictions of either of the strategies taken separately or as combined?

2. In terms of the pooled data, which strategy is stronger? Try to explain any discrepancies.

3. In your view, which of the two cognitive strategies is the more plausible? Explain why.

INSTRUCTIONS

On the following pages is a list of sixteen sentences, each of which contains a relative clause. Your task is to evaluate the relative naturalness of each of the sentences on a seven-point scale, where "1" is the *least* natural and "7" is the *most* natural.

First, read through the list of sentences.

Next, pick that sentence which is the *least* natural (e.g., the most awkward or clumsy). Make your judgements in terms of the forms of the sentences and not in terms of their meanings. Once you have picked the least natural sentence, circle "1" on the associated scale.

Next, select the *most* natural sentence on the list, again in terms of form. Circle "7" for that sentence. There may be more than one sentence for which you wish to assign a "7" or a "1."

Now, you have anchored your scale at either end. Judge the relative naturalness for each of the remaining sentences and indicate your judgements by circling one of the numbers from "1" through "7" inclusive.

COGNITIVE STRATEGIES STIMULI

1 = LEAST NATURAL   7 = MOST NATURAL

1. The dog chased the cat that scratched the man.
   1 2 3 4 5 6 7

2. The boy dropped the statue that his mother loved.
   1 2 3 4 5 6 7

3. The woman that baked the cake won the prize.
   1 2 3 4 5 6 7

4. The thief that the policeman shot wore a hat.
   1 2 3 4 5 6 7

5. The judge disliked the politician that the public elected.
   1 2 3 4 5 6 7

6. The boy that kissed the girl feared her father.
   1 2 3 4 5 6 7

7. The woman knew the boy that bought the car.
   1 2 3 4 5 6 7

8. The ball that the girl threw broke a window.
   1 2 3 4 5 6 7

9. The boy spanked the dog that chased the car. .
   1 2 3 4 5 6 7

10. The man that bought the tie knew the clerk.
    1 2 3 4 5 6 7

11. The teacher praised the story that the student wrote.
    1 2 3 4 5 6 7

12. The rabbit that the children caught bit the teacher.
    1 2 3 4 5 6 7

13. The dog that jumped the fence chased the postman.
    1 2 3 4 5 6 7

14. The guest liked the wine that the hostess served.
    1 2 3 4 5 6 7

15. The woman that the mayor trusted signed the petition.
    1 2 3 4 5 6 7

16. The woman kissed the man that sold the house.
    1 2 3 4 5 6 7

LABORATORY 10. SEMANTIC FIELDS

REFERENCES

Kess (1976, Ch. 7); Palermo (1978, Ch. 5)

INTRODUCTION

A semantic field is a group of lexical items which are related to each other by virtue of having certain semantic properties or elements in common. For example, color terms like *red, yellow, green* seem to be more closely related to each other, simply because they are color terms, than a series of words like *red, cat, swim*, which appear to have very little in common. Some examples of semantic fields are kinship terms, color terms, and verbs of judging (e.g., *blame, praise, accuse, judge,* etc.). One problem which arises in connection with the analysis of semantic fields concerns the interrelations among the various members of a particular field. Some elements tend to be judged closer to certain elements than to others. The perceived relationships among the elements within a semantic field may well vary from person to person. The investigation of semantic fields by means of experimental techniques is often referred to as the study of the subjective lexicon.

PURPOSE

The purpose of this laboratory is to investigate the structure of relationships among a set of English words, with the aim of establishing a semantic field and determining the relative distances among members of the field.

PROCEDURE

Students will act as subjects. Read the instructions and then carry out the experiment. In the laboratory session, your data will be pooled with that of the other students and the pooled data will be analyzed.

DATA

Pool your results with that of the other students, and for each of the 28 pairs of words, calculate a mean similarity score. Construct "TABLE 1. Pooled Data" in your lab notebook. This table should contain two columns, the first labelled "Pairs" and the second labelled "Mean Similarity." Enter the 28 pairs of words in the first column and the mean similarity score for each pair in the second.

RESULTS

1. Examine the data in Table 1 and identify the three pairs with the most similarity (e.g., the lowest similarity ratings). These should hopefully be the pairs ROBIN/HAWK, ROBIN/SPARROW, and HAWK/SPARROW. Calculate the mean ratings for these three pairs and call this the FOCUS of the semantic field.

2. The remainder of the words in this particular field can be conceived of as being relatively close to or distant from the semantic focus. Of the remaining words, PENGUIN should be semantically closer to the focus than the others. Calculate the mean for the pairs HAWK/PENGUIN, SPARROW/PENGUIN, and ROBIN/PENGUIN. Call this the BIRD/PENGUIN mean.

3. For the other words, calculate the distance from the focus by calculating the mean of HAWK/--; SPARROW/--, and ROBIN/-- for each of the words WHALE, MONKEY, TROUT, and CAT. Call these values the BIRD/WHALE, BIRD/MONKEY, BIRD/TROUT, and BIRD/CAT distances.

4. In your lab notebook construct "FIGURE 1. Semantic Distances." This figure will simply be a graduated straight horizontal line, with the left end defined as 0. Graduate the line into 1 cm units from "0" to "9" at the right. Label the *focus* at the appropriate point on the line. Plot each of the five distances calculated above on the line and label them.

CONCLUSIONS

1. Why do the three names of birds form the semantic focus? Why is PENGUIN a little further from the focus than the distances among each of the three more "central" birds?

2. Comment on each of the other four distances (BIRD / WHALE, BIRD / MONKEY, BIRD / TROUT, and BIRD / CAT). Why are these points situated as they are from the focus? In general, what features determine the relative distance from the focus?

3. If the items CROW, MOUSE, and LETTUCE had been included in the stimuli, where do you think they would have fallen in Figure 1 with respect to the other pairs? Why?

Laboratories

SEMANTIC FIELD EXPERIMENT INSTRUCTIONS

1. Scan the following list of English nouns:

CAT, HAWK, WHALE, SPARROW, MONKEY, TROUT, PENGUIN, ROBIN.

2. Scan the list again and pick that pair of words which you consider to be the *most similar* in meaning. Place a "1" in that cell corresponding to the pair you have just picked.

3. Scan the list again and pick that pair of word which you consider to be the *least similar* in meaning. Place a "9" in the cell corresponding to the pair you have just picked.

4. You have now secured your "anchor points" for the use of the scale from "1" to "9." For each of the remaining cells, compare each pair of words in terms of similarity of meaning. In each cell place a number from "1" to "9" inclusive, where the lower numbers correspond to relative similarity in meaning and the higher numbers to relative distance or dissimilarity.

MOST SIMILAR = 1   LEAST SIMILAR = 9

      hawk whale sparrow monkey trout penguin robin

cat — — — — — — —

hawk ·· — — — — — —

whale ········· — — — — —

sparrow ··············· — — — —

monkey ····················· — — —

trout ··························· — —

penguin ····························· —

STATISTICAL NOTIONS

In these laboratories, you will need only a very limited set of mathematical tools. These include the *mean, variance,* and *standard deviation* for a set of measurements. In order to understand each of these concepts, let us assume that we have taken a set of n measurements, and that a typical measurement is indicated by x_i. Thus, our measurements can be represented as:

$$x_1, x_2, \ldots x_i, \ldots x_n$$

The (arithmetic) *mean* is defined as the sum of all the measurements, divided by n, the number of measurements taken. This is calculated as follows:

$$\bar{x} = \frac{\Sigma x_1}{n}$$

To get an indication of the amount of variation within a given set of measurements, one can specify the *range*, which is simply the difference between the largest and the smallest measurements. A further measure of the variability within a set of measurements is the set of *deviation* scores, d_i, which are defined as:

$$d_i = x_i - \bar{x}.$$

A more useful measure of the variation within a set of measurements is the *variance*, s^2, defined as follows:

$$s^2 = \frac{\Sigma (x_i - \bar{x})^2}{n-1}$$

Statistics

The variance is defined as the sum of the squares of the differences between individual measurements and the mean (i.e., the deviation scores), divided by *n-1*, where *n* is the number of measurements taken. Finally, the *standard deviation* is defined simply as the square root of the *variance*, or

$$s = [\frac{\Sigma\ (x_i - \bar{x})^2}{n-1}]^{\frac{1}{2}}.$$

To illustrate these notions, consider the following example, in which four subjects (1 through 4) rated the relative acceptability of five different syntactic types (Ta through Te) on a nine point scale:

Subject	Ta	Tb	Tc	Td	Te	Mean
1	5	5	5	5	5	5
2	5	5	5	4	6	5
3	1	4	2	5	3	3
4	1	7	1	2	9	4

The (arithmetic) *mean* for each subject is easily calculated, using the formula on the previous page. The mean for each subject is indicated in the table. To get an indication of the variability within a given subject, we can calculate the deviation scores for each measurement. The deviations for each subject (from his own mean) are:

Subject	Ta	Tb	Tc	Td	Te
1	0	0	0	0	0
2	0	0	0	-1	1
3	-2	1	-1	2	0
4	-3	3	-3	-2	5

There is no variability in subject 1, some in subject 2, and more in subjects 3 and 4. The *standard deviation, s,* can be calculated for each subject, using the formula on the preceding page. The *variance* for subject 3 is 2.5, and the square root of 2.5, the *standard deviation*, is 1.58.

For each subject in the above example, calculate the *variance* and the *standard deviation*.

STATISTICAL TESTS

REFERENCES

Ferguson (1976, Chapters 11, 12, 13)

Three distinct statistical tests are outlined below. Each is used for a different purpose. Once the test is employed and the appropriate statistic has been calculated, its significance can be established by reference to the tables.

T-test for independent samples. If data from two treatments or conditions (*a* and *b*) are taken, with different subjects participating in each condition, the difference between the means for the two conditions can be evaluated by this test. It is necessary that subjects be randomly assigned to one or the other condition. We assume an equal number of *n* data points in each condition. The mean and the variance can be calculated for each of the conditions. The "within-group" variance for the pooled data can be calculated as follows, so long as the same number of entries *n*, is found in each condition:

$$s^2 = (s_a^2 + s_b^2)/2.$$

The *degrees of freedom, df*, for this situation is:

$$df = 2(n - 1).$$

Finally, the *standard error, SE*, is defined as:

$$SE = (2s^2/n)^{\frac{1}{2}}.$$

279

Statistics

To evaluate whether the difference between the two means is significant, the statistic t must be calculated. This statistic is defined as:

$$t = (\bar{x} - \bar{y}) / SE$$

Example. Suppose we have the two conditions A and B, each with n = 6 independent data points, as:

A	B
3	3
5	4
6	3
4	2
5	1
6	2

	A	B
sum	29	15
mean	4.83	2.50
variance	1.37	1.10

The pooled variance is calculated as:

$$s^2 = (1.37 + 1.10) / 2$$
$$s^2 = 1.24$$

and the standard error, SE, is:

$$SE = [(2 \times 1.24) / 6]^{\frac{1}{2}}$$
$$SE = .64.$$

Accordingly, t is calculated as:

$$t = (4.83 - 2.50) / .64$$
$$t = 3.64.$$

This value is then checked against the values in Appendix A and is found to be significant at the .05 level.

280

T-test for correlated samples. This test is used when the *same* subjects are tested under the two conditions. Here, we test whether or not the differences between the scores differ significantly from zero. In this case, we define D_i as the difference between a pair of scores for a particular subject. The *degrees of freedom, df,* for this test is the number of pairs of scores minus 1, or df = n-1, where *n* is the number of *pairs*. The variance for the differences is defined as:

$$s_D^2 = \frac{\sum (D_i - \bar{D})^2}{n-1}$$

The statistic *t* for correlated samples can be calculated using the following computational formula:

$$t = \frac{\sum D_i}{\left[\frac{n\sum D_i^2 - (\sum D_i)^2}{n-1} \right]^{\frac{1}{2}}}$$

Example. Six subjects are asked to assess the relative acceptability of two different syntactic types, *Ta* and *Tb* on a nine-point scale. Their scores, along with the sums and means, are:

Subject	Ta	Tb	D	D²
1	8	4	4	16
2	9	5	4	16
3	6	3	3	9
4	7	2	5	25
5	5	6	-1	1
6	7	3	4	16
sum	42	23	19	83
mean	7.0	3.8	3.2	

The statistic *t* is calculated as follows, from the above definition,

$$t = 19 \ / \ [\frac{6 \times 83 - (19)^2}{5}]^{\frac{1}{2}}$$

$$t = 3.63.$$

From Appendix A, the value is found to be significant at the .05 level.

Statistics

Chi-square test. This test is used in order to evaluate the difference between expected and observed frequencies. If O is the *observed* frequency of a given phenomenon and E is the theoretically predicted or *expected* frequency, chi-square can be calculated as follows:

$$X^2 = \sum \frac{(O-E)^2}{E}$$

The *degrees of freedom, df,* is equal to the total number of differences minus 1, or $df = n - 1$.

Example. A group of twenty subjects is given four pairs of supposedly synonymous sentences. In each pair, one member is of the form NP V NP to NP, as in "John gave the book to Mary," while the other member is of the form NP V NP NP, as in "John gave Mary the book." We call the first type A and the second B. The subject's task is to select the "better" member of each pair. If the two types are truly synonymous, it is expected that type A would be selected half of the time and type B half of the time. The results of the experiment are:

Type	O	E	O-E	$(O-E)^2$
A	49	40	9	81
B	31	40	-9	81
Total	80	80		

From these figures, the value of chi-square can be calculated. It is:

$$X^2 = 81/40 + 81/40$$
$$X^2 = 4.05.$$

The *degrees of freedom, df* is 1 in this case, since there are only two options. Accordingly, the value for chi-square, for df=1, is found to be significant at the .05 level from Appendix B.

APPENDIX A. CRITICAL VALUES FOR t

df	Level of significance for one-tailed test			
	.025	.01	.005	.0005
	Level of significance for two-tailed test			
	.05	.02	.01	.001
1	12.706	31.821	63.657	636.619
2	4.303	6.965	9.925	31.598
3	3.182	4.541	5.841	12.941
4	2.776	3.747	4.604	8.610
5	2.571	3.365	4.032	6.859
6	2.447	3.143	3.707	5.959
7	2.365	2.998	3.499	5.405
8	2.306	2.896	2.355	5.041
9	2.262	2.821	3.250	4.781
10	2.228	2.764	3.169	4.587
11	2.201	2.718	3.106	4.437
12	2.179	2.681	3.055	4.318
13	2.160	2.650	3.012	4.221
14	2.145	2.624	2.977	4.140
15	2.131	2.602	2.947	4.073
16	2.120	2.583	2.921	4.015
17	2.110	2.567	2.898	3.965
18	2.101	2.552	2.878	3.922
19	2.093	2.539	2.861	3.883
20	2.086	2.528	2.845	3.850
30	2.042	2.457	2.750	3.646
40	2.021	2.423	2.704	3.551
60	2.000	2.390	2.660	3.460
120	1.980	2.358	2.617	3.373
∞	1.960	2.326	2.576	3.291

APPENDIX B. CRITICAL VALUES FOR X^2

df	.05	.02	.01	.001
1	3.84	5.41	6.64	10.83
2	5.99	7.82	9.21	13.82
3	7.82	9.84	11.34	16.27
4	9.49	11.67	13.28	18.46
5	11.07	13.39	15.09	20.52
6	12.59	15.03	16.81	22.46
7	14.07	16.62	18.48	24.32
8	15.51	18.17	20.09	26.12
9	16.92	19.68	21.67	27.88
10	18.31	21.16	23.21	29.59

REFERENCES

American Psychological Association. *Publication manual* (2nd ed.), Washington, D.C.: American Psychological Association, 1974.

Anderson, B.F. *The psychology experiment: An introduction to the scientific method.* Belmont, CA.: Wadsworth, 1966.

Anglin, J.M. *Word, object, and conceptual development.* New York: Norton, 1977.

Anisfeld, M., & Tucker, G.R. The English pluralization rules of six-year-old children. *Child Development,* 1967, *38,* 1201-1217.

Anshen, F., & Aronoff, M. Morphological productivity and phonological transparency. *Canadian Journal of Linguistics,* 1981, *26,* 63-72.

Aronoff, M. *Word formation in generative grammar.* Cambridge, MA: The MIT Press, 1976.

Aronoff, M. Potential words, actual words, productivity, and frequency. In S. Hattori & K. Inoue (Eds.), *Proceedings of the XIIi International Congress of Linguists,* Tokyo, 1983, 163-171.

Aronoff, M., & Schvaneveldt, R. Testing morphological productivity. *Annals of the New York Academy of Sciences,* 1978, *318,* 106-114.

Baker, W.J. An 'information structure' view of language. *Canadian Journal of Linguistics,* 1976, *21,* 1-16. Reprinted in G.D. Prideaux, B.L. Derwing, & W.J. Baker (Eds.), *Experimental linguistics: Integration of theories and applications.* Ghent: E. Story-Scientia, 1980.

285

References

Baker, W.J., & Prideaux, G.D. Grammatical simplicity or performative efficiency. In G.D. Prideaux, B.L. Derwing, & W.J. Baker (Eds.), *Experimental linguistics: Integration of theories and applications*. Ghent: E. Story-Scientia, 1980.

Baker, W.J., Prideaux, G.D., & Derwing, B.L. Grammatical properties of sentences as a basis for concept formation. *Journal of Psycholinguistic Research*, 1973, *2*, 201-220. Reprinted in Prideaux, G.D., Derwing, B.L., & Baker, W.J. (Eds.),*Experimental linguistics: Integration of theories and applications*. Ghent: E. Story-Scientia, 1980.

Bartlett, F.C. *Remembering*. Cambridge: Cambridge University Press, 1932.

Berko, J. The child's learning of English morphology. *Word*, 1958, *14*, 150-177.

Berwick, R.C. Tansformational grammar and artificial intelligence: A contemporary view. *Cognition and Brain Theory*, 1983, *6*, 383-416.

Bever, T.G. A survey of some recent work in psycholinguistics. In W.J. Plath (Ed.), *Specification and utilization of a transformational grammar: Scientific report three*. Yorktown Heights, NY: Thomas J. Watson Research Center, IBC Corporation, 1968.

Bever, T.G. The cognitive basis for linguistic structures. In J.R. Hayes (Ed.), *Cognition and the development of language*. New York: John Wiley & Sons, 1970a.

Bever, T.G. The influence of speech performance on linguistic structure. In G.B. Flores D'Arcais & W.J.M. Levelt (Eds.), *Advances in psycholinguistics*. Amsterdam: North-Holland, 1970b.

Bever, T.G., Lackner, J.R., & Kirk, R. The underlying structures of sentences are the primary units of immediate speech processing. *Perception and Psychophysics*, 1969, *5*, 225-231.

Bever, T.G., Lackner, J.R., & Stolz, W. Transitional

probability is not a general mechanism for the segmentation of speech. *Journal of Experimental Psychology*, 1969, *79*, 387-394.

Bever, T.G., & Langendoen, D.T. A dynamic model of the evolution of language. *Linguistic Inquiry*, 1971, *2*, 433-463.

Bock, J.K., & Irwin, D.E. Syntactic effects of information availability in sentence production. *Journal of Verbal Learning and Verbal Behavior*, 1980, *19*, 467-484.

Bock, M. Levels of processing of normal and ambiguous sentences in different contexts. *Psychological Research*, 1978, *40*, 37-51.

Bransford, J.D., Barclay, J.R., & Franks, J.J. Sentence memory: A constructive versus interpretive approach. *Cognitive Psychology*, 1972, *3*, 193-209.

Bransford, J.D., & Franks, J.J. The abstraction of linguistic ideas. *Cognitive Psychology*, 1971, *2*, 331-350.

Bransford, J.D., & McCarrell, N.S. A sketch of a cognitive appeach to comprehension: Some thoughts about understanding what it means to comprehend. In W.B. Weimer & D.S. Palermo (Eds.), *Cognition and the symbolic processes*. Hillsdale, NJ: Lawrence Erlbaum, 1974.

Bresnan, J. An approach to universal grammar and mental representation. *Cognition*, 1981, *10*, 39-52.

Bresnan, J. The passive in lexical theory. In J. Bresnan (Ed.), *The mental representation of grammatical relations*. Cambridge, MA: The MIT Press, 1982.

Bresnan, J. & Kaplan, R.M. Introduction: Grammars as mental representations of language. In J. Bresnan (Ed.), *The mental representation of grammatical relations*. Cambridge, MA: The MIT Press, 1982.

References

Broadbent, D.A. Word-frequency effect and response bias. *Psychological Review*, 1967, *74*, 1-15.

Brown, H.D. Children's comprehension of relativized English sentences. *Child Development*, 1971, *42*, 1923-1926.

Brown, R. The development of Wh questions in child speech. *Journal of Verbal Learning and Verbal Behavior*, 1968, *7*, 279-290.

Brown, R. *A first language: The early stages*. Cambridge, MA: Harvard University Press, 1973.

Brown, R., Cazden, C.B., & Bellugi, U. The child's grammar from I to III. In J.P. Hill (Ed.), *Minnesota symposium on child psychology* (Vol. 2). Minneapolis: University of Minnesota Press, 1969, pp. 28-73.

Brown, R., & Fraser, C. The acquisition of syntax. In U. Bellugi & R. Brown (Eds.), *The acquisition of language. Monographs of the Society for Research in Child Development*, 1964, *29* (No. 92), 43-78.

Brown, R., & Hanlon, C. Derivational complexity and order of acquisition in child speech. In J.R. Hayes (Ed.). *Cognition and the development of language*. New York: John Wiley & Sons, 1970.

Bybee, J.L., & Modor, C.L. Morphological classes as natural categories. *Language*, 1983, *59*, 251-270.

Bybee, J.L., & Slobin, D.I. Rules and schemas in the development and use of the English past tense. *Language*, 1982, *58*, 265-289.

Cairns, H.S. Effects of bias on processing and reprocessing of lexically ambiguous sentences. *Journal of Experimental Psychology*, 1973, *97:3*, 337-343.

Carden, G. Backwards anaphora in discourse context. *Journal of Linguistics*, 1982, *18*, 361-387.

Carey, P.W., Mehler, J., & Bever, T.G. Judging the

288

veracity of ambiguous sentences. *Journal of Verbal Learning and Verbal Behavior,* 1970, *9,* 243-254.

Carpenter, P.A., & Just, M.A. Sentence comprehension: A psycholinguistic processing model of verification. *Psychological Review,* 1975, *82,* 45-73.

Carroll, J.B. Toward a performance grammar for core sentences in spoken and written English. In G. Nickel (Ed.), *Special issue of IRAL on the occasion of Bertil Malmberg's sixtieth birthday.* Heidelberg: J. Groos, 1973.

Catlin, J. On the word-frequency effect. *Psychological Review,* 1969, *76,* 504-506.

Chafe, W.L. *Meaning and the structure of language.* Chicago: University of Chicago Press, 1970.

Chapanis, A. Color names for color space. *Scientific American,* 1965, *53,* 327-346.

Chomsky, N. *Syntactic structures.* The Hague: Mouton, 1957.

Chomsky, N. *Current issues in linguistic theory.* The Hague: Mouton, 1964.

Chomsky, N. *Aspects of the theory of syntax.* Cambridge, MA: The MIT Press, 1965.

Chomsky, N. Deep structure, surface structure, and semantic interpretation. In R. Jakobson & S. Kawamoto (Eds.), *Studies in general and oriental linguistics presented to Shiro Hattori on the occasion of his sixtieth birthday.* Tokyo: TEC co., 1970a.

Chomsky, N. Remarks on nominalization. In R.A. Jacobs & P.S. Rosenbaum (Eds.), *Readings in English transformational grammar.* Waltham, MA: Ginn & Company, 1970b.

Chomsky, N. *Reflections on language.* New York: Pantheon Books, 1975.

Chomsky, N. *Rules and representations.* New York:

References

Columbia University Press, 1980.

Chomsky, N. *Lectures on government and binding.* Dordrecht: Foris, 1982a.

Chomsky, N. *Some concepts and consequences of the theory of government and binding. (Linguistic Inquiry Monograph Six).* Cambridge, MA: The MIT Press, 1982b.

Chomsky, N., & Miller, G.A. Introduction to the formal analysis of natural language. In R.D. Luce, R.R. Bush, & E. Galanter (Eds.), *Handbook of mathematical psychology 2.* New York: John Wiley & Sons, 1963.

Christensen, L.B. *Experimental methodology* (Second Edition). Boston: Allyn and Bacon, 1980.

Church, K.W. *On memory limitations in natural language processing.* Ph.D. dissertation, Massachusetts Institute of Technology, 1980. Reproduced by the Indiana University Linguistics Club, 1982.

Clark, E.V. On the acquisition of the meaning of *before* and *after. Journal of Verbal Learning and Verbal Behavior,* 1971, *10,* 266-275.

Clark, E.V. What's in a word? On the child's acquisition of semantics in his first language. In T.E. Moore (Ed.), *Cognitive development and the acquisition of language.* New York: Academic Press, 1973.

Clark, E.V. Some aspects of the conceptual basis for first language acquisition. In R.L. Schiefelbusch & L.L. Lloyd (Eds.), *Language perspectives: Acquisition, retardation, and intervention.* Baltimore: University Park Press, 1974.

Clark, H.H., & Card, S.K. The role of semantics in remembering comparative sentences. *Journal of Experimental Psychology,* 1969, *82,* 545-553.

Clark, H.H., & Clark, E.V. Semantic distinctions and memory for complex sentences. *Quarterly Journal of Experimental Psychology,* 1968, *20,* 129-138.

Clark, H.H., & Clark, E.V. *Psychology and language: An introduction to psycholinguistics*. New York: Harcourt Brace Jovanovich, 1977.

Clark, H.H., & Haviland, S.E. Psychological processes as linguistic explanation. In D. Cohen (Ed.), *Explaining linguistic phenomena*. Washington, D.C.: Hemisphere Press.

Clark, H.H., & Lucy, P. Understanding what is meant from what is said: A study in conversationally conveyed requests. *Journal of Verbal Learning and Verbal Behavior*, 1975, *14*, 56-72.

Clark, H.H., & Stafford, R.A. Memory for semantic features of the verb. *Journal of Experimental Psychology*, 1969, *80*, 326-334.

Clifton, C., & Odom, P. Similarity relations among certain English setnence constructions. *Psychological Monographs*, 1966, *80*, 1-35.

Coulter, G.R. A conjoined analysis of American Sign Language relative clauses. *Discourse Processes*, 1983, *6*, 305-318.

Cowper, E.A. *Constraints on sentence complexity: A model for syntactic processing*. Unpublished Ph.D. dissertation, Brown University, 1976.

Cutler, A. Productivity in word formation. *Papers from the Sixteenth Regional Meeting, Chicago Linguistics Society*. Chicago: Chicago Linguistics Society, 1980.

Cutler, A. Degrees of transparency in word formation. *Canadian Journal of Linguistics*, 1981, *26*, 73-76.

Deese, J. On the structure of associative meaning. *Psychological Review*, 1962, *69*, 169-175.

Deese, J. *The structure of association in language and thought*. Baltimore: Johns Hopkins Press, 1965.

Deese, J. *Psycholinguistics*. Boston: Allyn and Bacon, 1970.

References

Derwing, B.L. *Transformational grammar as a theory of language acquisition.* Cambridge: Cambridge University Press, 1973.

Derwing, B.L. Morpheme recognition and the learning of rules for derivational morphology. *Canadian Journal of Linguistics,* 1976, *21,* 38-66.

Derwing, B.L. Is the child really a "little linguist"? In J. Macnamara (Ed.), *Language learning and thought.* New York: Academic Press, 1977.

Derwing, B.L. Psycholinguistic evidence and linguistic theory. In G.D. Prideaux (Ed.), *Perspectives in experimental linguistics.* Amsterdam: John Benjamins B.V., 1979.

Derwing, B.L. English pluralization: A testing ground for rule evaluation. In G.D. Prideaux, B.L. Derwing, & W.J. Baker, (Eds.), *Experimental linguistics: Integration of theories and applications.* Ghent: E. Story-Scientia, 1980.

Derwing, B.L., & Baker, W.J. *Rule learning and the English inflections.* Final Report to the Canada Council, (File No. S73-0387), 1974.

Derwing, B.L., & Baker, W.J. *On the learning of English morphological rules.* Final Report ot the Canada Council, (File No. S73-0387), 1976.

Derwing, B.L., & Baker, W.J. The psychological basis for morphological rules. In J. Macnamara (Ed.), *Language learning and thought.* New York: Academic Press, 1977.

Derwing, B.L., & Baker, W.J. Recent research on the acquisition of English morphology. In P. Fletcher & M. Garman (Eds.), *Language acquisition.* Cambridge: Cambridge University Press.

Derwing, B.L., & Baker, W.J. Rule learning and the English inflections. In G.D. Prideaux, B.L. Derwing, & W.J. Baker (Eds.), *Experimental linguistics Integration of theories and applications.* Ghent: E. Story-Scientia, 1980.

Derwing, T.M. *The acquisition of WH questions.*

Unpublished M.Sc. thesis, University of Alberta, 1979.

Dik, S.C. *Functional grammar.* Amsterdam: North-Holland, 1978.

Donaldson, M., & Balfour, G. Less is more: A study of language comprehension in children. *British Journal of Psychology*, 1968, *59*, 461-472.

Dressler, W.U. (Ed.), *Current trends in linguistics.* New York: Walter de Gruyter, 1978.

Ervin, S.M. Imitation and structural change in children's language. In E.H. Lenneberg (Ed.), *New directions in the study of language.* Cambridge, MA: The MIT Press, 1964.

Ferguson, G.A. *Statistical analysis in psychology and education* (5th ed.). New York: McGraw-Hill, 1981.

Fillenbaum, S., & Rapoport, A. *Structures in the subjective lexicon.* New York: Academic Press, 1971.

Fillmore, C.J. The case for case. In E. Bach & R.T. Harms (Eds.), *Universals in linguistic theory.* New York: Holt, Rinehart, & Winston, 1968.

Fillmore, C.J. Verbs of judging: An exercise in semantic descriptions. *Papers in Linguistics*, 1969, *1*, 91-117.

Fletcher, P. On paraphrase. In G.D. Prideaux, B.L. Derwing, & W.J. Baker (Eds.), *Experimental linguistics: Integration of theories and applications.* Ghent: E. Story-Scientia, 1980.

Fodor, J.A., & Bever, T.G. The psychological reality of linguistic segments. *Journal of Verbal Learning and Verbal Behavior*, 1965, *4* 414-420.

Fodor, J.A, Bever, T.G., & Garrett, M. *The psychology of language: An introduction to psycholinguistics and generative grammar.* New York: McGraw-Hill, 1974.

293

References

Fodor, J.D. Parsing strategies and constraints on transformations. *Linguistic Inquiry*, 1978, *9*, 427-473.

Ford, M. Sentence planning units: Implications for the speaker's representation of meaningful relations underlying sentences. In J. Bresnan (Ed.), *The mental representation of grammatical relations*. Cambridge, MA: The MIT Press, 1982.

Ford, M., Bresnan, J., & Kaplan, R.M. A competence-based theory of syntactic closure. In J. Bresnan (Ed.), *The mental representation of grammatical relations*. Cambridge, MA: The MIT Press, 1982.

Foss, D.J., Bever, T.G., & Silver, M. The comprehension and verification of ambiguous sentences. *Perception and Psychophysics*, 1968, *4*, 304-306.

Francis, W.N. *The structure of American English*. New York: Ronald Press, 1958.

Franks, J.J., & Bransford, J.D. The acquisition of abstract ideas. *Journal of Verbal Learning and Verbal Behavior*, 1972, *11*, 311-315.

Frazier, L. *On comprehensing sentences: Syntactic parsing strategies*. Ph.D. dissertation, University of Massachusetts, 1978. Reprinted by the Indiana University Linguistics Club, 1979.

Frazier, L., & Fodor, J.D. The sausage machine: A new two-stage parsing model. *Cognition*, 1978, *6*, 291-325.

Fromkin, V.A. The non-anomalous nature of anomalous utterances. *Language*, 1971, *47*, 27-52.

Fromkin, V.A. (Ed.). *Speech errors as linguistic evidence*.The Hague: Mouton, 1973.

Fromkin, V.A. Slips of the tongue. *Scientific American*, December, 1973. Reprinted in William S.-Y. Wang (Ed.), *Human communication: Language and its psychobiological bases*. San Francisco: W. H. Freeman & Company, 1982.

Garrett, M., & Bever, T.G., & Fodor, J.A. The active use of grammar in speech perception. *Perception and Psychophysics*, 1966, *1* 30-32.

Gleason, H.A., Jr. *An introduction to descriptive linguistics*. Revised Edition. New York: Holt, Rinehart and Winston, 1961.

Glucksberg, S., & Danks, J.H. Grammatical structure and recall: A function of the space in immediate memory or recall delay? *Perception and Psychophysics*, 1969, *6*, 113-117.

Glucksberg, S., & Danks, J.H. *Experimental psycholinguistics: An introduction*. Hillsdale, NJ: Lawrence Erlbaum, 1975.

Grice, H.P. Logic and conversation. In P. Cole & J. Morgan (Eds.), *Syntax and semantics* vol. 3. New York: Academic Press, 1975.

Grimes, J. *The thread of discourse*. The Hague: Mouton, 1975.

Gruber, J.S. *Studies in lexical relations*. Unpublished Ph.D. dissertation, MIT, 1965.

Hakes, D.T. Effects of reducing complement constructions on sentence comprehension. *Journal of Verbal Learning and Verbal Behavior*, 1972, *11*, 278-286.

Halliday, M.A.K. Notes on transitivity and theme in English: I. *Journal of Linguistics*, 1967a, *3*, 37-81.

Halliday, M.A.K. Notes on transitivity and theme in English: II. *Journal of Linguistics*, 1967b, *3*, 199-244.

Halliday, M.A.K. Notes on transitivity and theme in English: III. *Journal of Linguistics*, 1968, *4*, 179-215.

Harner, L. Children's understanding of linguistic reference to past and future. *Journal of Psycholinguistic Research*, 1976, *5*, 65-84.

References

Hatch, E.M. *Psycholinguistics: A second language perspective*. Rowley, MA: Newbury House, 1983.

Henley, N.M. A psychological study of the semantics of animal terms. *Journal of Verbal Learning and Verbal Behavior*, 1969, *8*, 176-184.

Hörmann, H. *Psycholinguistics*. New York: Springer-Verlag, 1971.

Hörmann, Hans. *To mean, to understand*. New York: Springer-Verlag, 1981.

Hunter, P.J. *Verb-particle position in English: An experimental study*. Unpublished M.Sc. thesis, University of Alberta, 1981.

Hunter, P.J., & Prideaux, G.D. Empirical constraints on the verb-particle construction in English. *Journal of the Atlantic Provinces Linguistic Association*, 1983, *5*, 3-15.

Huttenlocher, J. The origins of language comprehension. In R.L. Solso (Ed.), *Theories in cognitive psychology*. Potomac, MD: Lawrence Erlbaum, 1974.

Innes, S. *Developmental aspects of the plural formation in English*. Unpublished M.Sc. thesis, University of Alberta, 1974.

Itagaki, N. *Contextual determinants of linguistic expressions*. Unpublished M.Sc. thesis, University of Alberta, 1982.

Itagaki, N., & Prideaux, G.D. Pragmatic constraints on subject and agent selection. In S.C. Dik (Ed.), *Advances in functional grammar*. Dordrecht, Holland: Foris, 1983.

Jackendoff, R. *Semantic interpretation in generative grammar*. Cambridge, MA: The MIT Press, 1972.

Jespersen, O. *The philosophy of grammar*. New York: Norton, 1965.

Kac, M.B. *Corepresentation of grammatical structure*. Minneapolis: University of Minnesota Press, 1978.

Kac, M.B. In defence of autonomous linguistics. *Lingua*, 1980, *50*, 243-245.

Kaplan, R.M., & Bresnan, J. Lexical-functional grammar: a formal system for grammatical representation. In J. Bresnan (Ed.), *The mental representation of grammatical relations*. Cambridge, MA: MIT Press, 1982.

Katz, J.J. *Semantic theory*. New York: Harper & Row, 1972.

Katz, J.J., & Fodor, J.A. The structure of a semantic theory. *Language*, 1963, *39*, 170-210.

Katz, J.J., & Postal, P.M. *An integrated theory of linguistic descriptions*. Cambridge, MA: MIT Press, 1964.

Kess, J.F. *Psycholinguistics: Introductory perspectives*. New York: Academic Press, 1976a.

Kess, J.F. Reversing directions in psycholinguistics. *Language Sciences*, 1976b, *42*, 1-5.

Kess. J.F., & Hoppe, R.A. *Ambiguity in psycholinguistics*. Amsterdam: John Benjamins B.V., 1981.

Kimball, J. Seven principles of surface structure parsing in natural language. *Cognition*, 1973, *2*, 15-47.

Kintsch, W. Notes on the structure of semantic memory. In E. Tulving & W. Donaldson (Eds.), *Organization of memory*. New York: Academic Press, 1972.

Kintsch, W. *The representation of meaning in memory*. Hillsdale, NJ: Lawrence Erlbaum, 1974.

Kintsch, W. Memory representations of texts. In R.L. Solso (Ed.), *Information processing and cognition*. Hillsdale, NJ: Lawrence Erlbaum, 1975.

Kintsch, W. Memory for prose. In C.N. Cofer (Ed.), *The structure of human memory*. San Francisco: W. H. Freeman, 1976.

References

Kintsch, W. *Memory, language, and thinking.* New York: John Wiley & Sons, 1977.

Kintsch, W., & Glass, G. Effects of propositional structure upon sentence recall. In W. Kintsch (Ed.), *The representation of meaning in memory.* Hillsdale, NJ: Lawrence Erlbaum, 1974.

Kintsch, W., & Keenan, J.M. Reading rate and retention as a function of the number of propositions in the base structure of sentences. *Cognitive Psychology,* 1973, *3,* 257-274.

Kiparsky, P., & Menn, L. On the acquisition of phonology. In J. Macnamara (Ed.), *Language learning and thought.* New York: Academic Press, 1977.

Klima, E.S., & Bellugi, U. Syntactic regularities in the speech of children. In J. Lyons & R. Wales (Eds.), *Psycholinguistic papers.* Edinburgh: Edinburgh University Press, 1966.

Koziol, S.M. The development of noun plurals during the primary grades. *Papers and reports on child language development.* Committee on Linguistics, Stanford University, 1970, *2,* 76-96.

Kuczaj, S. A. The acquisition of regular and irregular past tense forms. *Journal of Verbal Learning and Verbal Behavior,* 1977, *16,* 589-600.

Kuczaj, S.A. Children's judgement of grammatical and ungrammatical irregular past tense verbs. *Child Development,* 1978, *49,* 319-326.

Kuno, S. Constraints on internal clauses and sentential subjects. *Linguistic Inquiry,* 1973, *4,* 363-385.

Kuno, S., & Kaburaki, E. Empathy and syntax. *Linguistic Inquiry,* 1977, *8,* 626-672.

Ladefoged, P., Broadbent, D.E. Perception of sequence in auditory events. *Quarterly Journal of Experimental Psychology,* 1960, *13,* 162-170.

Lakoff, G. Stative adjectives and verbs in English.

Mathematical linguistics and automatic translation. NSF Report No. 17: I-1-15. The Computational Laboratory, Harvard University, 1966.

Lakoff, G. *Irregularity in syntax.* New York: Holt, Rinehart, & Winston, 1970.

Lakoff, G., & Johnson, M. *Metaphors we live by.* Chicago: University of Chicago Press, 1980.

Lakoff, G., & Thompson, H. Introducing cognitive grammar. In C. Cogen, H. Thompson, G. Thurgood, K. Whistler, & J. Wright (Eds.), *Proceedings of the First Annual Meeting of the Berkeley Linguistics Society.* Berkeley, CA: Berkeley Linguistics Society, 1975, pp. 295-313.

Langacker, R.W. Movement rules in functional perspective. *Language,* 1974, *50,* 630-664.

Lees, R.B. *The grammar of English nominalizations.* The Hague: Mouton, 1960.

Leopold, W.F. *Speech development of a vilingual child: A linguist's record.* Vol. 1 *Vocabulary growth in the first two years.* Vol. 2 *Sound-learning in the first two years.* Vol. 3 *Grammar and general problems in the first two years.* Vol. 4 *Diary from age 2.* Evanston, IL: Northwestern University Press, 1939, 1947, 1949a, 1949b.

Levelt, W.J.M. Psychological representations of syntactic structures. Heymans Bulletin HB-69-36 EX, Department of Psychology, Groningen University, 1967.

Levelt, W.J.M. A scaling approach to the study of syntactic relations. In G.B. Flores D'Arcais & W.J.M Levelt (Eds.), *Advances in psycholinguistics.* Amsterdam: North-Holland, 1970.

Limber, J. "Remind" remains. *Linguistic Inquiry,* 1970, *1,* 511-523.

Limber, J. The genesis of complex sentences. In T.E. Moore (Ed.), *Cognitive development and the acquisition of language.* New York: Academic

References

Press, 1974.

Lightfoot, D. *The language lottery*. Cambridge, MA: The MIT PRess, 1982.

MacKay, D.G. To end ambiguous sentences. *Perception and Psychophysics*, 1966, 1, 426-436.

MacKay, D.G., & Bever, T.G. In search of ambiguity. *Perception and Psychophysics*, 1967, 2, 193-200.

Magnera, G. *Variation in organizing the lexicon*. Unpublished Ph.D. dissertation, The University of Alberta, 1982.

Maratsos, M. How to get from words to sentences. In D. Aaronson & R.W. Rieber (Eds.), *Psycholinguistic research: Implications and applications*. Hillsdale, NJ: Lawrence Erlbaum, 1979.

Marckworth, M.L., & Baker, W.J. A discriminate function analysis of co-variation of a number of syntactic devices in five prose genres. In G.D. Prideaux, B.L. Derwing, & W.J. Baker (Eds.), *Experimental linguistics: Integration of theories and applications*. Ghent: E. Story-Scientia, 1980.

Marcus, M.P. *A theory of syntactic recognition for natural language*. Cambridge, MA: The MIT Press, 1980.

Marslan-Wilson, W. Speech understanding as a psychological process. In J.C. Simon (Ed.), *Spoken language generation and understanding*. Dordrecht: Reidel, 1980.

Martin, E. Towards an analysis of subjective phrase structure. *Psychological Bulletin*, 1970, 74, 153-166.

Matthews, P.H. *Generative grammar and linguistic competence*. London: George Allen & Unwin, 1979.

McCawley, J.D. English as a VSO language. *Language*, 1970, 46, 286-299.

McCawley, J.D. Prelexical syntax. In R.J. O'Brien

(Ed.), *Linguistic Developments of the Sixties--Viewpoints of the Seventies. Monograph Series in Languages and Linguistics,* 1971, *24,* 19-33.

McNeill, D. The creation of language by children. In J. Lyons & R.J. Wales (Eds.), *Psycholinguistic papers.* Edinburgh: Edinburgh University Press, 1966.

McNeill, D. *The acquisition of language: The study of developmental psycholinguistics.* New York: Harper & Row, 1970.

Mehler, J., & Carey, P. Role of surface and base structures in the perception of sentences. *Journal of Verbal Learning and Verbal Behavior,* 1963, *6,* 335-338.

Menn, L. Phonotactic rules in beginning speech. *Lingua,* 1971, *26,*225-251.

Miller, G.A. A psychological method to investigate verbal concepts. *Journal of Mathematical Psychology,* 1969, *6,* 169-191.

Miller, G.A., & McKean, K.E. A chronometric study of some relations between sentences. *Quarterly Journal of Experimental Psychology,* 1964, *16,* 297-308.

Miller, W., & Ervin, S. The development of grammar in child language. In U. Bellugi & R. Brown (Eds.), *The acquisition of language. Monograph of the Society for Research in Child Development,* 1964, *29,* 9-34.

Minsky, M. A framework for representing knowledge. In P. Winston (Ed.), *The psychology of computer vision.* New York: McGraw-hill, 1975.

Mistler-Lachman, J.L. Levels of comprehension in processing normal and ambiguous sentences. *Journal of Verbal Learning and Verbal Behavior,* 1975, *11,* 614-623.

Murrell, G.A., & Morton, J. Word recognition and morpheme structure. *Journal of Experimental*

References

Psychology, 1974, *24*, 19-33.

Natalicio, D.S. *Formation of the plural in English: A study of native speakers of English and native speakers of Spanish.* Unpublished Ph.D. dissertation, University of Texas, Austin, 1969.

Newmeyer, F.J. *Grammatical theory: Its limits and its possibilities.* Chicago: University of Chicago Press, 1983.

Osgood, C.E. The nature and measurement of meaning. *Journal of Experimental Psychology*, 1952, *49*, 197-237.

Osgood, C.E., Suci, G.J., & Tannenbaum, P.H. *The measurement of meaning.* Urbana, Ill.: University of Illinois Press, 1957.

Palermo, D.S. More about less. A study in language comprehension. *Journal of Verbal Learning and Verbal Behavior*, 1973, *12*, 211-221.

Palermo, D.S. Still more about the comprehension of "less." *Developmental Psychology*, 1974, *10*, 827-829.

Palermo, D.S. *Psychology of language.* Glenview, Ill.: Scott, Foresman & Company, 1978.

Patel, P.G. Perceptual chunking, processing time, and semantic information. *Folia Linguistica*, 1973, *6*, 152-166.

Perlmutter, D.M. Relational grammar. In E.A. Moravcsik & J.R. Wirth (Eds.), *Syntax and semantics, Volume 13: Current approaches to syntax.* New York: Academic Press, 1980.

Pinker, S. A theory of the acquisition of lexical interpretive grammars. In J. Bresnan (Ed.), *The mental representation of grammatical relations.* Cambridge, MA: The MIT Press, 1982.

Popper, K.R. *Conjectures and refutations: The growth of scientific knowledge.* New York: Basic Books, 1962.

Postal, P.M. On the surface verb 'remind'. *Linguistic Inquiry*, 1970, *1*, 37-120.

Prideaux, G.D. A functional analysis of English question formation: A response to Hurford. *Journal of Child Language*, 1976, *3*, 417-422.

Prideaux, G.D. The acquisition of relative clauses: A functional analysis. *Canadian Journal of Linguistics*, 1979a, *24*, 25-40.

Prideaux, G.D. A psycholinguistic perspective on English grammar. *Glossa*, 1979b, *13*, 123-157.

Prideaux, G.D. The role of perceptual strategies in the processing of English relative clause structures. *Proceedings of the Eighth International Conference on Computational Linguistics*. Tokyo: COLING 80, 1980, 60-67.

Prideaux, G.D. The processing of Japanese relative clauses. *Canadian Journal of Linguistics*, 1982, *27*, 23-30.

Prideaux, G.D. Positional tendencies of English relative clauses as evidence for processing strategies. In A. Makkai & A.K. Melby (Eds.), *Festschrift for Rulon Wells*. Lake Bluff, Ill.: Jupiter Press, 1984.

Prideaux, G.D., & Baker, W.J. The recognition of ambiguity. *Human Communication*, 1976, *4*, 51-58. Reprinted in Prideaux, Derwing, & Baker (Eds.), *Experimental linguistics: Integration of theories and applications*. Ghent: E. Story-Scientia, 1980.

Prideaux, G.D., & Baker, W.J. *Perceptual strategies and relative clause processing*. Final Report to the Social Sciences and Humanities Research Council of Canada, Research Grant No. 410-80-0343, 1982.

Prideaux, G.D., & Baker, W.J. An integrated perspective on cognitive strategies in language processing. *META*, 1984a,.

Prideaux, G.D., & Baker, W.J. Cognitive strategies and relative clause processing. Final Report to the

References

Social Sciences and Humanities Research Council of Canada, Research Grant No. 410-82-0153, 1984b.

Prince, E.F. A comparison of WH-clefts and *it*-clefts in discourse. *Language*, 1978, *54*, 883-906.

Randall, J.H. *-ity*: A study in word formation restrictions. *Journal of Psycholinguistic Research*, 1980, *9*, 523-534.

Reber, R.S. What clicks may tell us about speech perception. *Journal of Psycholinguistic Research*, 1973, *2*, 286-287.

Reber, A.S., & Anderson, J. R. The perception of clicks in linguistic and nonlinguistic messages. *Perception and Psychophysics*, 1970, *8*, 81-89.

Reid, J.R. Sentence type variables as aural concept formation dimensions. *Journal of Psycholinguistic Research*, 1974, *3*, 233-246.

Romney, A.K., & D'Andrade, R.G. Cognitive aspects of English kin terms. In A.K. Romney & R.G. D'Andrade (Eds.), *Transcultural studies in cognition*. *American Psychologist*, 1964, *66*, No. 3, Part 2.

Rosch. E. On the internal structure of perceptual and semantic categories. In T.E. Moore (Ed.), *Cognitive development and the acquisition of meaning*. New York: Academic Press, 1973.

Rosch, E. Cognitive representation of semantic categories. *Journal of Experimental Psychology*, 1975, *104*,192-233.

Rosch. E. Classification of real-world objects: Origins and representations in cognition. In P.N. Johnson-Laird & P.C. Wason (Eds.), *Thinking: Readings in cognitive science*. Cambridge: Cambridge University Press, 1977.

Rosch, E., & Mervis, C.B. Family resemblances: Studies in the internal structure of categories. *Cognitive Psychology*, 1975, *7*, 573-605.

Rubenstein, H., Lewis, S.S., & Rubenstein, M.A. Evidence for phonemic recording in visual word recognition. *Journal of Verbal Learning and Verbal Behavior*, 1971, *10*, 645-652.

Rummelhard, D.E. Notes on a schema for stories. In D. LaBerge & S.J. Samuels (Eds.), *Basic processes in reading*. Hillsdale, NJ: Lawrence Erlbaum, 1977.

Sachs, J.S. Recognition memory for syntactic and semantic aspects of connected discourse. *Perception and Psychophysics*, 1967, *2*, 437-442.

Savin, H.B., & Perchonock, E. Grammatical structure and immediate recall of English sentences. *Journal of Verbal Learning and Verbal Behavior*, 1965, *4*, 348-353.

Schank, R., & Abelson, R.P. Scripts, plans, and knowledge. In P.N. Johnson-Laird & P.C. Wason (Eds.), *Thinking: Readings in cognitive science*. Cambridge: Cambridge University Press, 1977.

Schlesinger, I.M. Production of utterances and language acquisition. In D.I. Slobin (Ed.), *The ontogenesis of grammar*. New York: Academic Press, 1971.

Schlesinger, I.M. *Production and comprehension of utterances*. Hillsdale, NJ: Lawrence Erlbaum, 1977.

Searle, R.J. *Speech acts: An essay in the philosophy of language*. Cambridge: Cambridge University Press, 1969.

Sheldon, A. The role of parallel function in the acquisition of relative clauses in English. *Journal of Verbal Learning and Verbal Behavior*, 1974, *13*, 272-281.

Sheldon, A. On strategies for processing relative clauses: A comparison of children and adults. *Journal of Verbal Learning and Verbal Behavior*, 1977, *6*, 305-315.

Siegel, D. *Topics in English morphology*. Unpublished Ph.D. dissertation, MIT, Cambridge, MA,

References

1974.

Slobin, D.I. Grammatical transformations and sentence comprehension in childhood and adulthood. *Journal of Verbal Learning and Verbal Behavior,* 1966, *5,* 219-227.

Slobin, D.I. Universals of grammatical development in children. In G.B. Flores D'Arcais & W.J.M. Levelt (Eds.), *Advances in psycholinguistics.* Amsterdam: North-Holland, 1970.

Slobin, D.I. Cognitive prerequisites for the development of language. In C.A. Ferguson & D.I. Slobin (Eds.), *Studies in child language development.* New York: Holt, Rineholt, & Winston, 1973.

Slobin, D.I. *Psycholinguistics* (2nd ed.). Glenview, IL: Scott, Foresman, and Company, 1979.

Slobin, D.I., & Welsh, C.A. Elicited imitation as a research tool in developmental psycholinguistics. In C.A. Ferguson & D.I. Slobin (Eds.), *Studies in child development.* New York: Holt Rinehart & Winston, 1973.

Smyth, R.H, Prideaux, G.D., & Hogan, J.T. The effect of context on dative position. *Lingua,* 1979, *47,* 27-42.

Spencer, N.J. Differences between linguists and non-linguists in intuitions of grammaticality-acceptability. *Journal of Psycholinguistic Research,* 1973, *2,* 83-98.

Stanners, R.F., Neiser, J.J., Hernon, W.P., & Hall, R. Memory representations for morphologically related words. *Journal of Verbal Learning and Verbal Behavior,* 1979, *18,* 399-412.

Taft, M., & Forster, K.I. Lexical storage and retrieval of prefixed words. *Journal of Verbal Learning and Verbal Behavior,* 1975, *14,* 638-647.

Tavakolian, S.L. (Ed.). *Language acquisition and linguistic theory.* Cambridge, MA: The MIT Press, 1981.

Thorkdike, E.L., & Lorge, I. *The teacher's word book of 30,000 words*. New York: Teachers College Press, 1944.

de Villiers, J.G., & de Villiers, P.A. *Language acquisition*. Cambridge, MA: Harvard University Press, 1978.

Wardhaugh, R. *Introduction to linguistics* (2nd ed.). New York: McGraw-Hill, 1977.

Watt, W.C. On two hypotheses concerning psycholinguistics. In J.R. Hayes (Ed.), *Cognition and the development of language*. New York: John Wiley & Sons, 1970.

Weinreich, U. *Languages in contact*. The Hague: Mouton, 1968.

Weir, R. *Language in the crib*. The Hague: Mouton, 1962.

Wheeler, C.J., & Schumsky, D.A. The morpheme boundaries of some English derivational suffixes. *Glossa*, 1980, *14*, 3-34.

Woodworth, R.S., & Schlosberg, H. *Experimental psychology* (revised edition). New York: Holt, Rinehart, & Winston, 1954.

Zimney, G.H. *Method in experimental psychology*. New York: Ronald Press, 1961.

Zwicky, A.M. An expanded view of morphology in the syntax-phonology interface. In S. Hattori & K. Inoue (Eds.), *Proceedings of the XIII International Congress of Linguists*, Tokyo, 1983, 198-208.

acceptability, 33-4,36-7,
215,218-9
acquisition, 39,57-8,67,
78-9,83,89,101-2,
119,122,156,206,
227,241
ambiguity, 9,25,110-1,
122,156,206,227,241
ambiguous, 4,37,41
anomaly, 43
anti-interruption, 130
argument, 31,32,51,178
associative theory
of meaning, 163

base component, 19
bracketing, 135,140,146

canonical form, 115
chronometric, 106,113,
155
chunking, 41
click(s), 109-10,114
closure, 47,134,136-8,
147,150,157,200,
263-4
competence, 25,34,100,
102,132,151,201,206
complementizer, 5
comprehension, 8,33,39,
40,44-7,49,53-4,56,
67,99,102,104,118,
143,183,202
concept formation, 113
confusability, 109

connotation, 193
context, 40,47-8,54,115,
164,188,215

data,
comprehension, 8,9
diachronic, 8
dialect, 7,6
experimental, 9
production, 9
text, 3
dative, 17,18,22,23,198
deep structure, 20,24,45,
102,109,112,150
deixis, 49
denotation, 193
denotative, 163
derivational morphology,
73,84,89,93-4
derivational theory of
complexity, 99,102-8,
111-3,122-3,153,155,
251
dialect, 4,7,8,215
differentiation, 63
direct object, 18,29,43,
139,142,178,261
discourse, 41,43-4,48,
54-5, 60,104,123,
143,147,191-3,198-9,
204-5
distractors, 13

editing, 8
elicited imitation, 66